SILVER·BURDETT

Making Music

Program Authors

Jane Beethoven
Susan Brumfield
Patricia Shehan Campbell
David N. Connors
Robert A. Duke
Judith A. Jellison

Rita Klinger
Rochelle Mann
Hunter C. March
Nan L. McDonald
Marvelene C. Moore
Mary Palmer
Konnie Saliba

Will Schmid
Carol Scott-Kassner
Mary E. Shamrock
Sandra L. Stauffer
Judith Thomas
Jill Trinka

PEARSON
Scott
Foresman

Editorial Offices: Glenview, Illinois • Parsippany, New Jersey • New York, New York
Sales Offices: Parsippany, New Jersey • Duluth, Georgia • Glenview, Illinois
Coppell, Texas • Ontario, California • Mesa, Arizona

ISBN: 0-382-36572-0
2008 Edition

Copyright © 2005, Pearson Education, Inc.

9 10 V063 09 08

Contributing Authors

Audrey A. Berger
Roslyn Burrough
J. Bryan Burton
Jeffrey E. Bush
John M. Cooksey
Shelly C. Cooper
Alice-Ann Darrow
Scott Emmons
Debra Erck
Anne M. Fennell
Doug Fisher
Carroll Gonzo
Larry Harms
Martha F. Hilley
Debbie Burgoon Hines

Mary Ellen Junda
Donald Kalbach
Shirley Lacroix
Henry Leck
Sanna Longden
Glenn A. Richter
Carlos Xavier Rodriguez
Kathleen Donahue Sanz
Julie K. Scott
Gwen Spell
Barb Stevanson
Kimberly C. Walls
Jackie Wiggins
Maribeth Yoder-White

Listening Map Contributing Authors

Patricia Shehan Campbell
Jackie Chooi-Theng Lew
Ann Clements
Kay Edwards
Sheila Feay-Shaw
Kay Greenhaw

David Hebert
Hunter C. March
Carol Scott-Kassner
Mary E. Shamrock
Sandra L. Stauffer

Movement Contributing Authors

Judy Lasko
Marvelene C. Moore
Dixie Piver

Wendy Taucher
Susan Thomasson
Judith Thompson-Barthwell

Recording Producers

Buryl Red, Executive Producer

Rick Baitz
Rick Bassett
Bill and Charlene James
Joseph Joubert
Bryan Louiselle
Tom Moore

J. Douglas Pummill
Michael Rafter
Mick Rossi
Buddy Skipper
Robert Spivak
Jeanine Tesori
Linda Twine

Contents
Steps to Making Music

 = **Core Lesson**
 = **Music Reading Lesson**

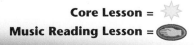

Core Lesson =
Music Reading Lesson =

⭐ = **Core Lesson**

✋ = **Music Reading Lesson**

Unit 4 Building Our Musical Skills 126

Unit Introduction

M*U*S*I*C M*A*K*E*R*S The Singers Unlimited

Core Lesson = ☆
Music Reading Lesson = ✋

✫ = **Core Lesson**
✋ = **Music Reading Lesson**

Core Lesson =
Music Reading Lesson =

Paths to Making Music

STEPS TO
Making
Music

Sounds Surround

Your journey with music is like a circle—it has no end. Step into the circle and **sing** "Turn the Beat Around."

As you sing, pass the beat around. **Clap** one beat, in turn, around the circle. **Create** different ways to pass the beat around.

Let the Music Begin!

Love to hear ___ it. Blow horns you sure sound pret -

- ty. Your vi - o - lins keep mov - in' to the nit - ty grit -

- ty. When you hear the scratch of the gui - tar scratch-ing, then you know that

rhy - thm cor - ners all the ac - tion, whoa ___ yeah.

Turn the beat _ a - round. _ Love to hear _ per - cus - sion.

Turn it up - side down, _ Love to hear _ per - cus -

_ sion. Love to hear _ it, love to hear _ it.

Well, the gui - tar play - er starts play - in' with the

syn - co - pat - ed rhy - thm, scratch, scratch, _ scratch.

Makes _ me want to move my bod - y, yeah, yeah, _ yeah. _

And when the drum - mer starts beat - in' that beat he

nails that beat with the syn - co - pat - ed rhy - thm and the

rat - tat - tat - tat - tat - tat on the drums _ hey, _ yeah.

Expression in Your Music

Listen to this song. What feelings, or emotions, do the words communicate? How does the music reflect these feelings? One way music suggests feelings is with **dynamics**.

> **Dynamics** are the different levels of loudness and softness of sound.

CD 1–3

Put a Little Love in Your Heart

Words and Music by Jimmy Holiday, Randy Myers, and Jackie De Shannon

VERSE

1. Think of your fel - low man, lend him a help - ing hand,
2. An - oth - er day ___ goes by, and still the chil - dren cry,
3. Take a good look ___ a - round, and if you're look - ing down,

Put a lit - tle love ___ in your heart. _____

If

You see, it's get - ting late, oh, please don't hes - i - tate,
you want the world ___ to know, we won't let ha - tred grow,
I hope when you ___ de - cide, kind - ness will be ___ your guide,

REFRAIN

Put a lit - tle love ___ in your heart. _____ And the world ___

The Language of Expression

Musicians usually use Italian words when they talk about dynamics.

p (piano) = soft
mp (mezzo piano) = medium soft
mf (mezzo forte) = medium loud
f (forte) = loud

< *(crescendo)* = gradually louder

> *(decrescendo)* = gradually softer

Use dynamics while you **sing**
"Put a Little Love in Your Heart."

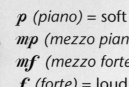

_____ will be a bet-ter place, And the world _ will be a

bet-ter place for you ___ and me. ___ You just wait _

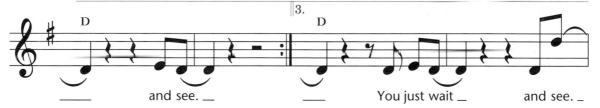

_____ and see. _ You just wait _ and see. _

mf 1st time, *p* 2nd time, *f* last time

_____ Put a lit-tle love _ in your heart. _____

Video Library View and listen to another version of "Put a Little Love in Your Heart," as performed by the Total Experience Gospel Choir on the *Singing Styles* video.

Expressive Music

"Put a Little Love in Your Heart" has been recorded by many singers. **Listen** for dynamic contrast in this version by the gospel singer Mahalia Jackson.

 CD 1–5
Put a Little Love in Your Heart

by Jimmy Holiday, Randy Myers, and Jackie De Shannon as performed by Mahalia Jackson

Mahalia Jackson (1912–1972) recorded this version of the song in 1969.

Mahalia Jackson ▶

Moving with Expression

As you **sing** "Put a Little Love in Your Heart," perform these signs each time this phrase is sung.

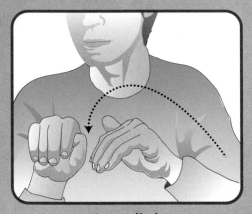

Put a little

love

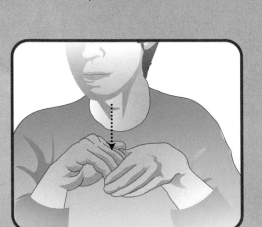

in your

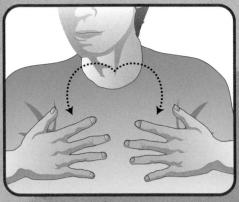

heart

A Dynamic Musician

Tony Bennett is famous for his smooth voice and singing style. Listen for his use of dynamic contrast as he sings *The Beat of My Heart*. When and where does he change the dynamics?

CD 1–6

The Beat of My Heart

by Johnny Burke and Harold Spina as performed by Tony Bennett

This song is performed in the swing style.

M·U·S·I·C M·A·K·E·R·S

Tony Bennett

Tony Bennett (Anthony Benedetto, born 1926) is originally from Astoria, Queens, New York. He attended the High School of Industrial Arts in Manhattan. Bennett got his break in music when comedian Bob Hope heard him singing at the Greenwich Village Inn. Hope was impressed and asked Bennett to sing with him at the Paramount Theater. Bennett later signed a record deal with Columbia Records and recorded hits such as *Boulevard of Broken Dreams, Rags to Riches,* and *I Left My Heart in San Francisco.* Bennett remains popular, and he has performed with rock groups such as the Red Hot Chili Peppers. He has received Grammy awards for Album of the Year and Best Traditional Pop Vocal.

ON THE ROAD TO RHYTHM

Look at the numbered rhythm patterns below. How many beats are in each pattern?

Using rhythm syllables, clap and count as you **read** your way down the rhythm road.

1.
2.
3.
4.
5.
6.
7.
8.

Look at the song on page 11. Find the time signature. How many beats are in each measure? **Listen** to "Soldier, Soldier" while you conduct a $\frac{4}{4}$ pattern.

A Girl and Her Soldier

Listen to this recording of *Lazy John*, a variation of "Soldier, Soldier." Then **compare** the two versions.

CD 1–14
Lazy John

arranged and performed by Jean Ritchie

Jean Ritchie is a folk singer from Kentucky. See page 349 for more information, including a recorded interview with this American legend.

Soldier, Soldier

CD 1–7

REFRAIN

Traditional Song from the United States and England

"Now, sol - dier, sol - dier, will you mar - ry me, with your mus - ket, fife, and drum?" "Oh, how can I mar - ry such a

rit. last time   *accel. last time*   Fine

pret - ty girl as you, when I've got no shoes to put on?"
when I've got no hat to put on?"
when I've got no coat to put on?"
when I've got a wife at ____ home?"

VERSE

Then off to the cob - bler ____ she did go, as
hat - ter ____
tai - lor ____

fast as she could run. She bought him a pair of the
hat
coat

D. C. al Fine

fin - est that there were, and the sol - dier put them _ on.
it ____
it ____

WORKING WITH RHYTHM

Have you ever rowed a boat or raked leaves? What is similar about these motions? Sea shanties like "Haul Away, Joe" were sung on large sailing ships in the 1700s and 1800s. They often accompanied repetitive motion. This song has a **strong and weak beat** in each measure to fit with the work being done. What kind of work on a ship would use this type of motion?

The **strong beat** is usually the first beat in a measure. The **weak beat** is usually the second or last beat in a measure.

Moving with a Sea Shanty

With a partner, **create** work movements to do while you **sing** "Haul Away, Joe."

CD 1–15

Haul Away, Joe

Sea Shanty from England

VERSE

1. Oh, when I was a lit - tle lad, or so my moth - er
2. Oh, once I was in Ire - land dig - gin' turf and
3. King Lou - ie was the King of France be - fore the re - vo -

told __ me,
'ta - ties, 'Way haul a - way, we'll haul a - way, Joe. That But
lu - tion, King

if I did not kiss a gal my lips would grow all
now I'm on a lime - juice ship __ haul - ing on the
Lou - ie got his head cut off which spoiled his con - sti -

mould - y,
brac - es, 'Way haul a - way, we'll haul a - way, Joe.
tu - tion,

REFRAIN

'Way haul a - way, we'll haul a - way for bet - ter weath - er,

'Way haul a - way, we'll haul a - way, Joe.

Dancing in DUPLE METER

"Gakavik" is a folk song from the Republic of Armenia, a country that became independent in 1991 after being part of the Soviet Union for seventy years.

This song is based on a strong and weak beat pattern known as **duple meter.** Clap the steady beat while you **sing** or **listen** to *"Gakavik."*

Duple meter is a basic pattern in which a measure has one strong and one weak beat.

CD 1–17

Gakavik

(The Partridge)

English Words by Mary Shamrock

Folk Song from Armenia

U - րեվ   բաց - վեց   թուխ __ ամ   պե - րեն,
A - rev   pats - vedz   tugh __ am   be - ren,
Threat-'ning clouds   hide the sky,   Soon the sun   breaks the gloom;

կա - քավ   թռ - ավ   կա - նաչ __ սա - րեն.
ga - kav   te - rav   ga - nach __ sa - ren.
Moun-tains high,   moun-tains green,   Ev - 'ry-where bright flow-ers bloom.

կա - նաչ __ սա - րեն'   սա - րի __ ծե - րեն,
Ga - nach __ sa - ren   sa - ri __ dze - ren,
Pret - ty   par - tridge through the air,   Feath-ers shin - ing   in the sun;

Duple Meter in Movement

Follow these steps to **create** a dance for *"Gakavik."*

- Step right, together, step right, easy kick
- Step left, together, step left, easy kick

Armenian
dancers ▶

Listening for Form

Follow the listening map as you **listen** to "Galop" from *Masquerade Suite*. Make up a story that involves a masquerade and fits with the music.

CD 1–24
Galop

from *Masquerade Suite*
by Aram Khachaturian

"Galop" is one section of music intended to be played at different points during a play titled *Masquerade*.

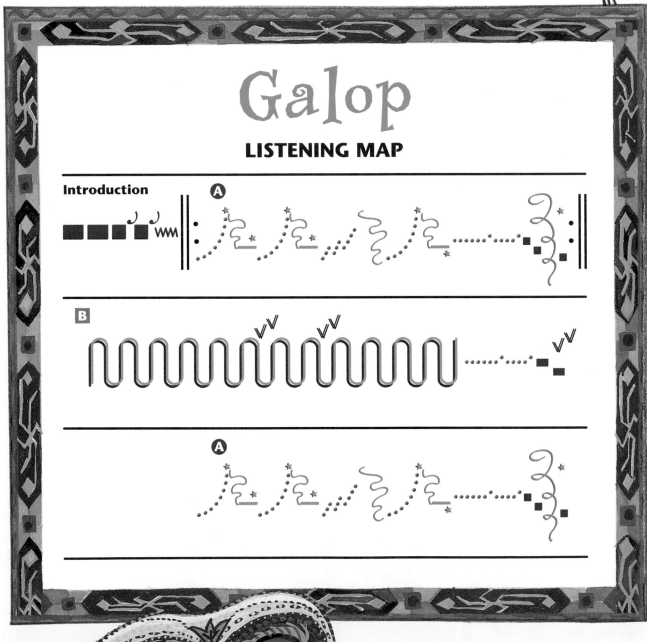

MUSIC MAKERS

Aram Khachaturian

Aram Khachaturian (1903–1978) is counted as one of the outstanding composers of the former Soviet Union. His music reflects his Armenian roots and background. Although he had great musical talent as a child, he did not begin formal training in music until he was nineteen years old. He drew upon the folk music of Armenia, as well as other countries in what was then the Soviet Union, to create a rich, colorful musical style.

Show What You Know!

1. Which of these rhythm patterns is the beginning of *"Gakavik"*? Which is the beginning of "Soldier, Soldier"?

A.

B.

2. Create a rhythm pattern in duple meter that is eight beats long using these note durations.

I Sing, You Sing

Some songs have parts for a solo and parts for a group to sing. This is known as **call and response,** and it is very similar to a conversation. The solo parts need to be completed by a response from the group.

Call and response is a musical device in which a portion of a melody (call) is followed by an answering portion (response).

Sing "Limbo Like Me" and take turns being the soloist.

CD 1–25

Limbo Like Me

Words and Music Adapted by Massie Patterson and Sammy Heyward

I want a girl to lim - bo like me; Lim - bo, lim-bo like me.
Lim - bo, __ lim - bo, lim - bo like me;

Ev - 'ry - bod - y lim - bo like me; Lim - bo, lim-bo like me.
My lit - tle goat can lim - bo like me;

Mon - key try to lim - bo like me; Lim - bo, lim-bo like me.
Mon - key no can lim - bo like me;

One an' all come lim - bo like me; Lim - bo, lim-bo like me.

Lim - bo, lim-bo like me; Lim - bo, lim-bo like me.

"Limbo Like Me" New words and new music adapted by Massie Patterson and Sammy Heyward. (Based on a traditional song) TRO-© 1963 (Renewed) Ludlow Music Inc., New York, N.Y. Used by permission.

18

Do the Limbo

This song and movement game come from the Caribbean calypso tradition. To play the game, two people hold a stick. The other players take turns bending backwards to go under the stick. The stick is lowered until the last player able to pass under the stick wins.

Move as you **listen** to Samaroo Jets perform *Brisad del Zulia*.

CD 1–27
Brisad del Zulia

**Traditional Caribbean Calypso
as performed by Samaroo Jets**

This performance features steel drums made from oil barrels.

MAKING A MELODY

Some songs express hope. "Gonna Ride Up in the Chariot" originated with African Americans during slavery when life was very harsh. It is a song of hope for freedom. **Sing** the song and then discuss the words.

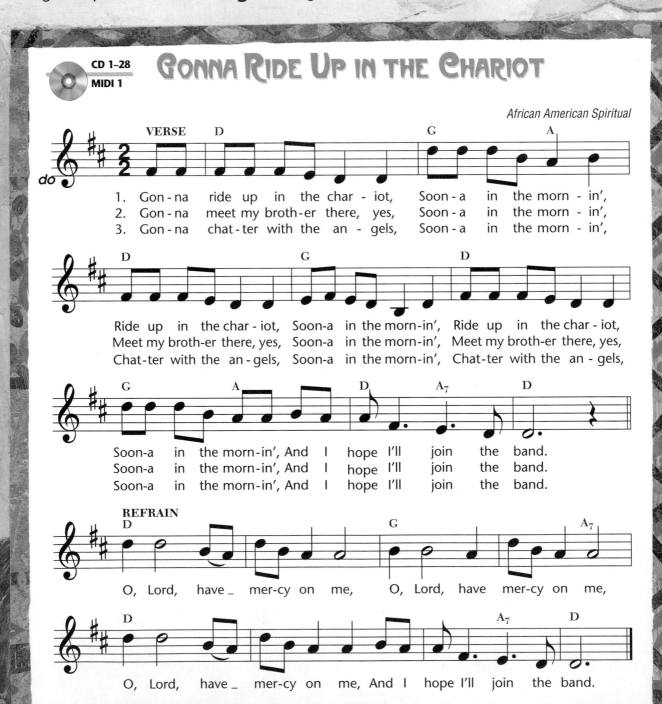

CD 1–28
MIDI 1

GONNA RIDE UP IN THE CHARIOT

African American Spiritual

do

VERSE D G A

1. Gon - na ride up in the char - iot, Soon - a in the morn - in',
2. Gon - na meet my broth-er there, yes, Soon - a in the morn - in',
3. Gon - na chat - ter with the an - gels, Soon - a in the morn - in',

D G D

Ride up in the char - iot, Soon-a in the morn-in', Ride up in the char - iot,
Meet my broth-er there, yes, Soon-a in the morn-in', Meet my broth-er there, yes,
Chat-ter with the an - gels, Soon-a in the morn-in', Chat-ter with the an - gels,

G A D A₇ D

Soon-a in the morn-in', And I hope I'll join the band.
Soon-a in the morn-in', And I hope I'll join the band.
Soon-a in the morn-in', And I hope I'll join the band.

REFRAIN
D G A₇

O, Lord, have _ mer-cy on me, O, Lord, have mer-cy on me,

D A₇ D

O, Lord, have _ mer-cy on me, And I hope I'll join the band.

Interval Practice

The melody of this song is composed of notes that either repeat, move by step, or move by skip. **Listen** to "Gonna Ride Up in the Chariot" and look for the **intervals** below in the melody.

An **interval** is the distance between two pitches.

1.   2.   3.   4.   5.   6.

What are the intervals shown above? To determine the interval, count the bottom tone as 1. Then count all lines and spaces up to the next pitch.

Sing "Gonna Ride Up in the Chariot" again and **read** the steps, repeats, and skips.

Compose Using Intervals

Compose an introduction for "Gonna Ride Up in the Chariot" to play on a melody instrument. Choose the notes from these pitches. Make sure you use a step, a skip, and a repeated tone in the melody.

Tune In

Africans who were brought to America created spirituals. The subject of spirituals was often freedom.

▲ State capitol,
Austin, Texas

Lone Star Intervals

From the time it was written, in 1941, "Deep in the Heart of Texas" has been an "unofficial" state song of Texas. Which songs represent your home state?

Listen to the song as you follow the notes on the staff. Now **sing** the song. Find the steps, skips, and repeated notes in the melody. Then answer these questions:

- How many different intervals can you **identify** in the melody? Which is the smallest? Which is the largest?

- Which intervals in this song were *not* used in "Gonna Ride Up in the Chariot," on page 20?

CD 1–33

DEEP IN THE HEART OF TEXAS

Words by June Hershey   *Music by Don Swander*

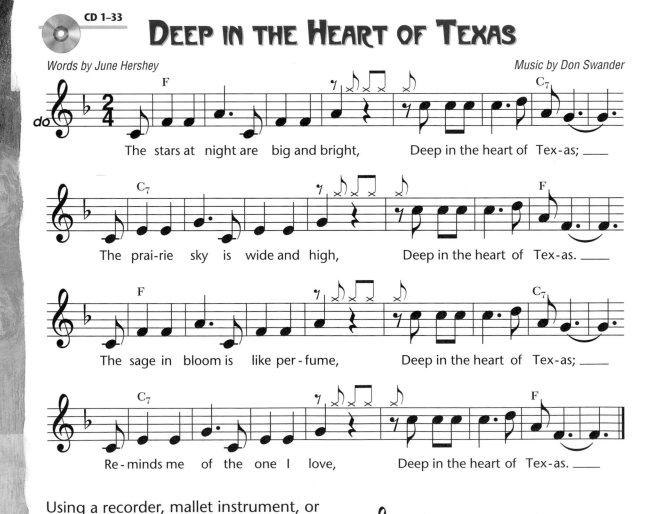

The stars at night are big and bright,   Deep in the heart of Tex-as; ____

The prai-rie sky is wide and high,   Deep in the heart of Tex-as. ____

The sage in bloom is like per-fume,   Deep in the heart of Tex-as; ____

Re-minds me of the one I love,   Deep in the heart of Tex-as. ____

Using a recorder, mallet instrument, or keyboard, **play** these repeated notes every time they appear in the song.

Baroque Melody

As you follow the listening map, **listen** for steps, skips, and repeated notes in the long, flowing melody, played by the first violins.

CD 1–35

"Air" in D

**from *Orchestral Suite No. 3*
by Johann Sebastian Bach**

In opera, an *aria* is an extended song for solo voice. Baroque composers used the term *air* to describe melodies modeled on Italian *arias*.

"Air" in D
LISTENING MAP

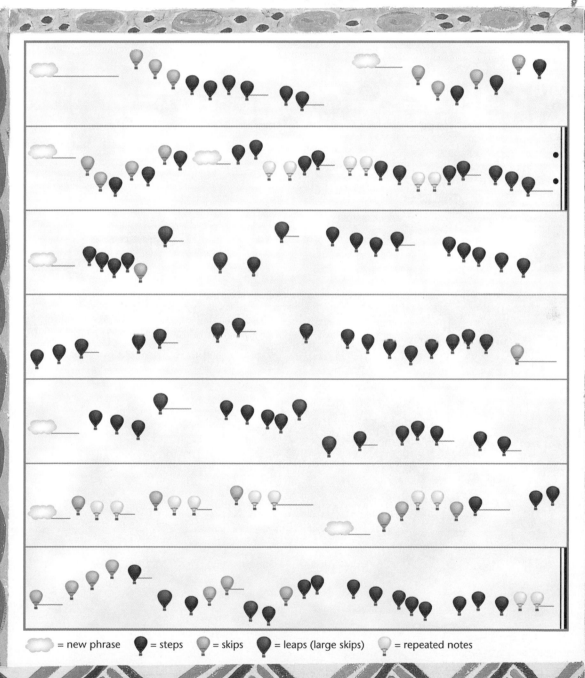

Pentatonic Patterns

Here is a Japanese melody made up of three melody patterns.
Follow its contour, or shape, as you **listen** to *"Tsuki."*

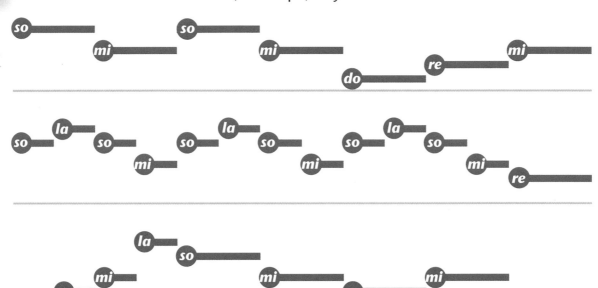

la
so
mi
re
do

Reading Pentatonic Scales

A song's notes make up its scale. **Read** the **pentatonic scale** on the syllable ladder. Find the steps and skips in the scale. Use hand signs as you **sing** the scale up and down.

> A **pentatonic scale** is a scale of five notes.

Read the pentatonic scale from the staff. The *do* symbol at the beginning of the staff will help you find your way around.

Now you are ready to **read** *"Tsuki"* from the staff.

CD 1–36

Tsuki
(The Moon)

English Words by Kazuo Akiyama   *School Song from Japan*

で　　た　　で　　た　　つ　　き　　が
1. De - ta,　de - ta,　tsu - ki　ga
1. Now　the　moon　is　com - ing　out!

ま＿＿る　い　ま＿＿る　い　ま　ん　ま　る　い
Ma - ru - i　ma - ru - i　ma - n　ma - ru - i,
Big and round, so　big and round, as　round＿ as a　tray.

ぼ　ん　の　よ　う　な　つ　き　が
Bo＿＿ n - no　yo - na　tsu - ki　ga.
Moon　is　big　and　round, just　like　a　tray.

2. *Kaku reta kumoni,*
   Kuroi, kuroi makuroi,
   Sumino yona kumoni.

2. Now the moon is hiding.
   Gone away, O gone away, O gone away so far.
   Up behind the clouds as black as tar.

♫rts Connection

◀ *Moonlight on Sebu River* (c. 19th century Japan) by Hiroshige

Tonal Center

Name the first and last note of this song. Count how many times this pitch occurs. Where does it occur most often? The pitch G is the **tonal center** of this song.

Now **listen** to the song's melody while humming G. Sometimes G fits with the melody, and sometimes it does not. Like a magnet, the melody always pulls back to G.

> A **tonal center** is a pitch that acts as a resting place or "home" for all of the other pitches that happen around it.

CD 1–43

Waitin' for the Light to Shine

from *Big River*

Words and Music by Roger Miller
Arranged by Linda Twine

VERSE

1. I have lived an un-di-rect-ed life, a cloud-y
2. Far be-yond hor-i-zons I have seen, be-yond the

way I know, the on-ly way I knew. So the
things I've done, be-yond the dreams I've dreamed. Are the

things I've done, in fact, each and ev-'ry one, are the
things I've done, in fact, each and ev-'ry one, are the

way that I was taught to run.
way that I was taught to run.

REFRAIN

I am wait - in' for the light to shine, I am

wait - in' for the light to shine.

I have lived in the dark - ness for so long, I am

1.
wait - in' for the light to shine.

2
2.
wait - in' for the light, I am wait - in' for the light, I am

wait - in' for the light to shine.

◀ "Jim" and "Huck"
in *Big River*

A Song of Revelation

In "Waitin' for the Light to Shine," the singer shares his feelings. Explain what he means by *darkness* and *light*.

A Light on Broadway

The American Broadway musical has been going strong for more than seventy years. The name *Broadway* comes from the famous New York City street where many of the musical theaters are located. Musicals are plays with speaking, singing, and dancing. The music is usually played by an orchestra in a pit in front of the stage. *West Side Story, The Sound of Music,* and *The Lion King* are famous Broadway musicals. Can you name others?

"Waitin' for the Light to Shine" is from the Broadway musical *Big River*. This show is based on Mark Twain's book *The Adventures of Huckleberry Finn.* In this book, set in the mid-1800s, the main characters, Huck and Jim, travel together on a raft down the mighty Mississippi River.

Tune In

Rene Auberjonois (Odo in *Deep Space 9*) and Brent Spiner (Data in *Star Trek—The Next Generation*) have both played the character Duke in *Big River* on Broadway.

ROGER MILLER AND LINDA TWINE

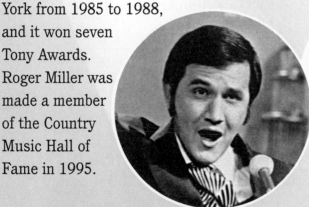

Roger Miller (1936–1992) wrote the music for *Big River*. He was famous as a country music singer and songwriter. *Big River* was his first attempt at writing a show for the stage, and the show was a big success. It had more than 1,000 performances in New York from 1985 to 1988, and it won seven Tony Awards. Roger Miller was made a member of the Country Music Hall of Fame in 1995.

Linda Twine began her career on Broadway as music director of *Big River*. After she graduated from the University of Oklahoma, she began teaching music in New York City public elementary schools. Roger Miller met her and discovered that she understood the style of music he wanted for *Big River,* so he asked her to be music director for the Broadway show.

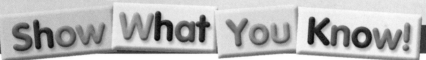

Show What You Know!

Read the following melodies using pitch syllables.

1. *do*

2. *do*

3. *do*

Look at the phrases above. How would you **identify** the tonal center of these phrases if the beginning were not marked with *do?*

MANY Voices

There are as many different "colors" in the sounds we hear as in the world we see. **Timbre** [TAM-ber] means "the color of a sound." Musicians use words such as *bright, dull, dark, mellow, clear, light, open,* and *shrill* to describe sound colors.

Timbre is the unique quality or tone color of sounds.

Every musical instrument has its own timbre, and each instrument can produce different shades of its own color. For example, just as you are able to see differences in shades of yellow or blue, musicians are able to hear differences in sounds.

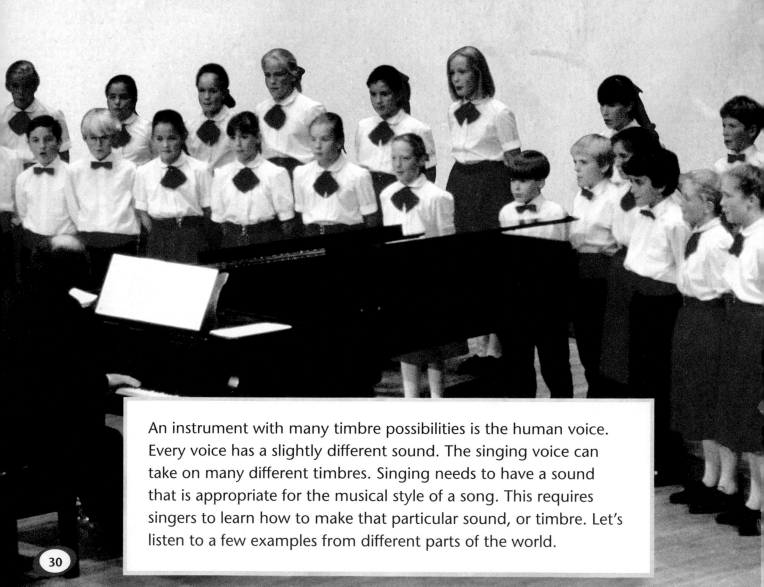

An instrument with many timbre possibilities is the human voice. Every voice has a slightly different sound. The singing voice can take on many different timbres. Singing needs to have a sound that is appropriate for the musical style of a song. This requires singers to learn how to make that particular sound, or timbre. Let's listen to a few examples from different parts of the world.

Voices Around the World

These people learn to sing with the sound typical of their culture. **Listen** to the timbre of the voices of these singers.

► Bulgarian singers

◄ Tuvinian musicians ▼

CD 2–1
Ghel moma

by S. Moutaftshiev
as performed by Le Mystère des Voix Bulgares

One quality of Bulgarian vocal music is harmony created by singing notes very close together, producing a special ringing sound.

CD 2–2
Sigit "Alash"

as performed by Tuvinian singers and musicians

This man from Tuva is singing *choomej* (singing technique). He changes the inside shape of his mouth to make the higher and lower pitched sounds.

CD 2–3
I Don't Want to Feel Like That

by Teresa Radigan and Donald Schlitz, Jr.
as performed by Patty Loveless

Loveless, a native of Kentucky, is known in country music for her soulful singing.

▲ Patty Loveless

CD 2–4
Powwow Song

Southern Plains Indians

This music accompanies a ceremonial social dance. Notice the quality of the performers' voices.

Jessye Norman ▼

CD 2–5
Nahandove

**from _Chansons madecasses_
by Maurice Ravel
as performed by Jessye Norman**

Jessye Norman is a well-known soprano who has performed all over the world.

CD 2–6
Rain, Rain, Beautiful Rain

**by Joseph Shabalala
as performed by Ladysmith Black Mambazo**

This South African group sings in simple harmony, with open and natural voices.

▼ Ladysmith Black Mambazo

Tune In

"Singing cleanses the soul; when the soul is clean, everything is open."
Joseph Shabalala

Your Voice—Your Song

Children's voices have a wonderful sound of their own—often clear and somewhat light. As you grow into your teenage years, you will develop the power and flexibility needed for adult singing. Here's a song about singing. As you **sing**, mix your own special vocal timbre with all the other timbres of your classmates to make a vocal rainbow.

CD 2–7
MIDI 2

I'm Gonna Sing

African American Spiritual

1. I'm gon - na sing when the spir - it says "Sing," _____
2. I'm gon - na shout when the spir - it says "Shout," _____
3. I'm gon - na pray when the spir - it says "Pray," _____
4. I'm gon - na sing when the spir - it says "Sing," _____

I'm gon - na sing when the spir - it says "Sing," _____
I'm gon - na shout when the spir - it says "Shout," _____
I'm gon - na pray when the spir - it says "Pray," _____
I'm gon - na sing when the spir - it says "Sing," _____

I'm gon - na sing when the spir - it says "Sing," _____
I'm gon - na shout when the spir - it says "Shout," _____
I'm gon - na pray when the spir - it says "Pray," _____
I'm gon - na sing when the spir - it says "Sing," _____

And o - bey the spir - it of the Lord. _____

LAYERED SOUNDS... CHA CHA CHA

Music has **texture.** It can be thick or thin, depending on the number of layers. The first two measures of *"Sonando"* are rhythm ostinatos you can **play** while you **sing** the song. Practice clapping each ostinato, then **perform** *"Sonando."*

Texture is the layering of sounds to create a thick or thin quality in music.

CD 2–9
MIDI 3

SONANDO

English Words by Alice D. Firgau

Words and Music by Peter Terrace
Arranged by Ted Solis, Adapted and Arranged by Kay Edwards

So - nan - do (clap)   pa - ra bai - lar,
They're play - ing   a cha - cha - cha.

Go - za (clap)   mi cha - cha - cha.
Come on,   let's have some fun.

Play 4 times (all instruments)

Sing 4 times

G   F   G

Lle - ga - ré Ma - rí - a, lle - ga - ré.
Here   I   am, Ma - ri - a, dance with me.

Play 2 times (all instruments)

G   F

So - nan - do (clap)   pa - ra bai - lar,
They're play - ing   a   cha - cha - cha.

G   F

Go - za (clap)   mi   cha - cha - cha.
Come   on,   let's have some fun.

Timbales ▼

More Layered Sounds

Listen for layered instruments in Poncho Sanchez's recording of *A Night in Tunisia*. How many instrument parts can you **identify**?

CD 2–14

A Night in Tunisia

by F. Paparelli and Dizzy Gillespie as performed by Poncho Sanchez

This version of *A Night in Tunisia* features a tenor saxophone and *timbales*. These instruments are part of the Latin/jazz fusion style.

How's the Texture?

When is a country a continent? When it's Australia. Australians have their own names for things found only in their country. "Tie Me Kangaroo Down, Sport" is an Australian song that plays with names.

Perform these ostinatos. Then **play** them as a layered accompaniment while you **sing** the song.

Aboriginal Australian playing the *didgeridoo*
▼

Woodblock
Doo did - ge - ri - doo doo,

Cabasa
Down, All to - geth - er now, Down, All to - geth - er now,

Temple Blocks
Cock - a - too cool, Cock - a - too cool,

Conga Drums
Down, Sport, Tie me kan - ga - roo,

Bass Drum
Keep cool, Keep cool,

Listen to *Brolga One* and notice the sound of the *didgeridoo* [DID-jeh-ree-doo]. The *didgeridoo* was invented and played by the aboriginal people of Australia. Now, everyone wants to play the *didgeridoo!* Wouldn't you?

CD 2–17
Brolga One

created and performed by aboriginal musicians with *didgeridoo*

This recording includes singing along with the *didgeridoo*.

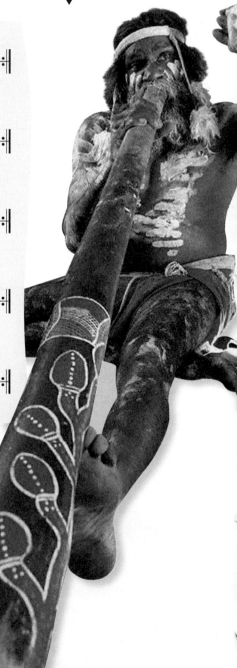

Tie Me Kangaroo Down, Sport

Words and Music by Rolf and Bruce Harris

VERSE

1. Watch me wal - la - bys feed, mate.
2. Keep me cock - a - too cool, Curl.
3. Take me ko - a - la back, Jack.
4. Mind me plat - y - pus duck, Bill.

Refrain Tie me kan - ga - roo down, sport.

Watch me wal - la - bys feed.
Keep me cock - a - too cool.
Take me ko - a - la back. He
Mind me plat - y - pus duck. Don't
Tie me kan - ga - roo down.

They're a dan - ger - ous breed, mate. So
Don't go act - ing the fool, Curl. Just
lives some - where on the track, Mac. So
let him go run - ning a - mok, Bill. So
Tie me kan - ga - roo down, sport.

watch me wal - la - bys feed. All to - geth - er now! *(to Refrain)*
keep me cock - a - too cool.
take me ko - a - la back.
mind me plat - y - pus duck.
Tie me kan - ga - roo down. *(to Verses)*

5. Play your didgeridoo, Blue.
   Play your didgeridoo.
   Keep playing 'til I shoot thro', Blue.
   Play your didgeridoo.
   All together now!   *Refrain*

6. Tan me hide when I'm dead, Fred.
   Tan me hide when I'm dead.
   So we tanned his hide when he died, Clyde.
   And that's it hanging on the shed.
   All together now!   *Refrain*

Power in Numbers
Layers of SOUND

"Pay Me My Money Down" is a work song originally sung by stevedores. The workers are singing about getting paid for their labor.

A solo voice sings the call. Many voices answer in the response and sing on the refrain to create a powerful sound. **Listen** for the layering of voices in the recording of "Pay Me My Money Down."

CD 2–18

Pay Me My Money Down

Work Song from the Georgia Sea Islands
Collected and Adapted by Lydia A. Parrish

VERSE *Call*

1. I thought I heard ___ the cap - tain say,
2. As soon as the boat was clear of the bar,

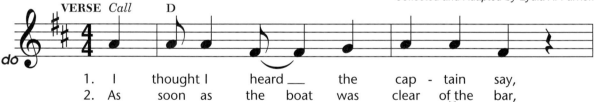

Response

"Pay me my mon-ey down," ___ To - mor - row is our
He knocked me down with the

Response

sail - ing day, ___
end of a spar,

"Pay me my mon-ey down." ___

Singing a Work Song

African Americans along the southeastern coast sang this song. **Listen** as the Georgia Sea Island Singers perform this song. **Create** work movements while you **sing** along.

CD 2–20

Pay Me My Money Down

Work Song Collected and Adapted by Lydia A. Parrish as performed by the Georgia Sea Island Singers

Notice the "work sounds" the performers are making while singing.

REFRAIN

"Pay me, __ oh, pay me, __ Pay me my mon-ey down. _

Pay me or go to jail, __ Pay me my mon-ey down." _

3. Well, I wish I was Mr. Steven's son,
   "Pay me my money down,"
   Sit on the bank and watch the work done,
   "Pay me my money down." *Refrain*

The Power of Layers of Percussion

Caribbean music is filled with layers of instruments. This includes the music of steel drums, made by layering many parts to create an exciting sound. About sixty years ago, musicians in Trinidad discovered how to make drums out of 55-gallon oil storage barrels. Steel drums can be tuned to specific pitches.

Many steel drum bands have fifty players or more! No matter what the size, every band has an "engine room" of instruments such as congas, drum sets, maracas, and claves. The engine room supplies a rhythmic background for the music.

Here is how steel drums are made.

▲ **1.** One end of the barrel is removed. The "skirt" of the barrel is cut to make a high-, medium-, or low-sounding drum.

◄ **2.** The top is hammered into a bowl shape with flat areas that produce definite pitches.

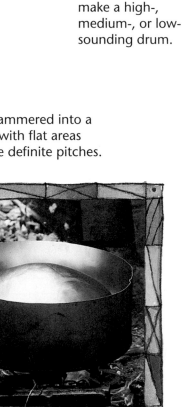

3. The entire drum is heated red-hot in a fire to cure the steel. ▶

Video Library Watch *Percussion Instruments: Tuned* to learn more about steel drum bands.

Classical Music with a Caribbean Flavor

Although steel drum bands are known for playing original calypso music, they also perform arrangements of many other musical styles. **Listen** to the calypso rhythms and layers in this version of *Eine kleine Nachtmusik (A Little Night Music)*.

 CD 2–21
Eine kleine Nachtmusik (A Little Night Music)

by Wolfgang Amadeus Mozart

Steel drum bands often play Caribbean versions of European classical orchestral works.

M·U·S·I·C M·A·K·E·R·S

AMOCO RENEGADES

Amoco Renegades is one of Trinidad's oldest steel drum bands. Jit Samaroo, director of the band, commented that the name of their group goes back to when "panmen" were considered ruffians more than musicians. The group had over 100 members when it was named champion in 1989 at the steel band competition called "Panorama." For the competition, Amoco Renegades performed *Somebody*.

Listen for layers of sound in this recording of *Somebody*.

 **CD 2–22**
Somebody

**by Winsford deVine
as performed by Amoco Renegades**

This recording was made three days before Amoco Renegades was named champion.

Review, Assess,

What Do You Know?

1. Look at the notation for *"Tsuki"* on page 25. Then answer these questions.

   a. Where is *do* located in the music?

   b. Point to all the notes named *so*. How many did you find?

   c. Do the same activity for the notes named *mi, re, la,* and *do.*

2. Name each dynamic symbol and point to the correct definition.

   a. *mf*   loud

   b. *p*   gradually louder

   c. *mp*   medium loud

   d. ——   soft

   e. *f*   medium soft

   f. ——   gradually softer

What Do You Hear? 1

  CD 2–23

Listen to these examples of vocal timbre. Briefly describe the timbre of each example using at least three adjectives in each description.

1. *Rain, Rain, Beautiful Rain*

2. *I Don't Want to Feel Like That*

3. *Nahandove*

4. *Sigit "Alash"*

Perform, Create

What You Can Do

Create Dynamics

Create a dynamics roadmap to follow while you sing "Waitin' for the Light to Shine" on page 26. Remember that dynamics should express the feelings and mood of the song.

Move to the Beat

Use movement to show strong and weak beats while you sing "*Gakavik*" on page 14. With a partner, create work movements to perform as you sing "Haul Away, Joe" on page 13.

Read a Melody

Read the notation for *"Tsuki"* on page 25, using pitch syllables and hand signs. Then perform the song again with the words.

Create Textures

Divide into two groups and perform "Pay Me My Money Down," on page 38, in call-and-response style. Sing the song again with only a few students singing the call and the rest of the class singing the response. Create additional verses to the song and perform them as a solo caller while the rest of the class sings the responses.

Sing and Swing

In the late 1950s and early 1960s, some songs with nonsense words were called doo-wop.

Sing "We Go Together," a song written in the style of 1950s rock 'n' roll. Then **identify** the nonsense words.

We Go Together

CD 2–27

from *Grease*

Lyrics and Music by Warren Casey and Jim Jacobs

1. We go to-geth-er, ___ like ra-ma la-ma la-ma ka
2. We're one of a kind _____ like dip da dip da dip

ding-a da ding ___ a-dong, Re-mem-bered for -
doo-wop ___ da doo-bee doo. Our names ___ are

ev - er _____ as shoo-bop sha wad-da wad-da
signed _____ boog-e-dy boog-e-dy boog-e-dy boog-e-dy

yip-pi-ty boom-de boom. Chang chang
shoo-by-doo-wop ___ she-bop Chang chang

EXPLORING MUSIC

chang-it - ty chang _ shoo-bop,   that's   the   way   it ____ should
chang-it - ty chang _ shoo-bop,   we'll al - ways   be _____ like

be. _____   wha - oooh,   yeah!   one, _____

wa   wa __   wa   waah. _____   When   we   go

out   at   night, _   and   stars   are   shin - in'   bright _

up   in   the   skies   a - bove, _____   or   at   the

high school dance, _   where you   can   find   ro - mance, _

may - be   it   might   be   lo - uh - uh - uh - uh - uh-ove.

Vocal Improvisation   Rama lama lama ka dinga da ding a dong,
Shoobop sha wadda wadda yippity boom de boom,
Chang chang changitty chang shoo bop,
Dip da dip da dip doo wap da doo bee doo,
Boogedy boogedy boogedy boogedy shooby doo wop shebop,
Sha na na na na na na na dinga da dinga dong
(Repeat)

Wop ba-ba loo-bop, a - wop bam boom   We're for each oth - er ___ like

wop   ba - ba   loo-bop,   a - wop   bam   boom. _   Just   like   my

broth - er ___   is   sha-na - na - na - na - na - yip - pi - ty dip __ de doom.

Chang chang   chang-it - ty chang _ shoo-bop,   we'll   al - ways

be _____ to - geth - er, _____   wha - oooh,   yeah!   We'll

al - ways ___   be to - geth - er. _____   We'll

al - ways ___ be to - geth-er. ___   Wop ba-ba, loo-bop, a-wop bam boom!

46

Doo-Wop Singing

Doo-wop groups usually had four or five vocalists and a rhythm section, which included guitar, bass, drums, and piano. The Four Tops, the Platters, and the Five Satins are three famous doo-wop groups. Can you name any others?

Listen to *In the Still of the Night,* the Five Satins' biggest hit.

CD 2–29
In the Still of the Night

by Fred Parris
as performed by the Five Satins

Forty years after this song's initial release, the group Boyz II Men recorded their own version of this doo-wop classic.

M·U·S·I·C M·A·K·E·R·S

The Five Satins

Fred Parris formed **The Five Satins,** a doo-wop singing group, in 1954 while he was still in high school. Parris wrote the song *In the Still of the Night* two years later. The song made the Five Satins famous.

Tempo Time

"Walk! Don't run!" When someone says that to you, what do you do? You change the speed of your movement. In music, **tempo** can help communicate the feeling of a song.

> **Tempo** is the speed of the beat.

Read the words of "Oh, Danny Boy." Before you **sing** the song, decide what tempo would be best.

CD 2–30

Oh, Danny Boy

Words by Thomas Moore

Folk Melody from Ireland

1. Oh, Dan-ny Boy, the pipes, the pipes are call-ing,
2. But when you come and all the flow'rs are dy-ing,

From glen to glen, and down the moun-tain side;
If I am dead, as dead I well may be;

The sum-mer's gone, and all the ros-es fall-ing,
You'll come and find the place where I am ly-ing,

'Tis you, 'tis you must go, and I must bide.
And kneel and say an A-ve there for me.

What's the Best Tempo?

"Oh, Danny Boy" is based upon a famous Irish melody. Composers and musicians from many different cultures have created their own arrangements of this tune. **Listen** to this version by the Australian composer Percy Grainger (1882–1961). Here are some words you can use to describe the tempo.

adagio—slow   *andante*—walking speed   *presto*—very fast

moderato—moderate   *allegro*—fast

 CD 2–32

Irish Tune from County Derry

**Folk Melody from Ireland
arranged by Percy Grainger**

This version of the "Oh, Danny Boy" melody
is performed by a wind ensemble.

Listening for Tempo

Listen to *Hungarian Dance No. 6*, a composition for orchestra. There are many tempo changes in this music. As you listen, point to the appropriate word in the tempo meter below.

Hungarian Dance No. 6

by Johannes Brahms

The *Hungarian Dances* were inspired by folk melodies of Eastern Europe.

Hungarian Dance No. 6

LISTENING MAP

76 · Adagio · Andante · Moderato · 108 · 120 · Allegro · 168 · Presto

speed indicator

bpm

Tempo Meter

50

Do the Chicken Dance!

Listen to *The Chicken Dance* and **move** with the music. Do your movements match the tempo of the music?

CD 3–1

The Chicken Dance

by Werner Thomas

The Chicken Dance is a favorite activity at celebrations and dances.

▲ **1.** Chirp with your hands.

▲ **2.** Flap your wings.

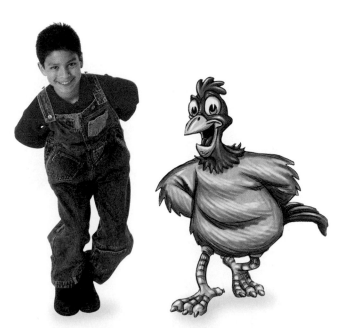

▲ **3.** Waddle downward.

▲ **4.** Clap four times.

The Score Is Tied

Rhythm is created by patterns arranged in many ways. What makes rhythm interesting is the way long and short sounds are arranged over the steady beat.

Listen to the rhythms in "Somebody's Knockin' at Your Door."

Using rhythm syllables, **read** the following rhythms. Then clap the rhythms as you **sing** the song. Are these rhythms the same as the rhythms in the song?

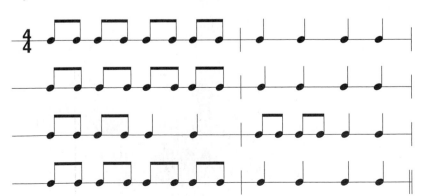

Somebody's Knockin' at Your Door

CD 3–3

African American Spiritual

Some - bod - y's knock - in' at your door,

Some - bod - y's knock - in' at your door.

Oh, _____ sin - ner, why don't you ans - wer?

Some - bod - y's knock - in' at your door.

Tie It All Together

We can notate the rhythm of the song words using the **tie**.

> A **tie** connects two notes of the same pitch.

tie   tie

Some-bod - y's knock-in' at your door, _____

Did you know tied notes can be written another way? For instance, these two rhythms sound the same:

For practice, let's add ties to the rhythms on page 52 to make them match the rhythm of the words. Be careful, the third line is tricky!

Rhythms of the Railroad

Rhythm has a powerful effect on people. Some rhythms make work easier and smoother. "Rock Island Line" is a railroad work song that uses rhythm to help everyone work together. ♪ ♩ ♪ is one important rhythm in the song. **Sing** "Rock Island Line" and **identify** this rhythm. How many times does it occur?

 CD 3–9

Rock Island Line

Edited with New Additional Material by Alan Lomax

Railroad Song
New Words and New Arrangement by Huddie Ledbetter

REFRAIN

I say the Rock Is - land Line is a might-y good road,

I say the Rock Is - land Line is the road to ride.

I say the Rock Is - land Line is a might-y good road,

If you want ___ to ride it, got to ride it like you find it,

Get your tick - et at the sta - tion for the Rock Is - land line.

VERSE

F

1. May be right and I may be wrong, —
2. A, B, C, dou - ble X, Y, Z, ——

F   C₇   F   *D.C. al Fine*

Know you're gon - na miss me ——— when I'm gone.
Cats —— in the cup - board, but they don't see me.

Syncopation is an arrange-ment of rhythm in which important notes begin on weak beats or weak parts of beats, giving an off-balance movement to the music.

All Aboard for Rhythm!

♪ ♩ ♪ is called **syncopation.**

Play these syncopated ostinatos on percussion instruments.

1.

2.

Form two groups. As everyone **sings** the song, group 1 **performs** the first ostinato, and group 2 performs the second.

Time for the Blues

If you say, "I feel blue," it usually means you feel sad about something. If you sing the blues, you are singing about your feelings.

A **time signature** is found at the beginning of most written music. Find the time signature in "Joe Turner Blues."

Perform this four-beat pattern while you **sing** "Joe Turner Blues."

1	2	3	4
pat	clap	snap	clap

The **time signature** tells how many beats are in each measure (top number) and the kind of note that gets one beat (bottom number).

CD 3–14
MIDI 5

Joe Turner Blues

Blues Song from the United States

1. They tell me __ Joe Turn-er's __ come and gone, __
2. He came here __ with for-ty __ links of chain, __
3. Joe Turn-er, __ he took my __ man a-way, __

They tell me __ Joe Turn-er's __ come and gone. __
He came here __ with for-ty __ links of chain. __
Joe Turn-er, __ he took my __ man a-way, __

He left me __ here to sing ____ this ____ song.

Singing the Blues

The first blues songs were recorded in the 1920s. **Listen** to another example of the blues. **Move** to the beat in $\frac{4}{4}$ meter. What is the performer of *St. Louis Blues* singing about?

CD 3–17

St. Louis Blues

by W.C. Handy; as performed by W.C. Handy's Memphis Blues Band

St. Louis Blues is one of many famous blues melodies. It was first published in 1914.

▲ In 1926, W.C. (William Christopher) Handy published a book of blues songs composed by himself and others. He is called the "Father of the Blues."

Show What You Know!

1. Clap and **perform** these rhythms using rhythm syllables. **Identify** the song.

2. Write your own rhythms in $\frac{4}{4}$ meter. Use one example of syncopation and one rest.

One Song—Two Sections

Think of a river in your town or state. **Listen** to the song "River," then **sing** along.

CD 3–18

River

Words and Music by Bill Staines

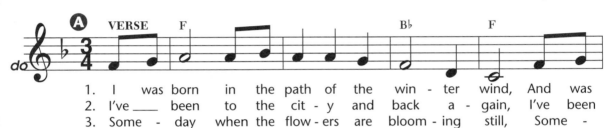

A VERSE

1. I was born in the path of the win - ter wind, And was
2. I've ___ been to the cit - y and back a - gain, I've been
3. Some - day when the flow - ers are bloom - ing still, Some -

raised where the moun - tains are old. _____ The
moved by some things _ that I've learned. _____ Met a
day when the grass _ is still green, _____ My

spring - time _____ wa - ters came danc - ing down, I re -
lot of ___ good peo - ple and I've called them my friends, Felt the
roll - ing _____ riv - er will round the bend And flow

mem - ber the tales they told. _____ The whis - tling ___
change when the sea - sons turned. _____ I've heard all the
in - to the o - pen sea. _____ So here's to the

ways of my young - er days Too quick - ly have
songs that the chil - dren sing And lis - tened to
rain - bow that's followed me here, And here's to the

Different Ways to Move

Move to show the different sections of "River." **Improvise** one motion for the **Ⓐ** section **(verse)** and one for the **Ⓑ** section **(refrain)**. Move as you **listen** to the song.

A **verse** is a section of a song where the melody stays the same when it repeats, but the words change.
A **refrain** is a section of a song that is sung the same way every time it repeats.

fad - ed on by. _____ But all of the mem - o - ries
love's _ mel - o - dies, _____ I've felt my own mus - ic with -
friends _ that I know, _____ And here's to the song that's with -

lin - ger still, Like the light in a fad - ing sky. _____
in me rise Like the wind in the au - tumn trees. _____
in me now; I will sing it where' - er I go. _____

REFRAIN

Riv - er, take me a - long, In your sun - shine sing me your

song. Ev - er mov - ing and wind - ing and _ free, You

roll - ing old riv - er, you chang - ing old riv - er, Let's

you and me, riv - er, Run down to the sea. _____

Sing It with Signing

Practice the signs below, then **sing** and sign the refrain of "River."

▲ river   ▲ sunshine   ▲ rolling

Flowing Along

Listen to *The Boatman's Dance*. This song has a verse and a refrain, as well as an introduction, **interludes,** and a *coda*. **Move** to show the different sections of the music. Here are some clues to help you.

Movement Clues

An **interlude** is a short musical connection between sections of a piece of music.

- The music for the introduction, interludes, and *coda* is slow.

- The music for the verse, section **A**, is fast.

- The music for the refrain, section **B**, has the word *boat* in it.

CD 3–20
The Boatman's Dance

from *Old American Songs*
by Aaron Copland

This piece was written for solo baritone voice, orchestra, and choir.

Read the poem "River." Think about how a river moves and how the poem is divided into sections (like the song in this lesson). Then **create** expressive movements while a friend reads the poem aloud.

River

by Lawrence Locke

The river moans.
The river sings.

Listen to the Fox, the Menominee,
The Susquehanna, Colorado, Platte,
The Ottowa, Snake, Bear,
And the Delaware.

Listen to the river.
The river moans.
The river sings.

The river is always going home.

Melody Goes 'Round

Ledger lines are extra lines for pitches above and below the staff.

"*Hashewie*" comes from Eritrea in North Africa. It is a pentatonic song. **Sing** the pentatonic scale as indicated in the color box. Remember to use hand signs.

so₁ la₁ do re mi so la

The notes outside the color box are low *la* and low *so*. When *do* is written in a space on the staff, low *la* is in the space below. In the scale above, *do* is in the bottom space. Low *la* must be written in a space below the staff and low *so* is written on a **ledger line.**

▼ Eritrean independence celebration

Sing these pentatonic patterns. Which ones can you find in *"Hashewie"*?

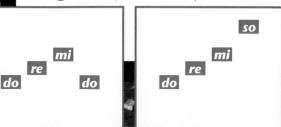

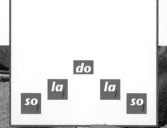

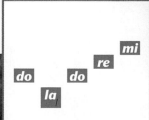

Reading low *la* and low *so*

Read "*Hashewie*" using pitch syllables and hand signs. Then **sing** the leader's part while your friends sing the response *Shewie*.

CD 3–21

Hashewie
(Going 'Round)

Tigrinya Words by Hidaat Ephrem

Folk Song from Eritrea, Africa

Call
Ha - shew - i - e_____
I will go 'round, _

Response
Shew - i - e
Shew - i - e

Call
Ha - shew - i - e_____
You will go 'round, _

Response
_____ Shew - i - e
_____ Shew - i - e

Call
Ha - shew - i - e
We all go 'round, _

Response
_____ Shew - i - e.
Shew - i - e.

Fine

Call (Tigrinya)
Bi - ha - de ha - bir - na
Ha-shew - ie e - na - bel - na
A - lem kit - fel - to
Ku - lu - me - nin - et - na
Ha-shew - i - e ni - bel
Nef' - lit - a - di - na
Bi - ha - de ha - bir - na

Response
Shew - i - e.

D. C. al Fine

Call (English)
All to - geth - er 'round,
Say - ing 'round and 'round,
So the world would know,
Who ____ we ____ are,
Let's ____ say ____ 'round,
All to - geth - er 'round,
Go - ing 'round and 'round,

Response
Shew - i - e.

D.C. al Fine

Tune In

"In Eritrea, you sing wherever you are. I'm used to singing when I'm walking, and learned many Eritrean values through song."
Hidaat Ephrem

Unit 2   63

Scale the Mountain

Have you ever climbed a mountain or been to the top of a tall building? You probably saw things from the top that you could never see from the bottom. Let's climb the pentatonic mountain below and discover what's at the top.

You already know some notes below *do.* Now **identify** the mystery note at the top of the pentatonic scale.

Sing the notes up and down the pentatonic scale. Then try skipping around from *do* to all the other notes.

Read this melody using pitch syllables and hand signs.

mi   do   re   do   la,   so,   do   re   mi   so   mi   re   do

so   so   la   do'   la   mi   so   so   so   la   mi   re   do

Sourwood Mountain

Folk Song from the Appalachian Mountains

1. Chic-ken crow-in' on Sour-wood Moun-tain, Hey, de-ing dang did-dle al-ly day.

So ma-ny pret-ty girls I can't count 'em, Hey, de-ing dang did-dle al-ly day.

My true love, she lives in Letch-er, Hey, de-ing dang did-dle al-ly day.

She won't come and I won't fetch her, Hey, de-ing dang did-dle al-ly day.

2. My true love's
   a blue-eyed daisy, Hey, . . .
   If I don't get her
   I'll go crazy, Hey, . . .
   Big dogs bark
   and little ones bite you, Hey, . . .
   Big girls court
   and little ones slight you, Hey, . . .

3. My true love
   lives by the river, Hey, . . .
   A few more jumps
   and I'll be with her, Hey, . . .
   My true love
   lives up in the hollow, Hey, . . .
   She won't come
   and I won't follow, Hey, . . .

Mountain Music

Create a pentatonic ostinato to accompany "Sourwood Mountain." Take turns playing the ostinato while others **sing** the song.

Tune In

"Sourwood Mountain" is from the Southern Appalachian Mountains and is often played on the fiddle. American pioneer fiddlers kept alive the traditional tunes of their ancestors from England, Ireland, and Scotland.

Melody Rhymes in Time

Humor can be expressed in any language. **Listen** for the humorous Spanish rhymes in this song.

CD 3–33
MIDI 6

Riqui rán

Translated by J. Olcutt Sanders   *Folk Song from Latin America*

1. A - se - rrín,   a - se - rrán. Los ma - de - ros de San Juan   co - men
1. A - se - rrín,   a - se - rrán. All the woods-men of San Juan   eat their

que - so, co - men pan. Los de Ri - que, al - fe - ñi - que; los de
cheese and eat their pan. Those from Ri - que, al - fe - ñi - que; Those from

Ro - que, al - fon - do - que, Ri - qui,   ri - que, ri - qui rán. 2. A - se -
Ro - que, al - fon - do - que, Ri - qui,   ri - que, ri - qui rán. 2. A - se -

rrín,   a - se - rrán. Las a - be - jas vie - nen, van; Miel la -
rrín,   a - se - rrán. Los chi - qui - llos ¿dón - de es - tán? To - dos
rrín,   a - se - rrán. All the bees fly hith - er, yon; Gath - er
rrín,   a - se - rrán. Where have all the chil - dren gone? They have

bo - ran pa - ra el pan. Li - ban flor - es las de Ri - que cual al -
a dor - mir se van. So - ña - rán con al - fe - ñi - que co - mo
nec - tar for their pan. Sip - ping from the flowers of Ri - que nec - tar
put their night-gowns on. They will dream of al - fe - ñi - que as the

66

mi - bar de al - fe - ñi - que, Y el pa - nal de los de Ro - que se pa -
sue - ñan los de Ri - que, Y ma - ña - na un al - fon - do - que co - me -
sweet as al - fe - ñi - que, Just as hon - ey combs of Ro - que look like
chil - dren dream in Ri - que, And to - mor - row al - fon - do - que they will

re - ce a un al - fon - do - que. Ri - qui, ri - que, ri - qui rán. 3. A - se -
rán con los de Ro - que. Ri - qui, ri - que, ri - qui rán.
loaves of al - fon - do - que. Ri - qui, ri - que, ri - qui rán. 3. A - se -
eat with those from Ro - que. Ri - qui, ri - que, ri - qui rán.

Name It and Play It

Name the notes in this melody for recorder. **Play** the melody with the first four measures of each verse of *"Riqui rán."*

Name the notes below and find these measures in *"Riqui rán."*

Show What You Know!

1. **Sing** this melody using pitch syllables.

2. Now **identify** the letter names for the pitches above. **Play** the melody on a xylophone or keyboard.

3. **Sing** this melody using pitch syllables. Then sing the notes using letter names and **play** the melody on recorder.

Each instrument has its own special sound, or timbre. To make a sound on most wind instruments, the player blows air into the instrument, causing the air to vibrate. The string instrument's sound is made by vibrating strings. **Sing** this Italian song about six instruments.

CD 3–37
MIDI 7

Eh, cumpari! (Hey, Buddy!)

Words and Music by Julius La Rosa and Archie Bleyer

Eh,   cum - pa   –   ri!   Ci   vo'   su   –   na   –   ri.
Hey,   good   bud   –   dy!   It's   time   to   play! _____

Chi   si   so   –   na

1. 'U   fris - ca   - let   –   tu?
2. 'U   sax   - o   - fo   –   na?
3. 'U   man - du   - li   –   nu?

Who   will   play   on

1. the   pic - co - lo? _____
2. the   sax   - o   - phone? __
3. the   man - do   - lin? _____

E   co - mu   si   so   –   na

'u   fris - ca   - let   –   tu?
'u   sax   - o   - fo   –   na?
'u   man - du   - li   –   nu?

And how   do   you   play   on

the   pic - co - lo? _____
the   sax   - o   - phone? __
the   man - do   - lin? _____

CD-ROM Using *Making Music* software, compose a piece of music with two different timbres. Think about how you can use timbre to organize your composition.

A - fu - mm'a - fu - mm'a la trom - bon', pa - pa pa - pa a la trum -
A-foom - a - foom on the trom-bone, pa - pa - pa - pa on the trum -

be - tt', a-zing - a - zing 'u vi - u - lin, a-pling - a - pling 'u man - du -
pet, a - dzing - a - dzing the vi - o - lin, a-pling - a - pling the man - do -

lin, tu - tu tu - tu 'u sax - o - fon, *(whistle)* _____ 'u fris - ca -
lin, too-too - too - too the sax - o - phone, the pic - co -

le - tt'e ti - pi - ti ti - pi - ti - ta.
lo and ti - pi - ti ti - pi - ti - ta.

4. . . . 'U viulinu? . . .   4. . . . the violin? . . .
5. . . . A la trumbetta? . . .   5. . . . the brassy trumpet? . . .
6. . . . A la trombona? . . .   6. . . . the slide trombone? . . .

One-Minute Woodwind Mysteries

Listen to the solo instrument in each piece of music. Find the picture of the woodwind instrument you hear playing the solo. You have one minute (or less) for each selection!

CD 4–1

One–Minute Woodwind Mysteries

B.B.'s Blues
by Branford Marsalis

"Serenata"
from *Pulcinella Suite*
by Igor Stravinsky

The Bee ("L'Abeille")
by Franz Schubert

"Vivace"
from *Sonata in F Minor*
by Georg Philipp Telemann

"Aviary"
from *Carnival of the Animals*
by Camille Saint-Saens

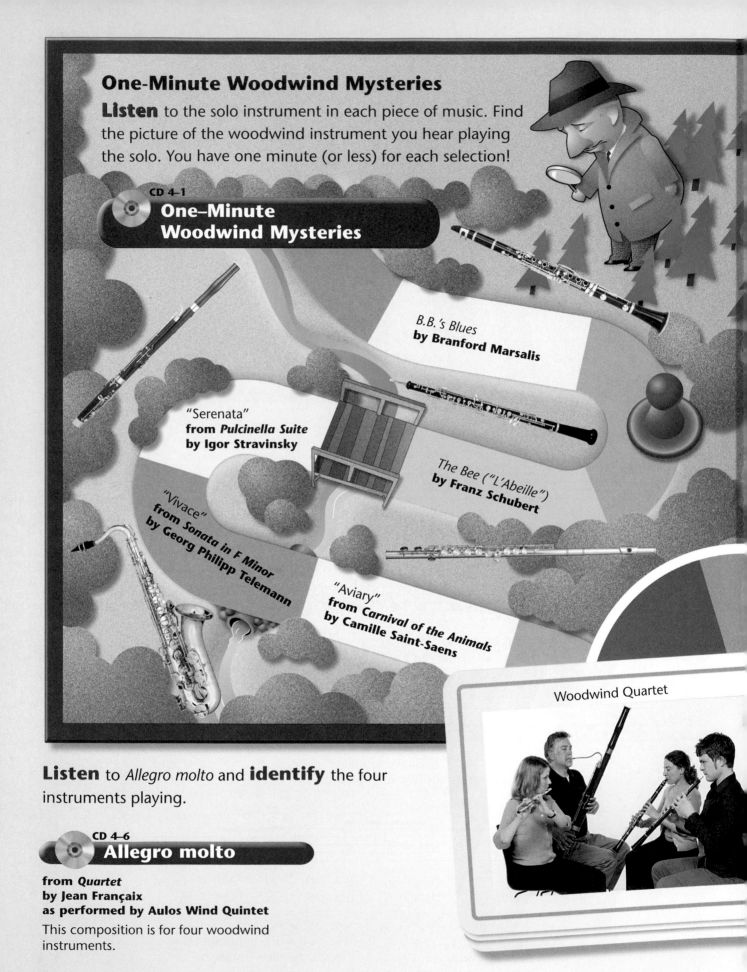

Woodwind Quartet

Listen to *Allegro molto* and **identify** the four instruments playing.

CD 4–6

Allegro molto

from *Quartet*
by Jean Françaix
as performed by Aulos Wind Quintet

This composition is for four woodwind instruments.

70

One-Minute Brass Mysteries

Listen to the solo instrument in each piece of music. Find the picture of the brass instrument playing the solo.

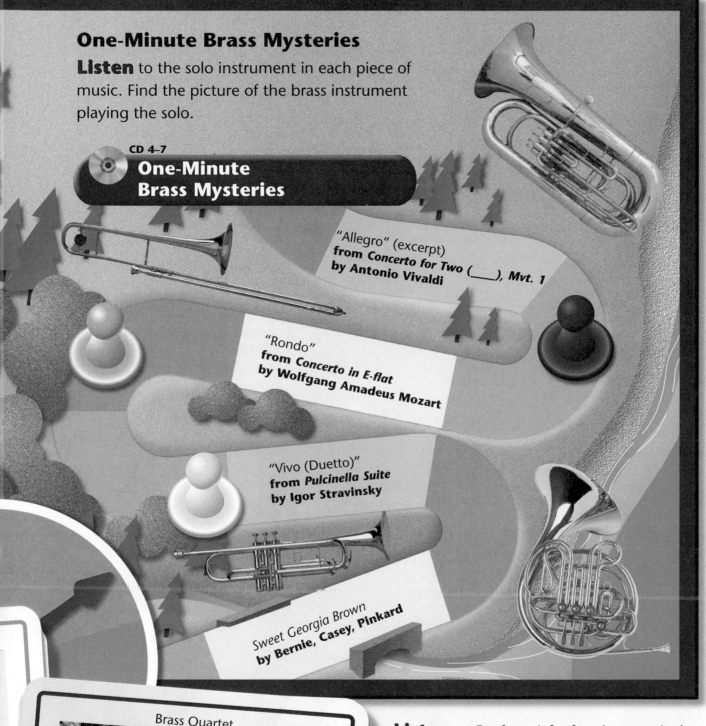

CD 4–7

One-Minute Brass Mysteries

"Allegro" (excerpt)
**from Concerto for Two (___), Mvt. 1
by Antonio Vivaldi**

"Rondo"
**from Concerto in E-flat
by Wolfgang Amadeus Mozart**

"Vivo (Duetto)"
**from Pulcinella Suite
by Igor Stravinsky**

Sweet Georgia Brown
by Bernie, Casey, Pinkard

Brass Quartet

Listen to *Fanfare*. A fanfare is a musical announcement, usually played by brass instruments. How would you **describe** this music?

CD 4–11

Fanfare

**from *La Peri*
by Paul Dukas**

Paul Dukas [doo-kah] also composed *The Sorcerer's Apprentice*, which is featured in the Disney movies *Fantasia* and *Fantasia 2000*.

Listening to Wind Instruments

Orchestras contain string, woodwind, brass, and percussion instruments. Look at this picture of an orchestra. How many woodwind and brass instruments can you **identify**?

Listen to this music for orchestra. After an introduction played by a snare drum, you will hear woodwind and brass instruments accompanied by string instruments. **Identify** the woodwind and brass instruments in the order you hear them played.

CD 4–12
Presentation of Pairs

**from *Concerto for Orchestra*
by Béla Bartók**

Concerto for Orchestra was Béla Bartók's last complete work for orchestra.

MUSIC MAKERS

Béla Bartók

Béla Bartók (1881–1945) was a composer, folk song collector, and pianist. He traveled through Hungary, Romania, Slovakia, Turkey, and North Africa recording on a phonograph and collecting thousands of songs. In his own compositions, Bartók often used the folk music he had collected—especially that of his native country, Hungary.

▼ The San Francisco Symphony Youth Orchestra, performing in Davies Symphony Hall under the direction of Resident Conductor, Edwin Outwater

Winds in the Band

Almost all of the instruments in a band are members of either the wind or percussion families. Look at this photo of a band and **identify** the various woodwind and brass instruments.

Now **listen** to this performance. Which instruments play first—woodwinds or brass?

CD 4–13
Lord Melbourne

from *Lincolnshire Posy*
by Percy Grainger

The selections in *Lincolnshire Posy* are based on folk melodies collected by Percy Grainger. Lincolnshire is a county in the eastern part of England.

MUSIC MAKERS

Marsalis Family

Ellis Marsalis ▶

◀ Wynton Marsalis

Branford, Wynton, Delfeayo, and Ellis Marsalis are members of a very musical family. Branford plays saxophone, Wynton plays trumpet, Delfeayo plays trombone, and Ellis (the father of the three brothers) plays the piano. When playing together, they make a jazz combo. As solo performers, Branford and Wynton have won several awards. They have performed on television shows such as Jay Leno's *Tonight Show*. Wynton also serves as the artistic director of "Jazz at Lincoln Center."

 CD 4–14
Knozz-Moe-King

written and performed by Wynton Marsalis

Wynton Marsalis is best-known as a jazz musician. In *Knozz-Moe-King*, he is playing a trumpet in a quartet.

▲ Delfeayo Marsalis

◀ Branford Marsalis

CD 4–15
Little Birdie

by Vince Guaraldi
as performed by the Ellis Marsalis Trio

Little Birdie is a reference to Woodstock, the bird character in the "Peanuts" cartoon strip.

CD 4–16
Allegro

from *Concerto for Two Trumpets*
by Antonio Vivaldi
as performed by Wynton Marsalis

Marsalis also performs classical music. Here, he is playing with an orchestra.

Paddle Along, Singing a Song

Have you ever paddled a canoe? To go forward, you pull the paddle through the water. You repeat this motion to keep the canoe moving. In "Canoe Song," repeated patterns help the song to move along. **Listen** to "Canoe Song" and **identify** the repeated patterns.

 CD 4–17

Canoe Song

Words and Music by Margaret E. McGhee

1. My pad - dle's keen and bright, Flash - ing with sil - ver,
2. Dip, dip and swing her back, Flash - ing with sil - ver,

Fol - low the wild goose flight, Dip, dip and swing.
Fol - low the wild goose track, Dip, dip and swing.

Sing this **ostinato** to accompany "Canoe Song."

Dip, dip and swing.

An **ostinato** is a repeated rhythm or melody pattern played throughout a piece or a section of a piece.

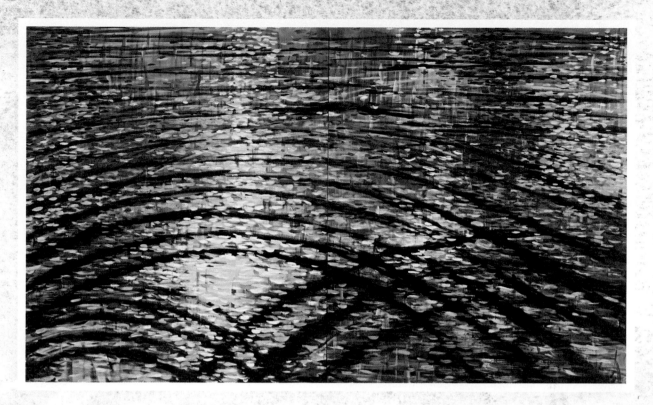

Arts Connection

▲ *Watercolor Ripple* (1995)
by the modern American artist
Gerrit Greve. What repeated
patterns do you see in this
painting?

Play an Ostinato

Adding melody ostinatos to a song changes the
musical texture. As more ostinatos are added, the
texture becomes thicker.

Practice these ostinatos for "Canoe Song." Then
perform them with the song to make the
texture thicker.

OSTINATOS EVERYWHERE

Look at the art around the edge of this page. How many repeated patterns can you find? Repeated patterns occur in music, too.

This repeated pattern is an ostinato. **Play** it on a melody instrument with *"Hey, m'tswala."*

Hey, m'tswala

Folk Song from Africa

do— Hey, m'tswa - la, ne - ye ti - pa ya - me tswa - la. ____

Create a Texture

To **create** a thicker texture, **play** these ostinatos as you **sing** "Hey, m'tswala."

Circlesong Ostinatos

Listen to *Circlesong 7*. The melody and ostinatos are by Bobby McFerrin and other musicians.

CD 4–22

Circlesong 7

by Bobby McFerrin

Bobby McFerrin says, "I've always felt that singing a song without words makes one song a thousand songs, because the people who hear it can bring their own stories to it."

M·U·S·I·C M·A·K·E·R·S

BOBBY McFERRIN

Bobby McFerrin (born 1950) began piano and music theory lessons as a child. He turned to singing in his twenties and soon became a leading vocal recording artist. Many of his recordings are *a cappella*—singing with no accompaniment. McFerrin performs in many styles, such as jazz, classical, and free improvisation. He has won many Grammy awards and is often a guest conductor of symphony orchestras.

Layers of Movement

How good are you at doing several movements at once?
Create a movement ostinato while you **listen** to
Circlesong 7. Be ready to **improvise** a movement solo
while your classmates **perform** the ostinato.

▲ Half the class improvises movements.

▲ Half the class performs the ostinato.

Patterns in Poetry

Read each of these poems from Africa.
Which poem uses a repeated pattern?

The Night

Poem of the Fipa, Africa

The night is over
before one has finished
counting the stars.

Enjoy the Earth

Poem of the Yoruba, Africa

Enjoy the earth gently
Enjoy the earth gently
For if the earth is spoiled
It cannot be repaired
Enjoy the earth gently

Review, Assess,

What Do You Know?

1. Look at the notation for "Joe Turner Blues" on page 56. Point to the time signature. How many beats are in each measure?

2. Name the title of a song in Unit 2 that has:

   a. Three beats in each measure

   b. Two beats in each measure

3. Reorder these musical terms for tempo from slowest to fastest.

   andante   presto   adagio   allegro   moderato

What Do You Hear? 2

 CD 4–23

Listen to these instrumental excerpts. Identify the instrument or instruments you hear.

1. brass	strings	woodwinds
2. brass	percussion	woodwinds
3. flute	oboe	clarinet
4. French horn	trumpet	trombone
5. clarinet	saxophone	bassoon
6. trumpet	trombone	tuba

Perform, Create

What You Can Do

Move with Rhythm

Sing "Somebody's Knockin' at Your Door," on page 53, and perform a four-beat body percussion ostinato as you sing.

Sing *"Riquirrán,"* on page 66, while performing small steady-beat movements during the verse.

Play the Notes

Play this recorder part with the recording of *"Riquirrán."* Play once through silently in chin position and then play aloud.

Move to Show Form

Listen to "River," on page 58, and create a movement for the **A** section and a different movement for the **B** section. Then perform the movements as you sing the song.

Song of Home

People often sing about places that are dear to them. In the United States, we sing our national anthem, or we sing a state song to express pride and love for our home.

"My Home's Across the Blue Ridge Mountains" is about fond memories of home. **Sing** the song and think of a place that is special to you.

CD 4–29

MY HOME'S ACROSS THE BLUE RIDGE MOUNTAINS

Collected by Louis Land Bascom

Folk Song from the Southern United States

REFRAIN
My home's __ a - cross __ the Blue Ridge Moun - tains.

My home's __ a - cross __ the Blue Ridge Moun - tains.

My home's __ a - cross __ the Blue Ridge Moun - tains.

And I may nev - er see you an - y - more.

Fine

VERSE
1. I'm go - in' back to North Caro - li - na.
2. I'm gon - na leave here Mon - day morn - in'.
3. One ____ more kiss be - fore I leave ____ you.

Learning the Language of Music

I'm go - in' back to North Caro - li - na.
I'm gon - na leave here Mon - day morn - in'.
One _____ more kiss be - fore I leave _____ you.

I'm go - in' back to North Caro - li - na.
I'm gon - na leave here Mon - day morn - in'.
One _____ more kiss be - fore I leave _____ you.

I may nev - er see you an - y - more.

D. C. al Fine

Music from the Ozarks

Listen to the Oak Ridge Boys sing about their home in *Ozark Mountain Jubilee.*

CD 4–31
Ozark Mountain Jubilee

by Roger Murrah and Scott Anders
as performed by the Oak Ridge Boys

This song is in the mountain style of the Ozarks.

M·U·S·I·C M·A·K·E·R·S

THE OAK RIDGE BOYS

This country music group consists of four main members: Joe Bonsall–tenor, Duane Allen–lead, Steve Sanders–baritone, and Richard Sterban–bass. Their music reflects the area where most of them were raised, the southern United States.

WALKING ALONG, SINGING A SONG

When people walk in groups, they sometimes like to sing walking songs. "The Happy Wanderer" is a walking song. **Sing** the two phrases in the verse of the song *legato.* In the refrain, **sing** the *ha-ha-ha's* *staccato.*

The term *legato* describes music performed in a smooth and connected style.
The term *staccato* describes music performed in a short and detached style.

Move with Expression

To help you **sing** the phrases in the verses smoothly, draw an arc in the air with your hand.

CD 4–32

THE HAPPY WANDERER

Words by Antonia Ridge

Music by Friedrich W. Möller

VERSE

1. I love to go a-wan-der-ing, A-long the moun-tain track,
2. I love to wan-der by the stream That danc-es in the sun.
3. I wave my hat to all I meet, And they wave back to me.
4. High o-ver-head, the sky-larks wing, They nev-er rest at home,

And as I go I love to sing, My knap-sack on my back.
So joy-ous-ly it calls to me, "Come! Join my hap-py song!"
And black-birds call so loud and sweet From ev-'ry green-wood tree.
But just like me, they love to sing, As o'er the world we roam.

REFRAIN

Val-de-ri (val-de-ri) val-de-ra, (val-de-ra) val-de-ri, (val-de-ri) val-de

ra, ha, ha, ha, ha, ha, Val-de-ri, (val-de-ri) val-de-ra, (val-de-ra)

My knap-sack on my back.
"Come! Join my hap-py song!"
From ev-'ry green-wood tree.
As o'er the world we roam.

Hear the Difference

Listen to a *legato* theme while you follow the notation. The curved lines in the score are called **slurs.**

A **slur** is a curved line connecting two or more notes of different pitch that tells the performer to play or sing the notes *legato.*

Joseph Haydn

CD 4–34

Serenade, Op. 3, No. 5

by Joseph Haydn

Serenade was written for string quartet.

In this piece, the violins always play *legato.* Sometimes they play two-note slurs, which connect the notes. Slurs above or below the noteheads look like this:

Now **listen** to the viola and cello. They are playing **pizzicato** [pit-see-KAH-toh].

The term **pizzicato** refers to plucking the strings instead of bowing.

Listen to the entire *Serenade.*
Create movements to show the difference between *legato* and *pizzicato.*

Listen to a string quartet movement that is played <u>only</u> *pizzicato.* How do the performers make the notes sound more expressive?

CD 4–35

Allegretto pizzicato

**from *String Quartet No. 4*
by Béla Bartók**

See page 73 for a Music Makers feature on this composer.

Franz Joseph Haydn

Joseph Haydn (1732–1809) was born in a small town in Austria, near the Hungarian border. He had a beautiful singing voice. At the age of eight, he was asked to go to Vienna and join the choir of St. Stephen's Cathedral. As an adult, he supported his family by serving as a royal court musician for a noble family named Esterházy. In this job, he wrote music to please the royal family. He had his own maid and footman, as well as a good salary. Haydn wrote more than 100 symphonies. He lived a long life and died a world-famous figure.

Rhythm and Dance

Listen to "Paw-Paw Patch," a popular game song. This version comes from the Ozark Mountains in Missouri, Arkansas, and Oklahoma. A paw-paw is a wild fruit that grows throughout the South.

Sing the words of "Paw-Paw Patch" as you tap a steady beat. Then **sing** them again as you clap the rhythm. How many sounds did you clap on the beats in the color boxes?

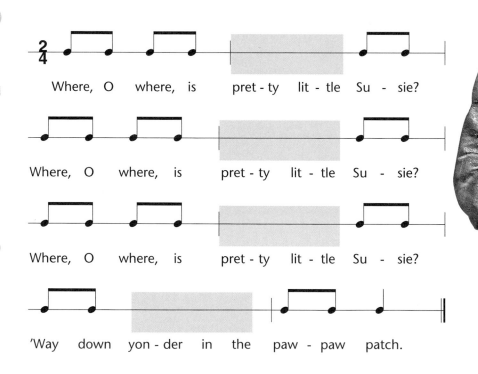

$\frac{2}{4}$ Where, O where, is pret - ty lit - tle Su - sie?

Where, O where, is pret - ty lit - tle Su - sie?

Where, O where, is pret - ty lit - tle Su - sie?

'Way down yon - der in the paw - paw patch.

Arts Connection

This wooden folk art carving of a fiddle player is from the Ozark Mountain region. ▶

Paw-Paw Patterns

When there are four even sounds on a beat, they can be notated like this.

Read the song again using rhythm syllables. **Perform** it with body percussion.

♩ stamp	♫ clap	pat

CD 4–36

Paw-Paw Patch

Play–Party Song from the United States

F

1. Where, O where, is pret - ty lit - tle Su - sie?
2. Come on, boys, ____ let's ____ go ____ find her,
3. Pickin' up paw - paws, put 'em in her pock - ets,

C₇

Where, O where, is pret - ty lit - tle Su - sie?
Come on, boys, ____ let's ____ go ____ find her,
Pickin' up paw - paws, put 'em in her pock - ets,

F

Where, O where, is pret - ty lit - tle Su - sie?
Come on, boys, ____ let's ____ go ____ find her,
Pickin' up paw - paws, put 'em in her pock - ets,

C₇   F

'Way down yon - der in the paw - paw patch.

Party Time

In the frontier days, before television and stereos were in most homes, the "play-party" was a popular singing and dancing game. Young people made up motions to familiar songs and accompanied their plays with singing. The fiddle and banjo were often used in play-parties.

Sing and **move** to "Paw-Paw Patch," and you'll see why it was one of the favorites.

▲ Lead girl walks around the lines.

▲ Lead girl walks around the lines and boys follow.

▲ Partners join hands and walk the same pathway.

▲ Partners take turns joining both hands and forming an arch while others pass under.

Listen to *College Hornpipe* and follow the  pattern throughout the music.

CD 5–1

College Hornpipe

Traditional

College Hornpipe features Yo-Yo Ma, cello; Edgar Meyer, bass; and Mark O' Connor, fiddle.

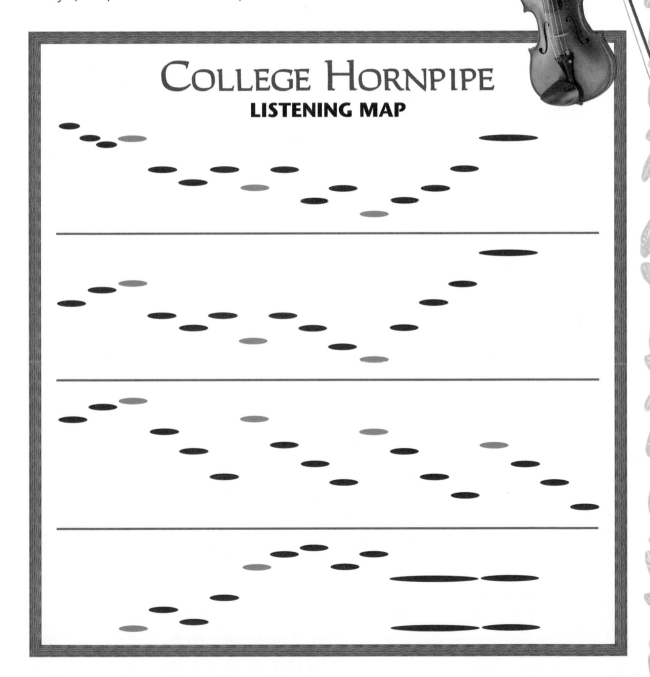

COLLEGE HORNPIPE
LISTENING MAP

Rhythm in the Wind

The song *"Ōsamu kosamu"* is about children facing the bitter cold wind.

Look at the music for *"Ōsamu kosamu."* How many groups of  can you find?

Listen for the pattern in the song *"Ōsamu kosamu."*

CD 5–2

Ōsamu kosamu (Biting Wind)

English Words by Gloria J. Kiester

Folk Song from Japan

1. Ō - sa - mu, ko - sa - mu, _____
   Bit-ing wind, __ bit-ing cold; _____

2. Ya - ma-ka-ra ko - zoo ga na - i - te - ki - ta ____
   Child-ren of the moun-tains are cry-ing from the cold; __

na - n to it - te na - i - te - ki - ta? _____
Why are they cry-ing, cry-ing from the cold? _____

"Sa-mu-i to it - te na - i - te - ki - ta!"
"We are in the wind; it's bit-ter, bit-ter cold!"

96

1 Ō - sa - mu ko - sa - mu. _____
  Bit - ing wind, __ bit - ing cold. _____

2 Ko - sa - mu. _____
  Bit - ing cold. _____

Practicing Rhythms

Play this percussion accompaniment while others
sing "Ōsamu kosamu" in two parts.

Xylophone

Metallophone

Finger Cymbal

Cymbal

Bass Metallophone

Tune In

The *koto*, featured in the recording of Ōsamu kosamu, is the national instrument of Japan. It generally has 13 strings. The sound is produced by plucking the silk strings.

SHINING WITH METER

The song "Rise and Shine" can make you want to sing and dance. The time signature is $\frac{4}{4}$. This tells you there are four beats in every measure. **Bar lines** divide the song into measures. Look at the rhythm below. Notice where the bar lines are placed.

> A **bar line** is the vertical line drawn through a staff to separate measures.

bar line

Clap the rhythm above. **Create** new measures in $\frac{4}{4}$ time by saying first names of classmates in rhythm.

Sing "Rise and Shine."

 CD 5–7

RISE AND SHINE

Folk Song from the United States

do

1. Rise ___ and shine ___ and give God the glo - ry, glo - ry.
2. God said to No - ah, "There's gonna be a flood - y, flood - y."
3. No - ah, he built him, he built him an ark - y ark - y.
4. Ani - mals, they came on, they came on by two - sies, two - sies.

Rise ___ and shine ___ and give God the glo - ry, glo - ry.
God said to No - ah, "There's gonna be a flood - y, flood - y."
No - ah, he built him, he built him an ark - y ark - y.
Ani - mals, they came on, they came on by two - sies, two - sies.

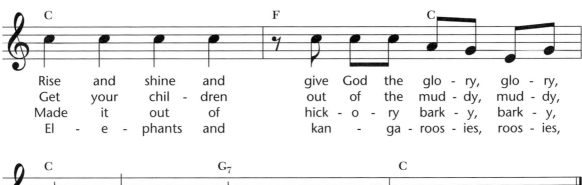

Rise and shine and | give God the glo - ry, glo - ry,
Get your chil - dren | out of the mud - dy, mud - dy,
Made it out of | hick - o - ry bark - y, bark - y,
El - e - phants and | kan - ga - roos - ies, roos - ies,

Chil - dren of the Lord.

5. Rained and rained
   for forty daysies, daysies.
   Rained and rained
   for forty daysies, daysies.
   Nearly drove those animals crazy, crazy, . . .

6. Noah, he sent out,
   he sent out a dovey, dovey.
   Noah, he sent out,
   he sent out a dovey, dovey.
   Sent him to the heavens abovey, bovey, . . .

7. Sun came out
   and dried off the landy, landy.
   Sun came out
   and dried off the landy, landy.
   Ev'rything was fine and dandy, dandy, . . .

8. This is the end,
   the end of my story, story.
   This is the end,
   the end of my story, story.
   Ev'rything is hunky-dory, dory, . . .

Show What You Know!

Move to show meter in 4. With a partner, **perform** this body percussion ostinato as you **sing** "Rise and Shine."

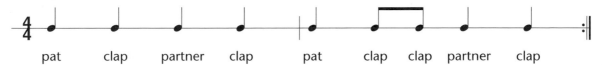

pat   clap   partner   clap   pat   clap   clap   partner   clap

BACK to the Beginning

The song "Walk in Jerusalem" is an African American spiritual. Look at the song. Notice that the **A** section is repeated after the **B** section. **Sing** "Walk in Jerusalem."

CD 5–12

WALK IN JERUSALEM

African American Spiritual

REFRAIN **A**

I want _____ to be read - y,

I want _____ to be read - y, _____

I want _____ to be read - y to

walk in Je - ru - sa - lem just like John.

Form in Movement

Show the four phrases of the **A** section by making an arc in the air. Then **create** your own movement for the **B** section.

VERSE **B**

1. John said the cit - y was just four square, _
2. John, oh, ____ John, __ what do you say? ____

Walk in Je - ru - sa - lem just like John, And
Walk in Je - ru - sa - lem just like John, That

he de - clared he'd meet me there! ___
I'll be there in the com - ing day, ____

D.C. al Fine

Walk in Je - ru - sa - lem just like John.
Walk in Je - ru - sa - lem just like John.

Add a Section and Mix

"Walk in Jerusalem" and the jazz song below are in different styles. But they do have something in common. **Listen** to "Cement Mixer" and **identify** the order of the Ⓐ and Ⓑ sections. How is this form similar to that of "Walk in Jerusalem"? How is it different?

CD 5–14

Cement Mixer

Words and Music by Slim Gaillard and Lee Ricks

Ce - ment mix - er! put - ti, put - ti,

Ce - ment mix - er! put - ti, put - ti,

Ce - ment mix - er! put - ti, put - ti,

A pud-dle o' voot - y, pud-dle o' goot - y, pud-dle o' scoot - y.

Picture This

Russian composer Modest Mussorgsky [moo-SORG-skee] (1839–1881) was inspired to write musical descriptions of a series of paintings. **Listen** to one example. It illustrates another variation of ABA form.

CD 5–16

The Hut of Baba Yaga

from *Pictures at an Exhibition*
by **Modest Mussorgsky (orchestrated by Maurice Ravel)**

Baba Yaga is a fiendish, terrifying figure from Russian folklore. How does Mussorgsky's music "paint" this image?

A pud-dle o' veet, Con - crete.

First you get some grav - el, Pour it in a vout;

To mix a mess o' mor - tar, you add ce - ment and wa - ter.

See the mel - low roon - y come out, ____ slurp, slurp, slurp.

Who wants a buck - et of ce - ment?

A Multiplication Melody

la
so

mi
re
do

la₁
so₁

This American play-party song is based on an old song from Scotland. "Charlie" is really Bonnie Prince Charles Stuart. Many songs have been written about his valiant, but unsuccessful, attempts to restore his family to the Scottish throne in the 1700s.

Do you recognize the scale shown on this pitch ladder? What kind of scale is it?

First, notice where *do* is placed on the staff. In this song, *do* is written on line two. **Identify** the other notes of the scale from the lines and spaces on the staff. **Read** the scale using pitch syllables and hand signs.

Twistification Hand Game

Sing "Weevily Wheat." The multiplication game mentioned in the last two lines of "Weevily Wheat" is known as "Twistification." **Create** your own verses using other multiplication tables.

CD 5–17

Weevily Wheat

Traditional

Don't want your wee-vi-ly wheat, Don't want your bar-ley.

Take some flour in half an hour and bake a cake for Char-lie.

Five times five is twen-ty-five, Five times six is thir-ty.

Five times sev'n is thir-ty-five, Five times eight is for-ty.

Twistification Hand Game ▼

A New Home Tone

mi
re
do

la,
so,

Even though "See the Children Playin'" uses the same notes as "Weevily Wheat" in its scale, it sounds very different. Can you figure out why?

"See the Children Playin'" uses the notes of the pentatonic scale, and its **tonic** note is low *la*. Its scale is called the *la*-pentatonic scale.

The **tonic** is the key, or home, tone in a scale.

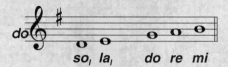

do   so, la,   do re mi

Arts Connection

▼ *Children Dancing* (1948) is by Robert Gwathmey. He is famous for painting scenes from African American life.

See the Children Playin'

Words by Reginald Royal

Folk Melody from Mississippi

1. See ___ the chil-dren play - in', two - by - two play - in',
2. Ma - ma calls the chil-dren, "Do ___ your chores now, chil-dren."

In ___ the fields play - in', and the work ain't done play - in'.
In ___ the fields chil-dren, dad-dy's com - in' home chil-dren.

Ma - ma she's watch-in', chil - dren play - in' watch-in',
See ___ the chil-dren play - in', with ___ their dad - dy play - in',

And it's get - tin' late watch-in' still the work ain't done watch-in'.
And their ma - ma too play - in', 'cause the work's all done play - in'.

Read the song using pitch syllables and hand signs. Use *do* to find your starting pitch.

Hear the Children Playin'

Perform these ostinatos with the song.

Follow that Melody!

"*Son macaron*" is believed to be a nonsense song. **Listen** to the song and follow the graph of the melody on the right.

Look at the song notation and use *do* to find your way around the staff. What is the starting pitch?

You may notice a note on the staff that you do not yet know. **Read** the song with pitch syllables and hum the mystery note. How many times does it occur in this song?

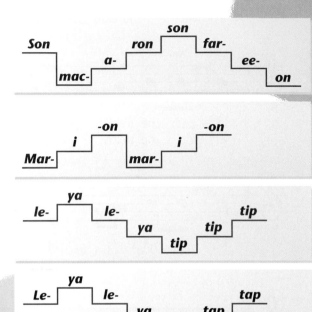

One beat, two beats, three beats. Catch!

Stay in the Game

Sing "*Son macaron.*" After you learn the song, play the game.

CD 5–27

Son macaron

Traditional

Son   ma - ca - ron,   son   far - ee - on.

Mar - i - on,   mar - i - on,   le - ya le - ya   tip tip tip.

Le - ya le - ya   tap tap tap.   One beat,   two beats,   three beats,   catch!

Show What You Know!

Identify whether these melodies are *do-* or *la-*pentatonic.

1.

2.

3.

4.

Compose a melody using the G-pentatonic scale. Choose either *do* or *la* as your tonic.

Strings and Things

Almost every culture has instruments that produce sound through the vibration of strings. Here are some examples of instruments from various cultures. **Listen** to *String Instrument Montage* to hear how these instruments sound.

CD 5–29
String Instrument Montage

▲ The **koto** [KOH-toh] is a Japanese zither with usually 13 strings. The body is a long rectangular box.

◄ The European **lute** [loot] was an important instrument of the Renaissance period (1450–1600).

The **sitar** [SIH-tahr] is a string instrument of north India. There are seven strings, which are plucked. Nine to 13 additional strings vibrate to give a special sound to the instrument. ▶

The **rebab** [REH-bahb] dates from the eighth century and is thought to be the ancestor of the violin. ▶

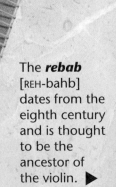

MUSIC MAKERS

Wolfgang Amadeus Mozart

Wolfgang Amadeus Mozart [MOHT-sahrt] (1756–1791) was a child prodigy who grew up in Salzburg, Austria. Many people consider him to be one of the greatest composers. His father, Leopold, was a musician who taught Wolfgang and his sister piano, violin, and music theory. When they were very young, Leopold took them all over Europe, where they played concerts. Wolfgang composed his first symphony at age eight, his first oratorio at age eleven, and his first opera at age twelve.

Strings of the Symphony Orchestra

Listen to Mozart's *Eine kleine Nachtmusik.* You will hear the traditional string instruments of the symphony orchestra—violin, viola, cello, and string bass.

 CD 5–30
Eine kleine Nachtmusik

by Wolfgang Amadeus Mozart
This piece is a minuet and trio. Minuets originally were courtly dances, and they are always in meter in 3.

Tune In

"I am never happier than when I have something to compose, for that, after all, is my sole delight and passion."
Wolfgang A. Mozart

Arts Connection

▲ *Danse dans un Pavillion*
by Jean Antoine Watteau
(1684–1721). The dancers in
this painting are performing
a courtly dance, similar to the
minuet.

W.A. Mozart

Moving to the Music

Hum this melody from *Eine kleine
Nachtmusik.* Choose a partner and walk
gracefully toward each other for two
measures and away for two measures.

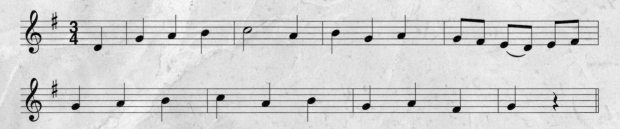

Tune In

When Mozart was a child, he enjoyed stunts such as playing piano with his hands hidden under a cloth so that he couldn't see the keys.

Classical Music—Here and Now

Many great classical composers are so widely respected that musicians today continue to perform their works. **Listen** to Bach's *Gigue* for solo violin, performed by Hilary Hahn.

CD 5–31
Gigue

from *Partita in E Major*
by **Johann Sebastian Bach**
as performed by **Hilary Hahn**

The *gigue,* or jig, is a dance originally from Ireland and England.

MUSIC MAKERS

Hilary Hahn

Hilary Hahn (born 1979) began playing violin at age four. Amazingly, she was playing the Bach Partitas by age eight. Two years later, she was admitted to the world-renowned Curtis Institute of Music in Philadelphia. Hahn enjoys taking time in her busy concert schedule to visit classrooms to play for students and to encourage them in their musical studies. While on tour, she keeps in touch with her fans through her Web site journal, where she also sends "postcards" from cities around the world.

Partners in Song

Calypso is a lively style of music from the Caribbean. This style has African roots, but it was developed in Trinidad. "Turn the World Around" is a calypso song with three melodies that are sung at the same time. Melodies that fit together in this way are known as **partner songs.**

Sing "Turn the World Around."

> **Partner songs** are two or more different songs that can be sung at the same time to create a thicker texture.

CD 5–32

Turn the World Around

Words by Harry Belafonte

Music by Robert Freedman

1. We come from _ the fire, ____ liv - ing in ___ the fire, ____
2. We come from _ the wa - ter, liv - ing in ___ the wa - ter,
3. We come from _ the moun - tain, liv - ing on ___ the moun - tain,

Go back to ____ the fire, ____ turn the world _ a - round.
Go back to ____ the wa - ter, turn the world _ a - round.
Go back to ____ the moun - tain, turn the world _ a - round.

4. Water make the river,
   river wash the mountain,
   Fire make the sunlight,
   turn the world around.

5. Heart is of the river,
   body is the mountain,
   Spirit is the sunlight,
   turn the world around.

6. We are of the spirit,
   truly can the spirit,
   Only can the spirit,
   turn the world around.

More Songs—More Texture

Sing "So Is Life" alone and then with "Turn the World Around."

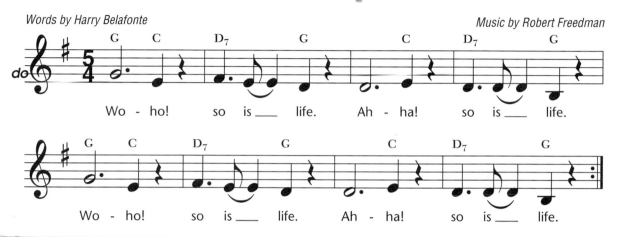

So Is Life

Words by Harry Belafonte

Music by Robert Freedman

Wo - ho! so is ___ life. Ah - ha! so is ___ life.

Wo - ho! so is ___ life. Ah - ha! so is ___ life.

Listen to the recording of "Turn the World Around." You will hear a third melody being sung to create a thicker texture. **Sing** "Do You Know Who I Am?" alone and then with "Turn the World Around" and "So Is Life."

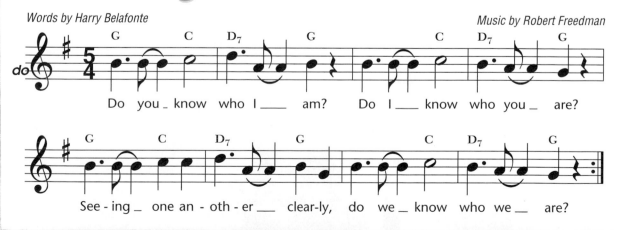

Do You Know Who I Am?

Words by Harry Belafonte

Music by Robert Freedman

Do you _ know who I ___ am? Do I ___ know who you _ are?

See - ing _ one an - oth - er ___ clear-ly, do we _ know who we _ are?

Playing Partners

Now that you can sing the partner songs, let's add some instruments. Practice each percussion part by clapping the rhythm. Now **play** an instrument.

Perform a different movement for each partner song.

▲ **1.** Move backward, then forward, and turn.

2. Touch your chest, reach up, and look side to side. ▼

The Man and His Music

Harry Belafonte is known for his performances of calypso music.

Listen to him perform *Jump in the Line.*

CD 5–34

Jump in the Line

by Harry Belafonte, Ralph DeLeon, Gabriel Oller, Steve Samuel

In this selection, Belafonte refers to getting up and dancing.

Harry Belafonte ▼

▲ **3.** Step out, raise your hands, and then step back.

Echo a Sentiment

"Over My Head" is a song strongly tied to the American Civil Rights movement.

Sing the song and make an arc in the air with one arm to help hold the long notes for four counts. During the long note held in each phrase, a second group of singers repeats the phrase. This is known as echo singing. Next, **sing** the song with a friend echoing the melody.

CD 5–35
MIDI 8

Over My Head

African American Spiritual

F

do

1. O - ver my head, (O - ver my head,) I hear mu - sic in the
2. O - ver my head, (O - ver my head,) I hear sing - ing in the

F   C₇

air. (I hear mu - sic in the air.) Yes, o - ver my head, (Yes, o - ver my
air. (I hear sing - ing in the air.) Yes, o - ver my head, (Yes, o - ver my

C₇   F

head,) I hear mu - sic in the air. (I hear mu - sic in the air.) O - ver my
head,) I hear sing - ing in the air. (I hear sing - ing in the air.) O - ver my

head, (O-ver my head,) I hear mu-sic in the air. (I hear mu-sic in the
head, (O-ver my head,) I hear sing-ing in the air. (I hear sing-ing in the

air.) There must be a God some - where.
air.)

3. Over my head,
   I hear freedom in the air . . .
   There must be a God somewhere.

4. Over my head,
   I hear victory in the air . . .
   There must be a God somewhere.

Echo Moving

Sing "Over My Head" and **create** a movement your partner can echo.

▲ 1. Create a movement.

▲ 2. Echo the movement of your partner.

Play F and C₇ Piano Chords

Follow the song notation and play these chords as you **sing**.

Element: TEXTURE/HARMONY | **Skill: PLAYING** | **Connection: SCIENCE**

MUSIC, MUSIC... EVERYWHERE

Music can be found in almost any place. Think about the sounds you hear at a construction site. The machinery creates sounds. These sounds can have a steady beat, or other rhythm pattern, and even pitch. When layered together, they create a unique texture that has a musical character. Many musicians are fascinated with these types of sounds and use them in their own compositions.

Listen to the recording of "Bundle-Buggy Boogie Woogie." Notice the layering of sounds to create texture.

CD 5–37

Bundle-Buggy Boogie Woogie

Poem by Dennis Lee   *Arranged by Konnie Saliba*

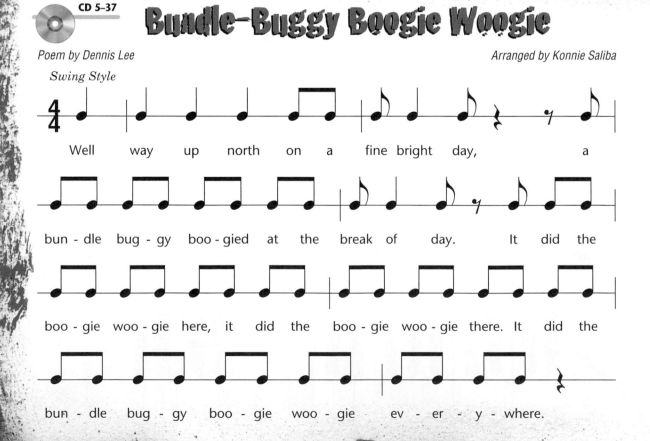

Layering with a Speech Piece

Voices can be used to create texture.

Perform "Bundle-Buggy Boogie Woogie."

TEXTURE

SOUNDS

Then an - oth - er bun - dle bug - gy did a boo - gie woo - gie hop. And an -

oth - er and an - oth - er in the bun - dle boo - gie bop. And it's

boo - gie woo - gie high and it's boo - gie woo - gie low, and it's

bun - dle bug - gy boo - gie woo - gie ev - 'ry - where you go.

Playing the Part

Create a thicker texture by adding these percussion parts to "Bundle-Buggy Boogie Woogie."

Swing Style

Listen for layers of sound and texture in this recording.

CD 5–39

Kitchen Stomp

from *Stomp Out Loud*
created by Luke Cresswell and
Steve McNicholas

Stomp Out Loud uses sounds found on the streets of New York in creative ways.

STOMP

Your Turn to Stomp

As the creators of *Stomp* know, sounds can be organized, and music can be made without traditional instruments. Let's create an indoor storm by performing these actions in sequence.

Action 1: Rub your palms together.

Action 2: Snap your fingers.

Action 3: Pat your legs lightly, getting faster.

Action 4: Stand and stamp your feet.

The storm can fade away if you reverse the order and end with rubbing your palms together.

Create another kind of composition by layering the sounds of things found in the room. Organize your composition with a beginning, a middle, and an end. Then teach the parts to your "stomp" group.

Perform your composition for your class.

M·U·S·I·C M·A·K·E·R·S

LUKE CRESSWELL and STEVE McNICHOLAS

In 1991, Luke Cresswell and Steve McNicholas created the percussion dance troupe known as *Stomp*. What is it that makes attending *Stomp* so special for people of any age? It is probably because the performers create their music from everyday items such as brooms, hubcaps, lids, and signs. They even make percussion instruments out of aluminum sinks tied around their shoulders! Both Cresswell and McNicholas believe that anyone can make music with common household items.

 Take It to the Net For more information about *Stomp*, visit *www.sfsuccessnet.com*.

Review, Assess,

What Do You Know?

1. Look at the notation for "Weevily Wheat," on page 105, and answer these questions.

   a. Where is *do* located in the music?

   b. What are the letter names for *do, re, mi, so,* and *la* in this song?

   c. Point to all the notes that are named *so$_l$* and *la$_l$*. How many did you identify?

2. Perform these examples using rhythm syllables and patting.

What Do You Hear? 3

 CD 5–40

Identify which string instrument is being played in each example.

1. *koto*   cello

2. violin   banjo

3. viola   *sitar*

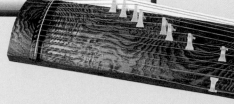

Perform, Create

What You Can Do

Read Melody

Read the notation for "See the Children Playin'," on page 107, and identify whether the song is *do*- or *la*-pentatonic. Sing the song using pitch syllables and hand signs. Sing the song again using the words.

Play Rhythms

Sing *"Ōsamu kosamu,"* on page 96. Perform the ostinato accompaniment on page 97 by patting the rhythms on your thighs. Then sing the song and play the accompaniment on the percussion instruments.

Find Sounds

Perform the speech piece "Bundle-Buggy Boogie Woogie," on page 120. Practice the rhythm ostinatos on page 122 and then perform them with the speech piece. Look around your classroom and home for materials that produce musical sounds when struck by a mallet. Create other ostinatos in $\frac{4}{4}$ time and play them using those sounds. Be sure to use the ♪♪♪♪♪ pattern. Perform these patterns with "Bundle-Buggy Boogie Woogie."

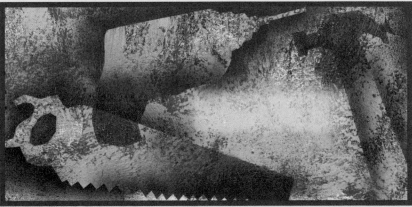

Swing It!

Listen for swing style in the Singers Unlimited version of *On Green Dolphin Street*.

CD 6–1
On Green Dolphin Street

**by Ned Washington and Bronislaw Kaper
as performed by the Singers Unlimited**
Many musicians perform *On Green Dolphin Street* because it is a jazz standard.

M·U·S·I·C M·A·K·E·R·S

The Singers Unlimited

The members of **The Singers Unlimited** are Gene Puerling (founding member), Don Shelton, Len Dresslar, and Bonnie Herman. The group gained popularity by singing jingles in the 1970s. Len Dresslar was the distinctive voice of the "green giant." Each member of the group is an accomplished vocalist. Using multiple track recording technology, the Singers Unlimited has produced amazing recordings in which the four performers sound like sixteen or more people.

Building Our Musical Skills

Swinging Music

Although swing **style** has its roots in 1930s-1940s jazz, today it is still a favorite style of music for performing, listening, and dancing.

Style is the special sound that is created when music elements such as rhythm and timbre are combined.

CD 6–2

Straighten Up and Fly Right

Swing Style

Words and Music by Nat King Cole and Irving Mills

A buz-zard took a mon-key for a ride in the air. __ The

mon-key thought that ev-'ry-thing was on the square. _ The

buz-zard tried to throw the mon-key off his back, __ but the

mon-key grabbed his neck and said, "Now lis-ten, Jack!"

Straight-en up and fly __ right. Straight-en up and fly _
Ain't no use in div - in'. What's the use in jiv -

__ right. Straight-en up and fly __ right. Cool _
- in'?

A DYNAMIC SONG

Listen for the changes in *dynamics* as you **sing** "The Lion Sleeps Tonight." When you have learned this song, **create** your own dynamic plan. Decide where the music should be softer or louder.

Playing Dynamics

Pick a percussion instrument to play one of the parts in this rhythm score. Practice playing your part. Then **perform** it with the other players. Plan different dynamics to make the piece more interesting. Now use it as an accompaniment to "The Lion Sleeps Tonight."

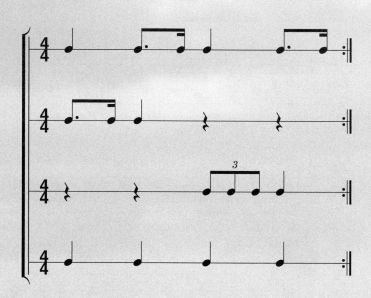

THE LION SLEEPS TONIGHT
(Wimoweh) (Mbube)

Words and Revised Music by George David Weiss,
Hugo Peretti, and Luigi Creatore

REFRAIN

Wim - o-weh, o-wim - o-weh, o-wim - o-weh, o-wim - o-weh, o-

wim - o-weh, o-wim - o-weh, o-wim - o-weh, o-wim - o-weh,

VERSE

1. In   the   jun - gle,   the   might - y   jun - gle,   the
2. Near   the   vil - lage,   the   peace - ful vil - lage,   the
3. Hush,   my   dar - ling,   don't fear,   my   dar - ling,   the

li - on   sleeps   to - night. _____
li - on   sleeps   to - night. _____
li - on   sleeps   to - night. _____

In   the   jun - gle,   the   qui - et   jun - gle,   the
Near   the   vil - lage,   the   qui - et   vil - lage,   the
Hush,   my   dar - ling,   don't fear,   my   dar - ling,   the

li - on   sleeps   to - night. _____
li - on   sleeps   to - night. _____
li - on   sleeps   to - night. _____

Lebo M.

Lebo M. (Lebo Morake, born 1966) is from South Africa. When he was fifteen, Morake left his home to pursue a music career in the United States. After studying at the Duke Ellington School of Music, he worked with the band Earth, Wind & Fire. One of his most famous projects was providing the authentic African instruments and singing for *The Lion King* Broadway production. He is a well-known musician in South Africa and the United States.

Listen for dynamic contrast as Lebo M. performs his version of *The Lion Sleeps Tonight*.

CD 6–6
The Lion Sleeps Tonight

by George David Weiss, Hugo Peretti, and Luigi Creatore as performed by Lebo M.

This version of the song is performed in the South African style of *a cappella* singing called *mbube*.

Another Dynamic Song

This lullaby from South Africa is in the Bantu language. Will you sing it loudly or softly? Why?

CD 6–7

T'HOLA, T'HOLA
(Softly, Softly)

Folk Song from South Africa

T'ho - la, t'ho - la ngoa-na - me; T'ho - la, t'ho - la ngoa-na - me,
Soft - ly, soft - ly, my ba - by; Soft - ly, soft - ly, my ba - by.

Di pe - re se - ra peng. ___ Ra - peng sa - ma ha - pu.
Hush, it is just the wind ___ Blow - ing through the branch - es.

Creating Dynamics

You can make sounds of many different dynamics with your voice. Look at these shapes on the right. First experiment with a vocal sound that each shape seems to suggest. Use a neutral syllable such as "ah." Then see how softly or loudly you can perform the sound. **Compose** a piece by putting the symbols in an order that you like. (Repeat any symbol as many times as you like.) Decide what dynamics will make your performance expressive and interesting.

FEELING UPBEAT

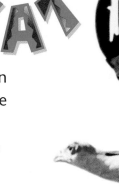

This song is about the *ochimbo* bird, which is found in Kenya and other central African countries. What is the message the singers are sending to the bird?

Sing "*Ochimbo*" and tap the strong, or first, beat of each measure.

CD 6–11
MIDI 9

OCHIMBO

Words by Margaret Marks

Folk Song from Kenya
As Sung by Ruth Nthreketha

Leader

O take your fair share, _ good fish - ing
good hunt - ing
O - chim - bo bird.

Chorus

O take your fair share, _ good fish - ing
good hunt - ing
O - chim - bo bird.

Leader

Take fish from the stream, _ good fish - ing
Take game from the plain, _ good hunt - ing
O - chim - bo bird.

Chorus

Take fish from the stream, _ good fish - ing
Take game from the plain, _ good hunt - ing
O - chim - bo bird.

Find the Upbeat

Look at the first phrase of "*Ochimbo.*" Does the phrase begin on the strong beat? When a phrase begins before a bar line, an **upbeat** occurs.

> An **upbeat** is one or more notes that occur before the first bar line of a phrase.

Play these ostinatos on drums or other percussion instruments to accompany "*Ochimbo.*" Find the upbeat in each ostinato.

Create your own ostinato to accompany "*Ochimbo.*"

This drummer belongs to the Kikuyu tribe, a farming group in Kenya. He is performing at a lodge in a game reserve. ▶

Discover a New Rhythm

Read the words of "*Ala Da'lona*." What feelings are expressed? In what way will this affect how you **sing** this song?

CD 6–18
MIDI 10

Ala Da'lona

English Words by Alice Firgau   *Arabic Folk Song*

A - la Da' - lo - na, A - la Da' - lo - na,

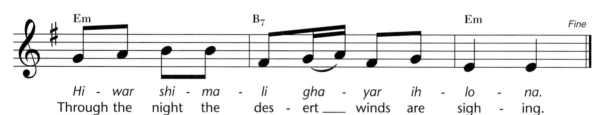

Hi - war shi - ma - li gha - yar ih - lo - na.
Through the night the des - ert ___ winds are sigh - ing.

Ma - ba - di i - mi ma - ba - di ba - yi;
Tell me where she's gone, My ___ fair Da' - lo - na,
Dark and love - ly braids,

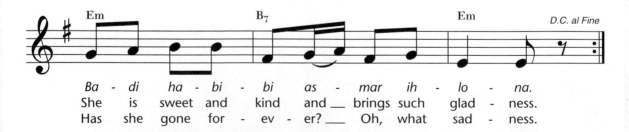

Ba - di ha - bi - bi as - mar ih - lo - na.
She is sweet and kind and ___ brings such glad - ness.
Has she gone for - ev - er? ___ Oh, what sad - ness.

Find the New Rhythm

Find the ♩♫ pattern in the song. **Read** this pattern with rhythm syllables.

Instruments of the Middle East

The recording of "*Ala Da´lona*" features an instrument called the *ud* [ood]. How does this instrument produce sound?

Listen for the *ud* and drums in the introduction of the recording of "*Ala Da´lona.*" The drums are the *tabl* [TAH-buhl] and the *darabukah* [dah-rah-BOO-kuh].

◀ The *ud* has been used in Middle Eastern music for more than 1,000 years.

Play these ostinatos on percussion instruments to accompany "*Ala Da´lona.*" Which ostinatos contain the new rhythm pattern you learned?

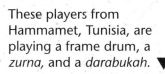

These players from Hammamet, Tunisia, are playing a frame drum, a *zurna,* and a *darabukah.* ▼

Finding New Rhythm Patterns

The Cumberland Gap is a passage through the Appalachian Mountains of Virginia, Kentucky, and Tennessee.

Look at the music for "Cumberland Gap" and find the ♪♫♪ rhythm pattern. Now **listen** carefully to hear this pattern in the song.

CD 6–22
MIDI 11

Cumberland Gap

Play-Party Song from Kentucky
Adapted by Jill Trinka

VERSE

1. Lay down, boys, take a lit-tle nap, lay down, boys, take a lit-tle nap,

Lay down, boys, take a lit-tle nap, for-ty-one miles to Cum-ber-land Gap.

REFRAIN

Cum-ber-land Gap, Cum-ber-land Gap, _____ Ooo, _____

Hoo, _____ Way low down in Cum-ber-land Gap. _____

2. Cumberland Gap is a mighty fine place, . . .
    (3 times)
   Three kinds of water to wash your face.
   Refrain

3. Cumberland Gap, with its cliffs and rocks, . . .
    (3 times)
   Home of the panther, bear, and fox.
   Refrain

4. Me and my wife and my wife's grandpap, . . .
    (3 times)
   We raise Cain at Cumberland Gap.
   Refrain

◀ *Daniel Boone Escorting Pioneers (1775)* by George Caleb Bingham (1811–1879). Boone, a legendary American frontiersman, helped blaze a trail through the Cumberland Gap.

Cumberland Patterns

Find the word *Cumberland* in the song. Ask yourself these questions.

- How many beats are used for the word *Cumberland*?

- How many sounds are on the beat?

- Does *Cumberland* have the same sound as ?

- What rhythm pattern fits with *Cumberland?*

Now **read** "Cumberland Gap" using rhythm syllables.

Show What You Know!

Show what you know and **read** the following rhythm patterns.

1.

3.

2.

4.

Create four rhythm patterns of your own using

Notate your patterns. Add words to match the rhythm. Then have a partner clap them with you.

Finding the Form

Have you ever had a day when nothing seemed to go right? In *The Wizard of Oz,* Dorothy is unhappy on her family's farm in Kansas. She sings of hope and looks for happiness "somewhere over the rainbow."

Sing Dorothy's song after listening to the recording.

CD 6–27

Over the Rainbow

Words by E. Y. Harburg

from *The Wizard of Oz*

Music by Harold Arlen

A

Some - where   o - ver the rain - bow,   way   up   high,

There's   a   land that I heard of   once in a lull - a - by.

Some - where   o - ver the rain - bow   skies   are   blue,

And   the   dreams that you dare to   dream real-ly do come true.   Some -

140

day I'll wish up-on a star and wake up where the clouds are far be-

hind me; _____ Where trou-bles melt like lem-on drops, a-

way, a-bove the chim-ney tops, that's where you'll find me.

Some - where o - ver the rain - bow blue - birds fly,

Birds fly o - ver the rain - bow, why, then, oh why, can't

Coda **3**

I? If hap-py lit-tle blue-birds fly be-

rit.

yond the rain-bow, why, oh why, can't I? _____

Find the Phrases

Find the phrases of "Over the Rainbow" that are the same. Look for a melody that repeats, even though the words are different. How many **A** phrases can you find? How many **B** phrases? What is the order of the **A** and **B** phrases in this song?

Tune In

The Wizard of Oz was just the first of many adventures for Dorothy. L. Frank Baum wrote 14 books about the "Wonderful World of Oz."

Move Over the Rainbow

As you **listen** to the recording of "Over the Rainbow" **move** to show the **A** and **B** phrases of the song.

A Make large, slow, circular motions by moving your arms through the air.

B Make small, quick, zigzag motions by moving your hand through the air in front of you.

Create your own motions to show the **A** and **B** phrases of the song. Then **move** as you **listen** to the recording again.

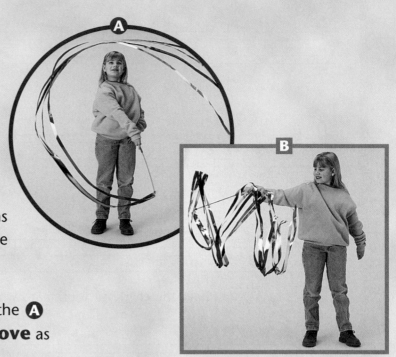

M·U·S·I·C M·A·K·E·R·S

Judy Garland

Judy Garland (1922–1969), born Frances Gumm, was one of the most famous movie stars of the 1930s and 1940s. Her career as an actress began when she was just two years old. It lasted for more than 40 years.

She was fourteen when she recorded her first album and just sixteen when the movie *The Wizard of Oz* was filmed. Her role as Dorothy made her a superstar, and her performance of *Over the Rainbow* made the song a hit. The song became her lifelong theme song.

142

Listen Over the Rainbow

Listen to two versions of "Over the Rainbow." **Describe** to a partner how they are the same, and how they are different.

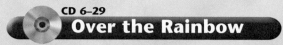

CD 6–29
Over the Rainbow

by E.Y. Harburg and Harold Arlen
as performed by Judy Garland from *The Wizard of Oz*

This song, which was almost cut from the movie, went on to win an Academy Award in 1939 for "Best Song."

CD 6–30
Over the Rainbow

by E.Y. Harburg and Harold Arlen
as performed by Aretha Franklin

This recording was made in 1960. Accompanying the 18-year-old singer, on piano, bass, and drums, is the Ray Bryant Trio. What other instruments can you hear playing softly in the background?

MUSIC MAKERS

Aretha Franklin

Aretha Franklin (born 1942), the "Queen of Soul," was born in Memphis, Tennessee. As a young girl, she sang at the Detroit church of her father, the Rev. C.L. Franklin. Her first recordings, made when she was 14, reflect her deep gospel roots. In the 1960s, high-energy, soul classics like "Respect" and "Chain of Fools" made her famous. During this period of the Civil Rights Movement, Franklin became a symbol of African Americans' growing confidence and pride.

IN SEARCH OF A New Note

Sing *Canción de cuna,* a lullaby from Latin America. The Cunas are Native Americans who live on the northern shore of Panama and the San Blas Islands.

 CD 6–31

Canción de cuna
(Cradle Song)

Folk Song from Latin America

Duer-me pron - to,　ni - ño mí - o,　Duer-me pron-to y　sin llo - rar.
Go　to sleep now,　go　to sleep now,　go　to sleep now,　lit - tle child.

Que_es - tás　en　los　bra - zos　de　tu　ma - dre, que　te　va_a can - tar.
You　are　in　your　moth-er's　arms. __　She will sing　a　lull - a - by.

A New Note

Read the five notes on the staff below. A new note goes in the color box.

la
so
fa
mi
re
do

The name of the new pitch, between *so* and *mi,* is *fa.* The step between *mi* and *fa* is called a half step because it is only half the distance of the whole steps between other pitches.

Using the pitch ladder, **sing** up and down the pitches from *do* to *la.* Now **identify** each *fa* in *"Canción de cuna."* Then **sing** the song again.

Arts Connection

▲ *Mola* textile pattern of the Cuna people

Cuna woman making a *mola* ▶

Focus on *Fa*

Find *fa* in the examples below. The *do* finder will help you find your way around the staff.

Here is another song with *fa*. The words of this song from Latin America send a silly message. **Listen** to *"Cantando mentiras."* What makes this song funny?

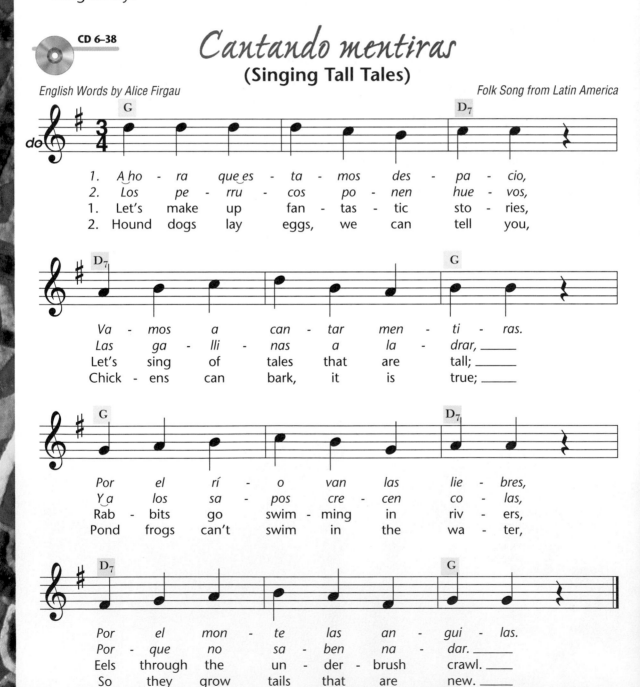

CD 6–38

Cantando mentiras
(Singing Tall Tales)

English Words by Alice Firgau

Folk Song from Latin America

1. A ho - ra que es - ta - mos des - pa - cio,
2. Los pe - rru - cos po - nen hue - vos,
1. Let's make up fan - tas - tic sto - ries,
2. Hound dogs lay eggs, we can tell you,

Va - mos a can - tar men - ti - ras.
Las ga - lli - nas a la - drar, _____
Let's sing of tales that are tall; _____
Chick - ens can bark, it is true; _____

Por el rí - o van las lie - bres,
Y a los sa - pos cre - cen co - las,
Rab - bits go swim - ming in riv - ers,
Pond frogs can't swim in the wa - ter,

Por el mon - te las an - gui - las.
Por - que no sa - ben na - dar. _____
Eels through the un - der - brush crawl. _____
So they grow tails that are new. _____

Practice *fa*

Now that you know *fa*, find the patterns below in "*Cantando mentiras.*" **Sing** the patterns as you **read** them from the staff.

1. so-fa-mi-fa   2. re-mi-fa-so   3. do-re-mi-fa-mi

One of the lines in the song contains a note you do not yet know. Point to the mystery note. You will learn about this note later.

◀ Latin guitarist

Latin Guitar

The guitar is a popular instrument throughout Latin America. You can accompany the two songs in this lesson, using just one or both chords shown below. Practice the chords first. Then **play** them as others **sing**.

MOVING A New Note

Let's see what happens to *fa* when a different note becomes *do*. Look at the half-steps and whole-steps on the keyboard below.

Fa is always a half-step above *mi*. When *do* is C, *mi* is E and *fa* is F. What happens when *do* is F? Find *fa* on the keyboard. Remember that *fa* is a half-step above *mi.*

To show this note on the staff, we mark it with a flat sign (♭) and call it B-flat.

do   re   mi   fa   so

If the flat sign is placed at the beginning of the staff, it is called a **key signature.** It means that all the Bs in this song are really B-flats.

key signature   do   re   mi   fa   so

A **key signature** tells which notes are to be performed with a flat or sharp throughout a piece of music.

whole-step

half-step   half-step   whole-step

D♭ E♭   G♭ A♭ B♭   D♭ E♭

C   D   E   F   G   A   B   C   D   E   F

What's for Sale?

Before the days of commercials, the street cry was a singing advertisement. You may have heard a similar cry from a vendor at a ball game. **Listen** to this song. What items are being advertised?

Look at the key signature of this song. Can you find *fa?* **Sing** "Chairs to Mend" using pitch syllables. Then you can sing this song as a round.

CD 7–1
MIDI 12

Chairs to Mend

Street Call from England

I
Chairs to mend, old chairs to mend.

II
Mack - er - el, fresh mack - er - el.

III
Rags? Rags? An - y old rags?

Show What You Know!

These melodies contain all of the notes you have learned. **Sing** each melody. Do any sound familiar?

1. $\frac{3}{4}$
   so so so so fa mi fa fa

2. $\frac{2}{4}$
   so mi fa so mi fa so so fa mi fa re

3. $\frac{4}{4}$
   mi fa so mi mi fa so mi mi fa so mi so fa mi

UNITED by *Melody*

At the opening ceremonies of the 1998 Winter Olympics, Seiji Ozawa [SAY-jee oh-ZAH-wah] conducted six performing groups at the same time. But this was no ordinary performance. The groups were on five different continents! Satellite technology allowed the musicians from all over the world to perform the fourth movement of Beethoven's *Symphony No. 9* together. Through this unique new way of performing, they delivered a powerful message of unity to the world.

New York

Berlin

Sydney

Beijing

Capetown

Nagano

◀ Conductor Seiji Ozawa

150

Follow that Melody!

Listen to "Ode to Joy" from Beethoven's *Symphony No. 9, Movement 4*. Follow the listening map below, and trace the **contour** of the melody with your finger.

Contour is the "shape" of a melody made by the way it moves upward and downward in steps, leaps, and repeated tones.

CD 7–6
Ode to Joy

**from *Symphony No. 9, Movement 4*
by Ludwig van Beethoven**

Beethoven [BAY-toh-vehn] had lost his hearing by the time he composed *Symphony No. 9*. This symphony was performed at the 1998 Winter Olympics in Nagano, Japan. Millions of people throughout the world heard the music that Beethoven himself heard only in his mind.

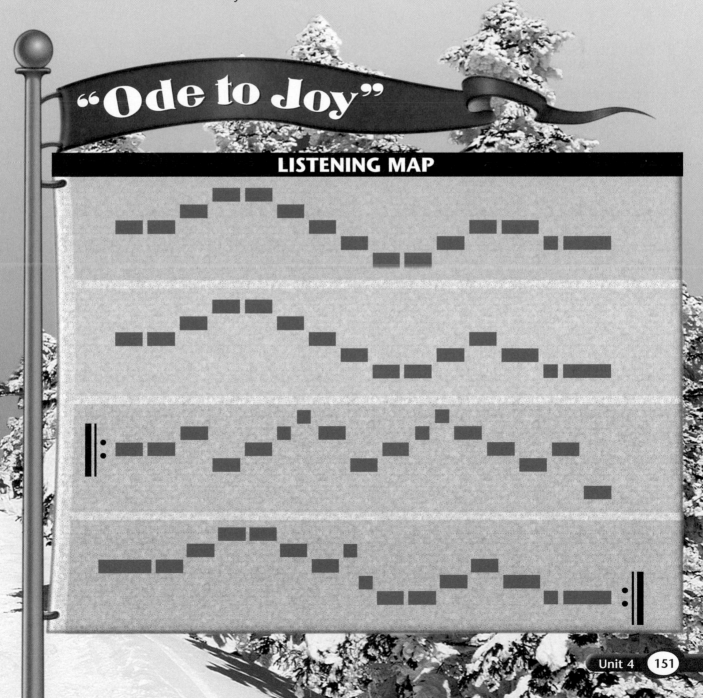

"Ode to Joy"

LISTENING MAP

A Message of Joy

Poet Friedrich Schiller (1759–1805) wrote the original German words for this song. **Sing** the message of "Ode to Joy" in English or in German.

CD 7–7

Ode to Joy

Words by Friedrich Schiller
English Words by Georgette LeNorth

Music by Ludwig van Beethoven

Freu - de, schön - er   Göt - ter - fun - ken,   Toch - ter aus E - ly - si - um,
Come and sing a   joy - ful cho - rus,   Lift your voic - es   to the sky.

wir be - tre - ten   feu - er - trunk - en,   Himm - li - sche, dein   Hei - lig-tum!
Help - ing hands now   join in friend-ship,   Keep-ing hearts and   spir - its high.

Dei - ne Zau - ber   bin - den ___ wied - er,   was die __ Mo - de   streng ge - teilt;
Sis - ter, broth-er,   care for each oth - er,   Care for the world and   keep it free.

al - le Men-schen wer-den Brüd - er,   wo dein sanf - ter   Flü - gel weilt.
Come __ to - geth - er, sing to-geth - er,   As a peace-ful   fam - i - ly.

Letter Names for Notes

Beethoven's melody has only six different notes. These notes are identified on the flags below. Find these notes in "Ode to Joy."

Review how to play the notes above on the recorder. Then **play** "Ode to Joy" along with the recording.

MUSIC MAKERS

Ludwig van Beethoven

Ludwig van Beethoven (1770–1827) is one of the most famous composers of all time. During his lifetime, Beethoven composed a variety of music including works for solo piano, small ensembles, and orchestra. He was born in Germany and began studying piano when he was very young. His first composition was published when he was only twelve years old. In his twenties, Beethoven gradually began to lose his hearing. Even after becoming completely deaf, he continued to write music.

Percussion on Parade

How do you think the first instruments were created? Long ago, people discovered that they could make sounds on objects they found around them. These objects developed into percussion instruments that we play today. You can also make sounds on objects you find around you.

Crash! Boom! Clang!

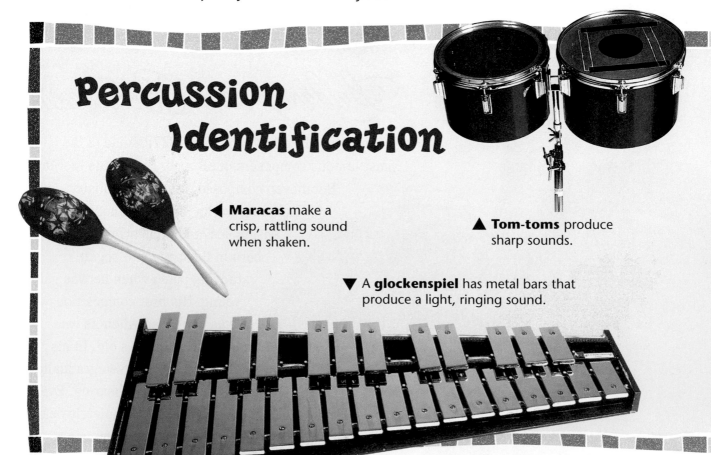

Percussion Identification

◄ **Maracas** make a crisp, rattling sound when shaken.

▲ **Tom-toms** produce sharp sounds.

▼ A **glockenspiel** has metal bars that produce a light, ringing sound.

Listen to *Toccata for Percussion.*
Identify the percussion
instruments as you hear them.

CD 7–11
Toccata for Percussion, Movement 3

by Carlos Chávez

Chávez [CHAH-vehs] (1899–1978) traveled all over Mexico learning about Mexican-Indian music. Much of the music he composed was influenced by the rhythms of these cultures.

◄ A **snare drum** can make a long, raspy roll or a sharp, short sound.

◄ **Claves** produce a bright, hollow sound when struck together.

A **bass drum** produces a deep boom or a soft "thudding" sound. ▶

▲ **Timpani,** also called kettledrums, can sound like a roll of thunder or a quiet "thump."

These instruments are featured in the Sound Bank on page 466.

Percussion in China

Percussion instruments play an important role in many types of music, including marching bands. Where have you heard a marching band perform? At a parade? At a football game? Children in Chinese communities hear *luogu* [loo-OH-goo] percussion ensembles at parades, festivals, and concerts. The sound of the *luogu* ensemble is as familiar in China as the sound of a marching band is in the United States.

▲ A *luogu* ensemble includes gongs, drums, cymbals, bells, and woodblocks.

As you **listen** to the percussion piece *Wu long,* follow the notation on the next page.

CD 7–13

Wu long (Dragon Dance)

Traditional Dance from China

Wu long is played for the Dragon Dance, a traditional dance often performed in parades for Chinese New Year. It is performed by a *luogu* ensemble using Chinese instruments.

In the Dragon Dance, many people carry a fabric dragon on sticks. As they move in a spiraling pattern, the dragon's body appears to slither down the street. ▶

156

Your Turn to Play

You can play *Wu long* with your class. Practice each part below using rhythm syllables. Then **play** the parts on percussion instruments. The ♩ in the drum part indicates that you play on the rim of the drum.

Listen to another *luogu* piece. How is it different from *Wu long?* How is it the same?

CD 7–14
Lian xi qu (étude)

Traditional Arrangement from China

This *étude*, or practice exercise, is from the south-central area of China. It features two pairs of cymbals that sound quickly, one after the other.

America in Two Parts ~ Melody and

Katharine Lee Bates was feeling pride for her country when she wrote the words to "America, the Beautiful" in 1893. She found her inspiration for the song as she stood on the top of Pikes Peak in Colorado.

CD 7–15
MIDI 13

America, the Beautiful

Words by Katharine Lee Bates

Music by Samuel A. Ward
Countermelody by Buryl Red

1. O beau-ti-ful for spa-cious skies, For am-ber waves of grain,
2. O beau-ti-ful for Pil-grim feet, Whose stern im-pas-sioned stress
3. O beau-ti-ful for pa-triot dream That sees be-yond the years

For pur-ple moun-tain maj-es-ties A-bove the fruit-ed plain!
A thor-ough-fare for free-dom beat A-cross the wil-der-ness!
Thine al-a-bas-ter cit-ies gleam, Un-dimmed by hu-man tears!

A-mer-i-ca! A-mer-i-ca! God shed His grace on thee
A-mer-i-ca! A-mer-i-ca! God mend thine ev-'ry flaw,
A-mer-i-ca! A-mer-i-ca! God shed His grace on thee

And crown thy good with broth-er-hood From sea to shin-ing sea!
Con-firm thy soul in self con-trol, Thy lib-er-ty in law!
And crown thy good with broth-er-hood From sea to shin-ing sea!

Countermelody

Sing the melody of "America, the Beautiful."
Then **sing** the **countermelody** below. Adding
a countermelody creates a thicker texture than either
part sung alone.

> A **countermelody** is a
> contrasting melody that is
> played or sung at the same
> time as the main melody.

Countermelody

O _____ beau-ti-ful,   O _____ beau-ti-ful,

O _____ beau-ti-ful,   O _____ beau-ti-ful,

A-mer-i-ca,   A-mer-i-ca,   A-mer-i-ca, the beau-ti-ful.

We sing A - mer - i - ca.   We sing A - mer - i - ca.

Patriotic Countermelodies

Listen for two countermelodies in *The
Stars and Stripes Forever.*

CD 7–17

The Stars and Stripes Forever

by John Philip Sousa

Sousa [soo-zah] (1854–1932) composed more than 100
marches in his lifetime. *The Stars and Stripes Forever* was
his favorite. It is played today by high school, college,
and community bands throughout the United States.

View from Pikes Peak, Colorado ▲

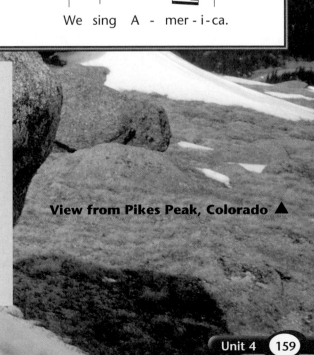

One Song, DIFFERENT TEXTURES

John Newton was a slave trader. When he realized slavery was wrong, he expressed his feelings through lyrics. Later, his lyrics were used with this early American hymn. **Listen** to the song and **describe** the texture.

CD 7–18

Amazing Grace

Words by John Newton

Early American Melody

1. A - maz - ing ___ grace, how sweet the sound, That
2. 'Twas grace that ___ taught my heart to fear, And

saved   a ___ wretch   like   me! _____   I
grace   my ___ fears   re - lieved; _____   How

once ___ was ___ lost, but now ___ am ___ found, Was
pre - cious ___ did that grace ___ ap - pear The

blind,   but ___ now   I   see. _____
hour   I ___ first   be - lieved! _____

3. Through many dangers, toils, and snares,
   I have already come;
   'Tis grace has brought me safe thus far,
   And grace will lead me home.

Sing "Amazing Grace." Then sing this countermelody with a small group while the rest of the class sings "Amazing Grace." How does the texture change?

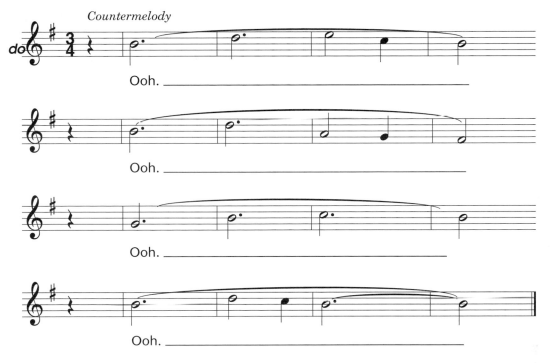

Ooh. _____

Ooh. _____

Ooh. _____

Ooh. _____

Comparing Textures

A thicker texture can be created by adding voices to the same melody line.

Listen to *Amazing Grace.*
Compare the texture of the recording with the texture of the song.

CD 7–20
Amazing Grace

as performed by Judy Collins

This recording by Judy Collins has two distinct textures—solo and chorus.

Painting by Michele Wood from *I See Rhythm* by Toyomi Igus ▶

Reprinted with permission of the publisher, Children's Book Press, San Francisco, CA. Art copyright © 1998 by Michele Wood

HARMONY TONES

Listen to "Dry Bones." Where does the **harmony** change in the song?

Harmony is two or more different tones sounding at the same time.

 CD 7–21
MIDI 14

DRY BONES

African American Spiritual

A

C — G₇ — C

E - ze-kiel cried, "Them dry __ bones!" E - ze-kiel cried, "Them dry __ bones!"

C — G₇ — C

E - ze-kiel cried, "Them dry __ bones!" Now hear the word of the Lord.

B

C

The foot bone con-nect - ed to the leg ____ bone,

C♯

The leg bone con-nect - ed to the knee ____ bone,

D

The knee bone con-nect - ed to the thigh ____ bone,

D♯

The thigh bone con-nect - ed to the hip ____ bone,

E

The hip bone con-nect - ed to the back ____ bone,

The back bone con-nect-ed to the shoul - der bone,

The shoul - der bone con-nect - ed to the neck ___ bone,

The neck bone con-nect - ed to the jaw ___ bone,

The jaw bone con-nect - ed to the head ___ bone, Now

hear the word of the Lord. Them bones, them bones gon - na
Them bones, them bones, them ___

walk a - round, Them bones, them bones gon - na
dry ___ bones, Them bones, them bones, them ___

walk a-round, Them bones, them bones gon - na walk a-round
dry ___ bones, Them bones, them bones, them ___ dry ___ bones.

Now hear the word of the Lord.
Now hear the word of the Lord.

Playing Harmony

Sing "Dry Bones." Then **play** C and G₇ **chords** in the Ⓐ section of the song on the Autoharp or keyboard.

> A **chord** is three or more notes arranged in intervals of a third, sounded at the same time.

Review, Assess,

What Do You Know?

1. Which symbol below is called *fortissimo*? What does it mean?

pp   p   mp   mf   f   ff

2. If you saw this symbol (*p*), how would you perform the music?

What Do You Hear? 4

CD 7–23

Point to the line below that matches the rhythms performed on the recording.

1. a.   b.

2. a.   b.

3. a.   b.

Perform, Create

What You Can Do

Move to Show Contour

Sing "Amazing Grace," on page 160, with eyes closed. Move your hand in an arc to show the contour of the melody.

Play Rhythms

Perform all four of the percussion lines of "*Wu long,*" on page 157, using rhythm syllables. Perform the piece as a group using body percussion. Have different people play each part. Perform the piece again using percussion instruments.

Move to Show Form

Sing "Ode to Joy," on page 152. Perform small, steady-beat movements during the **a** phrases and different movements during the **b** phrase.

Sing with Texture

Sing "America, the Beautiful," on page 158. Create a thick texture by singing the melody and the countermelody together.

This Music Is Hopping

In the early days of rock 'n' roll, music dance parties called hops were often held in the local school gym. Instead of a DJ, a hop would usually feature a live band. *At the Hop* is one of the songs a band might have performed at the dance.

M·U·S·I·C M·A·K·E·R·S

Danny & the Juniors

Danny & the Juniors was originally a high school quartet started by Danny Rapp at his Philadelphia high school. He and his three friends—David White, Frank Maffei, and Joe Terranova—exploded onto the national music scene with their first Billboard Top 40 hit, *At the Hop*. Danny & the Juniors reached the Top 40 eight more times with songs like *Twistin' U.S.A.* and *Rock and Roll Is Here to Stay*.

Listen to Danny & the Juniors as they perform *At the Hop*.

CD 7–26
At the Hop

by J. Medora, A. Singer, and D. White as performed by Danny & the Juniors

The best-selling record for Danny & the Juniors was *At the Hop*, which rocketed to the number one spot in 1957.

Discovering New Musical Horizons

At the Hop

CD 7–27

*Words and Music by A. Singer,
J. Medora, and D. White*

1. Well, you can rock it, you can roll it, do the stomp and e-ven stroll it at the
   swing it, you can groove it, you can real - ly start to move it at the

hop.　　　　When the rec-ord starts a spin - nin', you ca -
hop.　　　　Where the jump-in' is the smooth-est and the

lyp - so when you chick-en at the hop.　　Do the
mu - sic is the cool-est at the hop.　　All the

dance sen - sa - tion that is sweep-in' the na - tion at the hop.
cats and the chicks ___ can ___ get their ___ kicks ___ at the hop.

REFRAIN

Let's go to the hop! Let's go to the hop!

(Oh, ba - by!) Let's go to the hop! (Oh, ba - by!)

Let's go to the hop! Come on.

1. Let's go to the hop!   2. Well, you can Let's go to the hop!

Row with the TEMPO

The tempo, or speed of the beat, plays a big role in giving music mood or feeling. Listen to the following speech piece. Notice the tempo changes. Raise your hand when you hear the tempo change.

CD 7–29

Can You Canoe?

Words by Dennis Lee

Speech Piece

Can you ca - noe in Kal - a - ma - zoo?
I can ca - noe in Kal - a - ma - zoo;

Can you ca - noe in Kam - loops?
I can ca - noe in Kam - loops; but I

Can you ca - noe at a quar - ter to two in a
can - not ca - noe at a quar - ter to two in a

van when the traf - fic jam loops?
van when the traf - fic jam loops.

Continue Canoeing

Use the speech piece for your own experiments with tempo.
Perform "Can You Canoe?" at an easy flowing tempo, called *andante.* Next **perform** the piece in a medium tempo, *moderato.* Now, repeat the speech piece in a rapid, lively tempo, *allegro.*

Perform these rhythm patterns with "Can You Canoe?"

Listen to the following piece. Notice the tempo changes and suggest names for these tempos.

CD 7–31

Hungarian Dance No. 19

by Johannes Brahms

Brahms wrote the *Hungarian Dances* for piano four hands. This orchestral setting of No. 19 was arranged by Antonín Dvořák.

M·U·S·I·C M·A·K·E·R·S

Johannes Brahms

Johannes Brahms (1833–1897) was born in Hamburg, Germany, to a musical family. He began piano lessons at an early age and was admired as a composer and pianist. He composed piano works, four symphonies, four concertos, choral works, and many songs.

Element: RHYTHM | **Skill: MOVING** | **Connection: CULTURE**

Doin' Fine in Triple Time

The song *"Santa Clara"* is from the Philippine Islands in the South Pacific. The text of this song is written in a language of the Philippines called *Tagalog* [ta-GAH-log].

CD 7–32

Santa Clara

English Words by Alice Firgau

Folk Song from the Philippines
As sung by Sonny Alforque

San - ta   Cla - rang, ____ pi - nung   pi - no
San - ta   Cla - ra, ____ this   I   will   do.

Ang   pa - nga - ko   ko   ay   ga - ni - to.
In   my   heart   I   vow and prom - ise   you,

Pag - da - ting   ko po ____ sa U - ban - do.   Ay mag -
On   the road   I'll go ____ to U - ban - do;   While I'm

Feeling Strong

Listen to the strong triple feeling in this song: ONE-two-three, ONE-two-three. As you listen, **move** to show meter in 3 by performing these repeated motions: PAT-clap-snap.

Create hand movements of your own to go with the song. Always use the same movement for the strong beat.

◀ Filipino classical dancers

sa - sa - yaw _____ ng pan - dang - go.   A - ru -
there   I'll   dance ___ the fan - dan - go.   A - ru -

ray, a - ra - ru - ray, Ang pa - nga - ko'y tu - tu - pa - rin. A - ru -
ray, a - ra - ru - ray, And may my prom - ise   be ful - filled. A - ru -

ray, a - ra - ru - ray, Ang pa - nga - ko'y tu - tu - pa - rin. _____
ray, a - ra - ru - ray, And may my prom - ise   be ful - filled. _____

Make Mine ¾ Time

Listen to the Korean song "*Doraji*," another song in ¾. Unlike most other Asian cultures, Korea has folk songs in ¾ time. Is the tempo faster or slower than the tempo of "*Santa Clara*"?

CD 7–36

Doraji (Bluebells)

English Words by Patricia Shehan Campbell

Folk Song from Korea

Do - ra - ji, do - ra - ji, pek do - ra - ji,
Blue - bells, blue - bells, Love - ly blue - bells,

Sim - sim san - chuh __ neh __ pek do - ra - ji.
Deep in the moun - tains __ my __ blue - bells grow.

Hahn du bu - ri - man keh - yuh - do _____
Gather - ing blue - bells in wide val - leys.

Teh kwang - chu - ri su - ri - sal __ sal __ num - nun - goo - na.
Bas - kets of __ blue - bells __ will __ o - ver - flow.

Folk Melody, Folk Instruments

Listen for meter in 3 in this version of *Doraji*.

CD 7–40
Doraji

Folk Song from Korea

This version of *Doraji* is played on traditional Korean instruments and is sung in Korean folk style.

Sanjo is a traditional Korean instrumental form that has been used for centuries. **Listen** to this modern interpretation by Hi-za Yoo. She is playing the *kayagum* [ki-AH-gum], a Korean string instrument.

CD 7–41
Sanjo

written and performed by Hi-za Yoo

This excerpt is one of five sections. In *Sanjo* form, each section becomes faster and more complex.

MUSIC MAKERS
Hi-za Yoo

As a child in Korea, **Hi-za Yoo** studied traditional dance and instruments, and she became an outstanding performer. She has performed mainly in the Los Angeles area, where she has established an institute for teaching Korean music and dance.

Element: RHYTHM | **Skill: READING** | **Connection: CULTURE**

Sounds of Spain

The music of Spain has been influenced by many different cultures. The Moors, an Arabic people, lived in southern Spain for nearly seven centuries. They brought with them the *vihuela* [vee-HWAY-la], an ancestor of the guitar.

Listen for the sound of the *vihuela* in "*La Tarara*."

▲ *Castanets*

CD 8–1

La Tarara

English Words by Alice D. Firgau

Folk Song from Spain

REFRAIN   Em   B₇

La Ta - ra - ra,   sí,   la Ta - ra - ra,   no,
La Ta - ra - ra,   yes,   La Ta - ra - ra,   no,

Em   B₇   Em   *Fine*

La Ta - ra - ra,   ma - dre,   que la   bai - lo   yo.
La Ta - ra - ra,   ma - ma,   is a   dance I   know.

VERSE   Em   B₇

1. Tie - ne la Ta - ra - ra un jar - dín   de flo - res y me
2. Tie - ne la Ta - ra - ra un ces - to   de fru - tas y me
1. If I want to wan-der in her gar - den bow-ers, La Ta -
2. If I want a bas-ket of the fruit she'll har-vest, La Ta -

D. C. al Fine

Em   B₇

da, si quie - ro, siem - pre las me - jor - es.
da, si quie - ro, siem - pre las ma - du - ras.
ra - ra al - ways gives me her best flow - ers.
ra - ra al - ways gives me just the rip - est.

Arts Connection

◀ *Girl with a Guitar* by Jan Vermeer (1632–1675). How is the instrument in this painting similar to the *vihuela* shown below?

It's All the Same

Say the words to the refrain in rhythm and tap the beat with your foot. Now clap the rhythm pattern below while you say the words.

La Ta - ra - ra sí,

You can use the tie to show the sound that lasts for one and a half beats.

La Ta - ra - ra sí,

There is an easier way to write the same rhythm, using

La Ta - ra - ra sí,

Vihuela ▶

Identify and **read** the new rhythm pattern in *"La Tarara."*

TEARING THROUGH RHYTHM

Have you ever tried singing a song to pass the time while you work? Songs have long been used to make work go faster. **Sing** the song "Old House, Tear It Down!" Notice how the rhythms give the song energy.

CD 8–8

OLD HOUSE, TEAR IT DOWN!

Collected by John Work

African American Work Song

Em   Am   Em

1. Old house, tear it down! Who's gon-na help me tear it down?
2. New house, build it up! Who's gon-na help me build it up?

Em   Am   Em

Bring me a ham-mer, tear it down! Bring me a saw, __ tear it down!
Bring me a ham-mer, build it up! Bring me a saw, __ build it up!

Em   Am   Em Am Em

Next thing you bring me, tear it down! Is a wreck-ing ma-chine, tear it down.
Next thing you bring me, build it up! Is a car-pen-ter man, build it up.

Rewriting Rhythms

Read the first line of the song. Then clap part 2 of the rhythm pattern below while you say the words.

Old   house,   tear it __ down.

You can use ♪ ♩. to write the same rhythm.

Old   house,   tear it   down.

Read the entire song using rhythm syllables.

Two Patterns Alike and Different

The two patterns below are alike because both patterns are made up of two sounds: one long and the other short.

1.    2.

How are they different?

Sing "All Night, All Day."

Conduct the song in a four-beat pattern.
Identify the lines that contain one or both of the rhythm patterns above.

CD 8–13

ALL NIGHT, ALL DAY

African American Spiritual

REFRAIN

All night, all ____ day, An-gels watch-ing o-ver me, my Lord. _

All night, all ____ day, An-gels watch-ing o-ver me.
Fine

VERSE *Call*   *Response*

1. Now I lay me down _ to sleep, An-gels watch-ing o-ver me, my Lord. _
2. If I die be-fore _ I wake,

Call   *Response*   *D. C. al Fine*

Pray the Lord my soul _ to keep, An-gels watch-ing o-ver me.
Pray the Lord my soul _ to take,

Arts Connection

▲ *Mother and Child* (1919) by Martha Walter. How would the music change if a mother were to sing "All Night, All Day" as a lullaby to her young child?

Show What You Know!

Perform these rhythms using rhythm syllables.

1.

2.

Using the rhythms above, **compose** your own rhythm pattern. Make it four measures long. Be sure there are four beats in each measure. **Perform** it for the rest of the class.

KNOW the RONDO

"Heave–Ho," "Going, Going, Gone," and "The Snow" are speech pieces. Each has different rhythm patterns. Keep a steady beat as you **perform** these speech pieces.

CD 8–15

A Heave-Ho

Words by Dennis Lee   *Speech Piece*

Heave - Ho,   buck-ets of snow, the   gi - ant is comb-ing his beard.   The

snow is   as high as the   top of the sky, and the world has dis - ap - peared.

B Going, Going, Gone

Words by Dennis Lee   *Speech Piece*

Go - ing, go - ing, gone,   your dad - dy won't be   long.

Where did he go? To shov-el the snow.   Go - ing, go - ing, gone.

The Snow

Words by Clifford Dyment

Speech Piece

In no way that I chose to go could I es-cape the fall-ing snow. My

foot-steps made a shal-low space and then the snow filled up the place.

Accompaniment Rhythms

Learn these rhythms. Then **play** them on a percussion instrument. **Perform** the rhythms as an accompaniment for the three speech pieces.

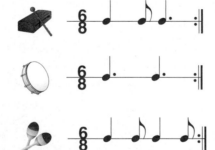

Now the Rondo

Now that you know three speech pieces, **perform** them in ABACA order. This order is a **rondo** form.

A **rondo** is a musical form in which the first section always returns. A common rondo form is ABACA.

A Mondo Rondo

Listen to *ABACA Dabble.* Remember the first melody—that's the **Ⓐ** section. Raise your hand each time you hear the **Ⓐ** section.

CD 8–17
ABACA Dabble

by Bryan Louiselle

This rondo is in a big band, swing style.

After each **Ⓐ** section, you hear a different section. The new sections are labeled **B** and **Ⓒ**.

Now **listen** to *ABACA Dabble* again and **move** to show rondo form.

A

Create a movement for the **Ⓐ** section that uses your entire body.

B

Move only your legs for the **B** section.

C

Create a movement for the **Ⓒ** section that uses your torso.

Follow the Form

Listen to this rondo for piano by Ludwig van Beethoven (1770–1827). As you follow the listening map, **identify** each appearance of section **A**.

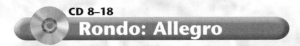

CD 8–18
Rondo: Allegro

from *Piano Sonata in C Minor, Op. 13* **("Pathétique")**
by Ludwig van Beethoven
as performed by Vladimir Horowitz

Rondo: Allegro is the third movement of this piano sonata, originally published in 1799.

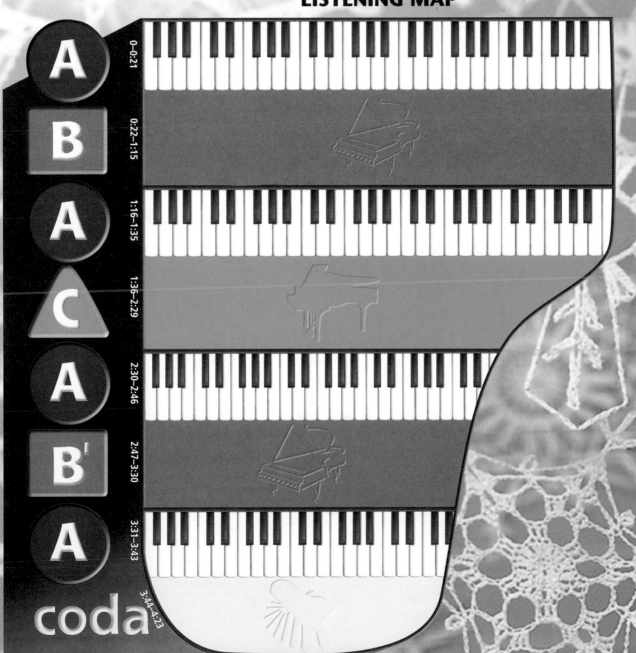

Rondo: Allegro
LISTENING MAP

A   0–0:21
B   0:22–1:15
A   1:16–1:35
C   1:36–2:29
A   2:30–2:46
B'   2:47–3:30
A   3:31–3:43
coda 3:44–4:23

Laugh and Sing

Do you know that the kookaburra is a bird? It's called "the laughing bird" because its song sounds like a hilarious cackle! Of course, you know that a gum tree doesn't really grow bubble gum. It's actually a eucalyptus tree. And the bush in Australia isn't like the bush in your mother's rose garden—it's another name for the forest.

Sing this silly song from Australia.

CD 8–19
MIDI 15

Kookaburra

Words and Music by Marion Sinclair

Kook - a - bur - ra sits on the old gum tree, _____

Mer - ry, mer - ry king of the bush is he. _____

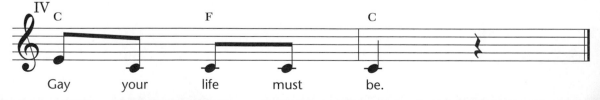

Laugh, kook - a - bur - ra, laugh, kook - a - bur - ra,

Gay your life must be.

Kookaburra Rhythm

Perform this pattern using rhythm syllables.

Which line of "Kookaburra" matches this rhythm?

Kookaburra Pitch

Sing the melody below, using pitch syllables and hand signs. As you can see, there is a note missing! Hum the missing note. How does the new note sound compared to *la?* Compared to high *do?* How does this melody relate to the rhythm pattern above?

do'

la   do'

?

la

so

WHERE'S THE NEW NOTE?

Have you ever lost something, only to find it right under your nose? Sometimes things seem to turn up where you least expect to find them.

Listen to "Missy-La, Massa-La." Learn to **sing** the song and then play the game with your friends.

CD 8–25

MISSY-LA, MASSA-LA

Game Song from the Caribbean

Mis - sy - la, ___ mas - sa - la, ___ Mis - sy lost _ her gold ring, go 'way.

Mis - sy - la, ___ mas - sa - la, ___ Mis - sy lost _ her gold ring. I got to

find 'em, find 'em, find 'em, find 'em, Find 'em, let me see ___ la, la, la, la

find 'em, find 'em, find 'em, find 'em, Find 'em, let me see.

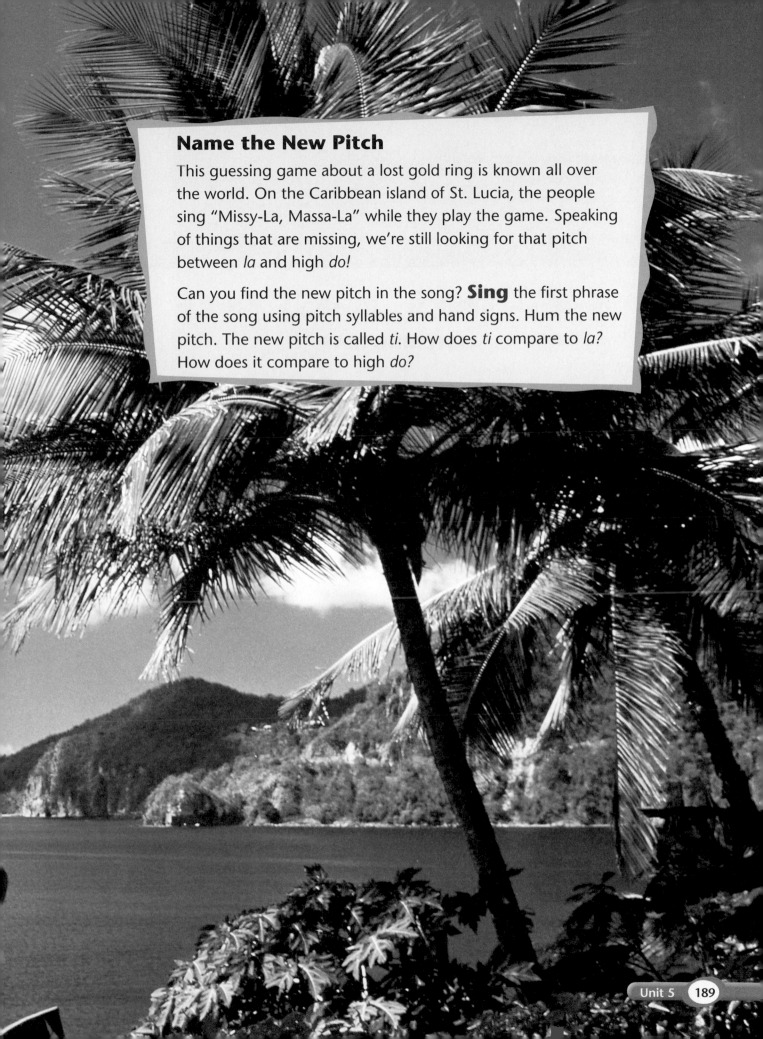

Name the New Pitch

This guessing game about a lost gold ring is known all over the world. On the Caribbean island of St. Lucia, the people sing "Missy-La, Massa-La" while they play the game. Speaking of things that are missing, we're still looking for that pitch between *la* and high *do!*

Can you find the new pitch in the song? **Sing** the first phrase of the song using pitch syllables and hand signs. Hum the new pitch. The new pitch is called *ti*. How does *ti* compare to *la?* How does it compare to high *do?*

Hear the New Note

As you **listen** to *A-Cling, A-Cling,* follow the map and **perform** the hand signs for *ti* and *do*.

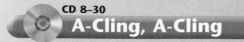

CD 8–30
A-Cling, A-Cling

Traditional Melody from Nevis

This selection is from Nevis, an island in the West Indies.

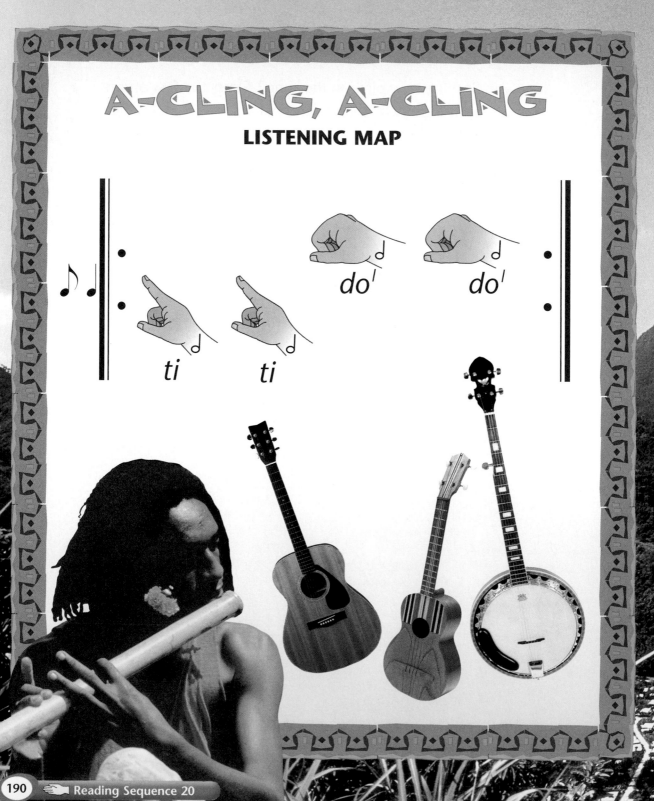

Arts Connection

▲ Mural of musicians playing
traditional Caribbean
instruments (Anonymous)

Show What You Know!

1. **Identify** the note *ti* in these examples. Then **sing** each example
   using pitch syllables.

   1. *do* 𝄞 o o o   2. *do* 𝄞 o o o   3. *do* 𝄞 o o o

2. **Identify** the songs or listening selections that have these patterns.
   Find other songs in the book that use the new note *ti*.

Performing Together

Performing with others is a fun part of making music. Rock, pop, classical—just about any style of music can be performed by a group. Musicians use the French word **ensemble,** meaning "together," to talk about group performance. Everyone in an ensemble pays special attention to what every member of the group is doing. Everyone in an ensemble must listen to each other to perform well together.

In music, an **ensemble** is a group of musicians who perform together.

Listen to these examples of ensembles performing.

CD 8–31
Scherzo

from *Piano Trio No. 2 in E-flat Major, Op. 100* by Franz Schubert

In Western classical music, a piano trio is not three pianos. It is a piano, cello, and violin.

CD 8–32
Rag puria kalyan

Raga from North India as performed by David Trasoff and Zakir Hussein

This Indian classical music ensemble plays the *sarod*, a string instrument, and the *tabla* (drums).

Piano trio ▲

▼ Classical Indian musicians

CD 8–33
Canzoni prima a 5

from *Canzoni et Sonate*
by Giovanni Gabrieli
as performed by Canadian Brass

This brass piece is performed by two groups, one echoing the other. This is called antiphonal style.

► Canadian Brass

CD 8–34
That's the Way

by Greg Clark and Scott Leonard
as performed by Rockapella

This selection features close harmony and vocal percussion.

MUSIC MAKERS
Rockapella

Vocalists Scott Leonard (high tenor), Kevin Wright (tenor), Elliott Kerman (baritone), Barry Carl (bass), and Jeff Thacher (vocal percussion) are the group **Rockapella**. The group started out singing barbershop and doo-wop on the streetcorners of Manhattan, a borough of New York City. After some time, they began to sing contemporary music and recorded *Zombie Jamboree.* The group is best-known for recording the soundtrack to *Where in the World Is Carmen Sandiego?*

Playing Together

Here is an instrumental selection for your class to play as an ensemble.
Listen to all the parts and stay together. **Perform** the three sections in the following order: ABACA. Do you remember the name of this musical form? If not, the title of the piece will give you a clue.

Orfferondo

Music by Mary Shamrock

B

Soprano Glockenspiel

Soprano Xylophone

Alto Xylophone

Bass Xylophone

C

D. C. al Fine

Sound of a Round

"Ah, Poor Bird" is a folk song from England. What do you think the lyrics mean?

Sing the song in unison.

CD 8–36

Ah, Poor Bird

Traditional Round from England

I
Dm

Ah,   poor   bird,   take   your   flight.

III

Far a - bove the sor - rows of this sad night!

Learning to Sing a Round

Let's add layers to the song. First **sing** measure 1 as an ostinato. Do the same with measures 2 and 3. **Perform** the ostinatos, together in groups.

Now that your ear is able to hear the harmony created by the ostinatos, **perform** "Ah, Poor Bird" as a **round.** Each part must wait one measure before beginning.

> A **round** is a follow-the-leader process in which all perform the same melody but start at different times.

Parts to Play

Add more layers to "Ah, Poor Bird" to **create** a thicker texture.
Perform this accompaniment as you **sing** the song.

Glockenspiel (play 3 times)

Alto Metallophone

Bass Xylophone

Another Round

This next round is from Mexico.
First **sing** it by layering line 1
and line 2. Then sing the entire
song as a round.

CD 8–38

Los niños en España cantan
(In Spain, the Children Sing)

English Words by S. T.   *Folk Song from Mexico*

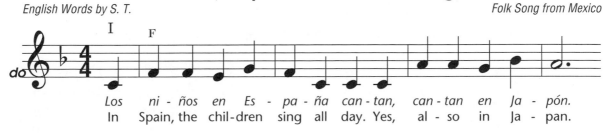

I F

do

Los   ni - ños   en   Es - pa - ña   can - tan,   can - tan   en   Ja - pón.
In   Spain, the   chil - dren   sing   all   day.   Yes,   al - so   in   Ja - pan.

II

Los   pa - ja - ri - tos   can - tan, can - tan   to - dos   su   can - ción.
Oh,   ev - 'ry - where the   birds join   in   with   wom - an, child, and   man.

ROUND AND A ROUND

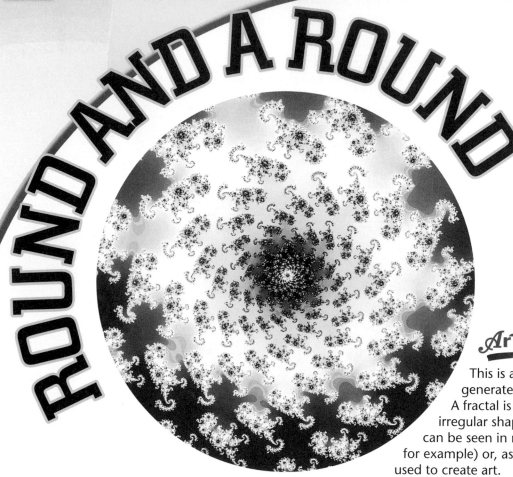

Arts Connection

This is a computer-generated fractal image. A fractal is any repeated, irregular shape. Such designs can be seen in nature (clouds, for example) or, as in this case, used to create art.

Have you ever held down a letter key on a computer? The key keeps repeating until you move your finger. Rounds are like that too. They don't end until a decision is made to stop.

Sing "The Computer" in unison. Then decide how many times you will **perform** it as a round.

Accompany "The Computer" on the keyboard using the chords C and G₇. **Play** the chords when they appear in the music.

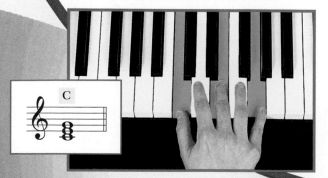

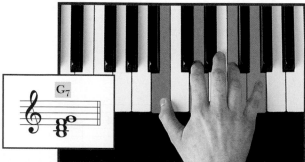

CD 8–42

THE COMPUTER

Words by Fitzhugh Dodson

Music by Mary Shamrock

A com-put-er is a think-ing ma-chine, the smart-est one you've

ev - er seen, but ev-'ry com-put-er can on - ly do ____

what some per - son has told it to.

Describing Texture

Listen to "Orbital View" from *Mars Suite*. **Describe** the texture of this computer music.

Computer music workstation ▼

CD 8–44
Orbital View

**from *Mars Suite*
by Michael McNabb**

Mars Suite was composed for the NASA movie *Mars in 3-D*. Images from the film were sent by the Viking lander during its mission to Mars.

CALLING ALL CHORDS

Believe it or not, frogs are a popular subject for song lyrics. **Sing** this song and **listen** to the accompaniment.

FROG MUSIC

Folk Song from Canada

There once was a frog who jumped in a bog, And played the bass

fid - dle in the mid - dle of a pud - dle, What a mud - dle!

"Bet - ter go 'round! Bet - ter go 'round!" _____

The Chord

Listen to the song again and raise your hand when you hear the chords change. Then point to the places in the music where the chords change.

Play these ostinatos with the song.

Glockenspiel

Alto Metallophone

Alto Xylophone

Bass Xylophone

His mu - sic was short, For soon he was caught, And now in the mid - dle

of a grid - dle he is fry - ing and is cry - ing:

"Rath - er be drown'd! Rath - er be drown'd!" _____

CHORDS IN A DIDDY

"Do Wah Diddy Diddy" has been a popular song for several decades. It has even been used in movie soundtracks. **Sing** the song and **listen** for the chord changes.

Play the Chords

Sing the lowest note of the A chord, then the D chord. Find these notes on a melody instrument. Now **play** them as an accompaniment to the song by following the chord symbols in the music.

Perform this accompaniment with the first eight measures of the song.

DO WAH DIDDY DIDDY

Words and Music by Jeff Barry and Ellie Greenwich

CD 8–47

There he was _____ just a - walk - in' down the street,
fore I knew __ it he was walk - in' next to me,

Sing-in' Do wah did - dy did-dy down did-dy do, Pop - pin' his fin - gers and a-
Took __ my hand __ just as

shuf - fl - in' his feet, Sing - in' Do wah did - dy di ddy
nat - ural as can be,

down did - dy do. He looked good, (yeah, yeah) He looked
We walked on, (yeah, yeah) To my

fine, (yeah, yeah) He looked good, he looked fine, and I
door, (yeah, yeah) We walked on to my door, and he

1.
near - ly lost my mind. Be -

2.
stayed a lit - tle more, Sing - in'

3 times
Do wah did - dy did - dy down did - dy do.

Review, Assess,

What Do You Know?

1. Look at the notation for "The Computer," on page 199.

   a. What pitch is named *do* in this song?

   b. Point to all the pitches that are called *ti*. How many did you identify?

   c. Do the same activity for the pitches named *so*, *fa*, *mi*, *la*, *re*, and *do*.

2. Match each of these tempo words with the correct definition.

   a. *andante*   very fast

   b. *moderato*   slow

   c. *allegro*   moderate

   d. *adagio*   walking speed

   e. *presto*   fast

▲ Brass quintet

What Do You Hear? 5

 CD 8–49

Listen to these examples and point to the picture of the ensemble you hear.

▲ Classical music trio

▲ Pop group

Indian classical music ensemble ▶

Perform, Create

What You Can Do

Sing Rounds and Rhythms

Sing "*Los niños en España cantan,*" on page 197, as a round. Create and perform steady-beat movement patterns that reflect the tempo and meter of the song.

Read and Sing *ti*

Sing "Missy-La, Massa-La," on page 188, from the notation using hand signs and pitch syllables. Then sing the song again using the words.

Play Chords

Practice the rhythm patterns for the accompaniment to "Do Wah Diddy Diddy," on page 202. Then sing the song and play the accompaniment on mallet instruments.

Move to Show Form

Perform a rondo speech piece by combining "Heave-Ho," "Going, Going, Gone," and "The Snow," on pages 182–183. Create a different steady-beat movement to accompany each section of the speech piece.

Making a New Place Your Own

As we know, musicians sing, play, listen to, and create music. Our music is based on our own ideas, experiences, and the special people and places in our lives. What people and places have influenced your own ways of making music?

Sing "America," a song about leaving a familiar place to find a new home. What do the words and music mean to you?

Create movements to add to your performance of the song.

▲ Immigrants arriving on Ellis Island, New York Harbor (May 27, 1920)

CD 9–1

America

Words and Music by Neil Diamond

Far, we've been trav-el-ing far, __ with-out __ a home, __ ____ but not with-out a star. __ Free,

on-ly want __ to be free, __ we hud-dle close, __

hang on __ to a dream. __

Making Music Our Own

On the boats and on ___ the planes,   they're com - ing to A -
Nev-er look-ing back __ a - gain,   they're com - ing to A -

mer - i - ca.   Home,   don't it seem so ___ far ___
mer - i - ca.   Home,   to a new and __ shin-

___ a-way,   oh, we're trav - el - ing light __ to - day,
- y place,   make our bed and we'll say ___ our grace,

New U.S. citizens celebrate after taking the oath of citizenship. ▶

Arts Connection

America (1985) by Chinese-American artist Diana Ong (born 1940) ▶

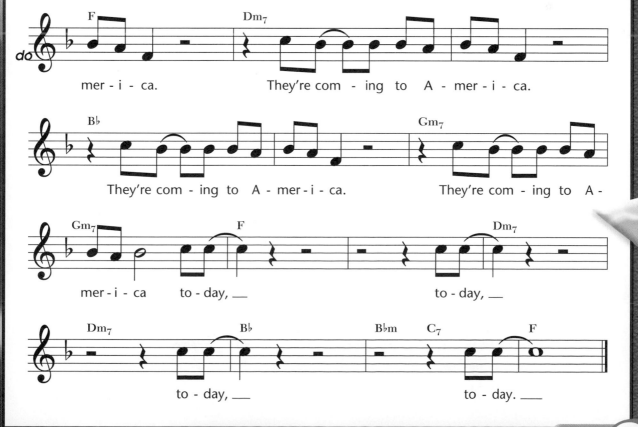

mer - i - ca.   They're com - ing to A - mer - i - ca.

They're com - ing to A - mer - i - ca.   They're com - ing to A -

mer - i - ca   to - day, __   to - day, __

to - day, __   to - day. __

Accent on Freedom

An **accent** indicates to play or sing a note with more emphasis than the other notes.

A musical **accent** (>) gives special importance or stress to certain notes. Find the accents in this patriotic song. Then perform them as you sing the song.

CD 9–3

America, the Free

Words and Music by Phyllis Wolfe-White (adapted)

C · · · · · · · · · · · Bb · Bb
do · I am the voice of A - mer - i - ca, · I am free-dom's song.

C · · · · · · · · · · · F > > > > · G >
I am the wings of an ea - gle, · I am proud and strong! · A -

F · G · Am · · · · F · C > Bb >
mer - i - ca, the beau - ti - ful, · A - mer - i - ca, the free, · A -

F · G · Am · · Bb · · · · *Last time to Coda* ⊕
mer - i - ca, the hope of all I ev - er dream to be. ____
· · · · · · · ev - 'ry op-por - tu - ni - ty. ____

Solo 1
C · · · Bb
Solo 2
F · · · G
Solo 3
C · · · Bb
I can be _____ · I can be _____ · I can be _____
(a doc - tor,) · (an ar - tist,) · (a bank - er,)

Arts Connection

▲ *Three Musicians* (1921) by Pablo Picasso. Many of Picasso's works
feature musical subjects. *Three Musicians* is in the "cubist" style.
Artists who painted in this style used geometric shapes such as
circles, squares, and triangles in abstract forms.

Accents Everywhere

Accents can be found everywhere in music, poetry, art, and dance. Look
at the painting by Picasso. How did the artist use such elements as shape
and color to give the impression of accents? What instruments are
depicted in *Three Musicians*?

Accents Make the Difference

Listen for accents in this instrumental piece. What instruments play the accents?

CD 9–5

Thunder and Lightning Polka

by Johann Strauss

Johann Strauss lived in Austria where German is spoken. The words for thunder and lightning in German are *Donner und Blitz*.

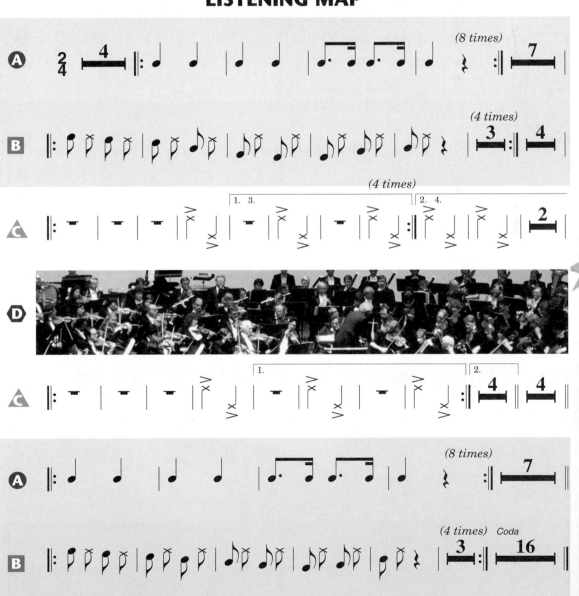

Rhythms on the Ranch

What is a ranch? Who lives there? What does a rancher do?
Sing "*El rancho grande,*" a song about life on a ranch.

Working with Rhythm

Identify the time signature in "*El rancho grande.*" How many beats are there in each measure of this song? **Move** to show the meter.

Clap and say the rhythm below. Then find it in "*El rancho grande.*" How many times does it occur?

Play these rhythm ostinatos to accompany the song.

El rancho grande
(The Big Ranch)

English Words by Alice D. Firgau

Music by Silvano R. Ramos

VERSE

A - llá en el ran - cho gran - de, A - llá don - de vi -
Out yon - der on a prai - rie, The ranch where I was

ví - a, _____ Ha - bía u-na ran-che - ri - ta, Que a-
liv - ing, _____ I heard a pret-ty cow-girl, Who

le - gre me de - cí - a, Que a - le - gre me de - cí - a: _____
hap-pi - ly was sing-ing, Who hap-pi - ly was sing - ing: ____

REFRAIN

Te voy ha - cer tus cal - zo - nes,
A pair of chaps I will make you,

Co - mo los u - sa el ran - che - ro;
Just like the ones for a ranch - er;

Te los co - mien - zo de la - na,
With wool and leath - er I'll make them.

Te los a - ca - bo de cue - ro.
Oh, do please give me your an - swer.

LESSON 3

Element: RHYTHM | Skill: SINGING | Connection: RELATED ARTS

Ringing Rhythm

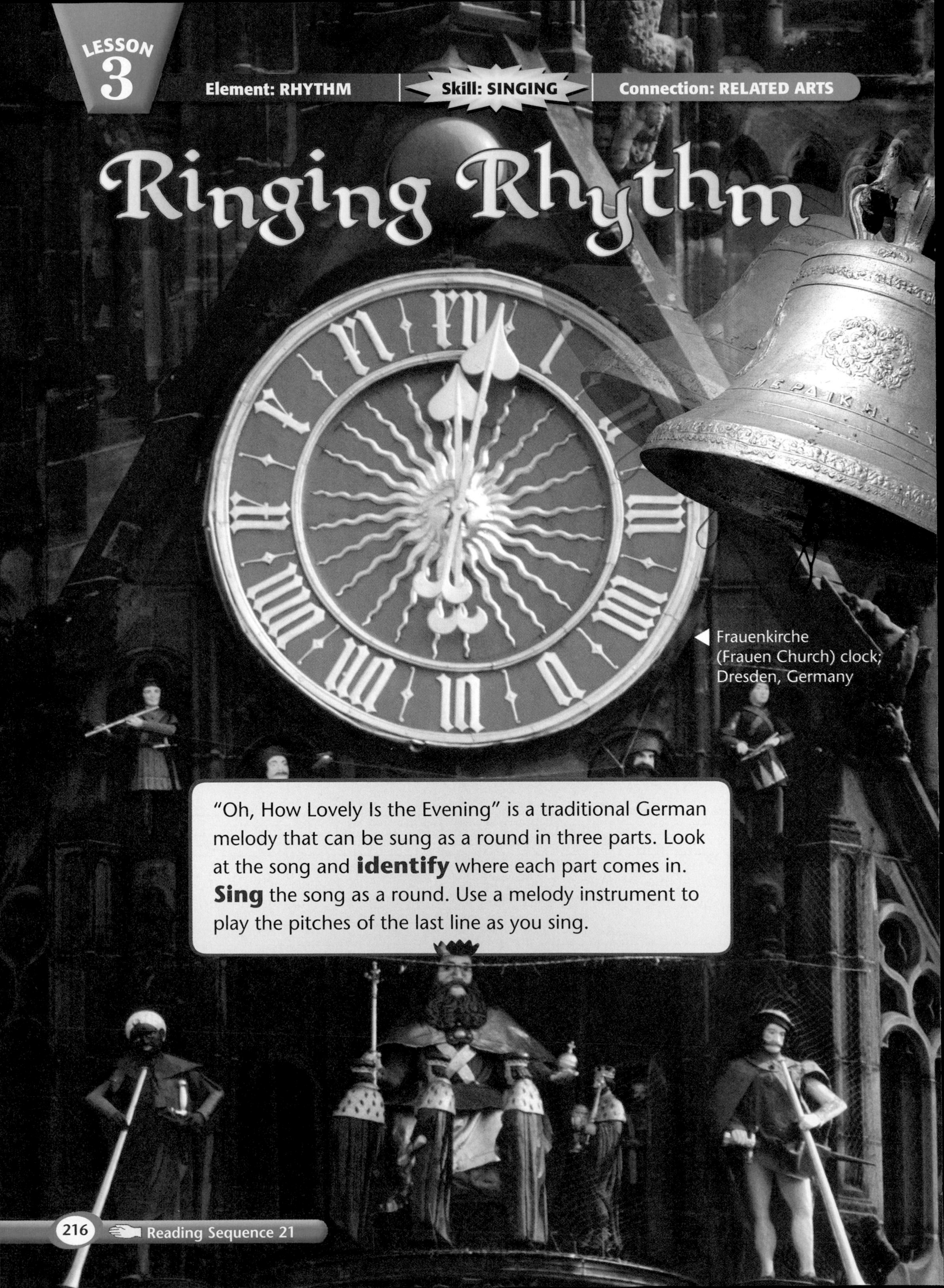

Frauenkirche (Frauen Church) clock; Dresden, Germany

"Oh, How Lovely Is the Evening" is a traditional German melody that can be sung as a round in three parts. Look at the song and **identify** where each part comes in. **Sing** the song as a round. Use a melody instrument to play the pitches of the last line as you sing.

CD 9-10

Oh, How Lovely Is the Evening

Traditional German Melody

I F — Bb — F — Bb — F
Oh, how love - ly is the eve - ning, is the eve - ning,

II F — Bb — F — Bb — F
When the bells are sweet - ly ring - ing, sweet - ly ring - ing,

III F — Bb — F — Bb — F
Ding, dong, ding, dong, ding, dong!

Rhythms in Time

- Look at the song again. **Identify** the rhythms you already know.

- Clap a steady beat and say the first two lines of "Oh, How Lovely Is the Evening" using rhythm syllables.

- How many notes are in the last line? How many measures? How many notes are in each measure?

- This song has three beats in each measure. How many beats is each note of the last line?

- Clap a steady beat and say the whole song using rhythm syllables.

Ringing and Singing

One group can **sing** the last line of the song as an ostinato, while others sing the entire song. Then sing the song as a three part round. **Create** your own instrumental accompaniment.

Skipping with Rhythms

Look at the first line of "Dry Bones Come Skipping" and **identify** the rhythms you know. Tap and say each rhythm. **Compare** the first line to the rest of the song. What did you discover? Now **sing** "Dry Bones Come Skipping."

How many bones are in your body? Can you name any of them?

CD 9–15

Dry Bones Come Skipping

Traditional Song from the United States

Dry bones come skip-ping up the val - ley.   Some of them bones are   mine. ___

Dry bones   come skip-ping up the val - ley.   Some of them bones are mine.

Some of them bones are   'Ze - kiel's   bones. _   Some of them bones are   mine. ___

Some of them bones are   'Ze - kiel's   bones. _   Some of them bones are mine.

Connect the Bones

Create a *bones* composition. Use the same meter and Ⓐ Ⓑ Ⓐ form as "Dry Bones Come Skipping."

Ⓐ **Compose** four measures of rhythm in meter in 4. Use rhythms you know. Look at "Dry Bones Come Skipping" for ideas. Decide how you will perform your rhythm. Will you use an instrument or body percussion?

Ⓑ Choose one of the poems below for the Ⓑ section. Read the poem, then decide how you will **perform** it. Will you speak it or sing it? Will you use movements or instruments to accompany the poem? Will you perform the poem once or more than once?

Ⓐ Repeat your Ⓐ section rhythm!

Bones
by Jeff Moss

Bones are important,
They do a big job.
Without them, you'd be just
A big squooshy blob.

A Poem to Help You Figure Out What Bone the Patella Is
by Jeff Moss

A hairy young primate named Stella
Once yelled, "Ow, I hurt my patella!"
So her mom chimpanzee
Simply bandaged her knee
And made well a patella of Stella.

Old Bones

When plants or animals died, they sometimes were buried in layers of soil that eventually became stone. As the soil turned to stone, the plants or animal skeletons left fossils. Fossils are traces of plants' and animals' remains that have been preserved in the earth. **Listen** to *Fossils*.

CD 9–20
Fossils

**from *Carnival of the Animals*
by Camille Saint-Saëns**

French composer Camille Saint-Saëns used xylophones to represent bones.

Say the rhythm below using rhythm syllables.
Listen for this rhythm in *Fossils*. Then
perform the pattern, using body percussion.

Snap
Clap
Pat
Stamp

MUSIC MAKERS

Camille Saint-Saëns

French composer **Camille Saint-Saëns** [san(n)-sa(hn)] (1835–1921) learned to play the piano and organ when he was young. Many of his compositions are for piano or organ with orchestra. In addition to performing and composing, Saint-Saëns was a writer. He wrote about music, history, and science.

Create a Fossil Rap

Fossils give us clues about plants and animals that lived many years ago. Much of what we know about dinosaurs comes from studying their fossilized bones.

Use "Gotta Find a Footprint" to **create** a rap in **A B A C A D A** form.

Gotta Find a Footprint

by Jeff Moss

A
Gotta find a footprint, a bone, or a tooth
To grab yourself a piece of dinosaur truth.
All the dino knowledge that we've ever known
Comes from a footprint, a tooth, or a bone.

B
A tooth can tell you what a dino would eat,
A sharp tooth tells you that he dined on meat.
A blunt tooth tells you that she dined on plants.
No teeth at all? Well, perhaps they slurped ants.

C
Footprints can tell you a dinosaur's size,
And how fast he ran when he raced with the guys.
Count all the footprints, you'll easily see
If he traveled alone or with a family.

D
Her bones will tell you if she stood up tall,
If she had a big tail or no tail at all.
Put the bones together and see how they'll look—
Pretty enough to get their picture took.

Show What You Know!

Speak "Gotta Find a Footprint" and pay attention to the rhythm of the words. Then **notate** the rhythm of the first two lines of the poem. Next **perform** the words using your notated rhythms.

Theme and Variations

A *balalaika* [bah-lah-LIE-kah] is a Russian folk instrument. Look at the pictures of the *balalaikas*. Then **describe** how they are the same and how they are different.

Listen to "*Minka*," a song from Ukraine about a soldier and the girl he left behind.

CD 9–21
MIDI 16

Minka

English Words by Margaret Marks

Folk Song from Ukraine

Ти ж ме-не під-ма-ну -ла, Ти ж ме-не під-ве-ла ——

1. Said the Cos-sack to the maid-en, "Love, my heart is heav-y lad-en.
2. Off the Cos-sack went to bat-tle, all a-lone poor Mink-a sat e-

Ти ж ме-не мо-ло-до-го, З у-ма ра-зу-ма зве-ла.

Du-ty calls so I'm a-fraid, en-chant-ress, we must part. _____

lev-en years and she grew fat, al-though her heart was true. _____

Variety Is the Spice of Life

Sing *"Minka."* The melody of the song can be called a **theme.** Now think of a way to vary or change *"Minka."* How will you make the theme different? Will you change the dynamics, tempo, melody, rhythm, or timbre of the music? Practice your **variation,** then **perform** it for the class. Be ready to explain how you made your variation.

> **Theme** is an important melody that occurs several times in a piece of music. **Variation** is music that is repeated, but changed in some important way.

A♭   E♭

Ти ж ме - не під - ма - ну - ла,   Ти ж ме - не під - ве - ла ___
I be-seech you fair - est Mink - a,   wait for me, I hate to think an -
When at last her Cos-sack lov - er   came back home and looked her o - ver,

Fm   C₇   Fm

Ти ж ме - не мо - ло - до - го,   З у - ма ра - зу - ма зве - ла.
oth - er man might come and tink - er   with your faith - ful heart!" ___
he be - gan to court an - oth - er.   Broke her heart in two! ___

MIDI Use the *"Minka"* song file with sequencing software to create variations of the melody.

Matreshka dolls
(nesting dolls) ◄

Russian Variations

Tap the rhythm of Glière's theme as you **listen** to *Russian Sailors' Dance.*

CD 9–26
Russian Sailors' Dance

from *The Red Poppy*
by Reinhold Glière

In this piece, Russian composer Reinhold Glière wrote variations on a theme.

> **Theme and variations** is a musical form in which each section is a variation of the original theme.

Move to the rhythm of the theme using body percussion.

clap
pat
stamp

Now **listen** for the **theme and variations.**
How many variations do you hear?

224

Reinhold Glière

Reinhold Glière [glee-EHR] (1875–1956) was a student and then a composition professor at the Moscow Conservatory in Russia. He wrote operas, symphonies, music for ballets, and piano music. Glière often used Russian folk melodies in his music. His operas and ballets included stories and themes of central Asia.

FIND THE SEQUENCE

Be a melody detective. Investigate the melody of "*Thula, thula, ngoana*" to find *fa* and *ti*. Here's a clue. This melody ends on *do*.

Listen to "*Thula, thula, ngoana*," an African lullaby and work song. **Sing** the melody with pitch syllables. Then **sing** the words.

CD 9–27

THULA, THULA, NGOANA
(Sleep, Sleep, Baby)

Folk Song from the Lesotho Region of South Africa

Thu - la, thu - la, ngoa - na, — thu - la, thu - la, ngoa - na, —
Sleep my lit - tle ba - by, — sleep my lit - tle ba - by, —

Thu - la, thu - la, ngoa - na, — thu - la, thu - la, ngoa - na. —
Sleep my lit - tle ba - by, — sleep my lit - tle ba - by. —

Sing and Sequence

Sing *"Thula, thula, ngoana"* again. Trace the shape of the melody as you sing. Notice the shape, or contour, of the first two measures. How many times does this contour occur in the rest of the melody?

Describe what happens to the starting note each time the contour pattern is repeated. The pattern you have found is a **melodic sequence.**

> A **melodic sequence** is a melody pattern that begins on a different pitch each time it is repeated.

Create movements to show the melodic sequence of *"Thula, thula, ngoana."*

Hear a Sequence

Listen for melodic sequences in this music. The most obvious sequence starts immediately after the loud opening chord.

CD 9–34
Slavonic Dance, Op. 46, No. 1

by Antonin Dvořák

The folk dances of Bohemia inspired Dvořák to compose this music. This region is now part of the Czech Republic.

Tengo una secuencia (I Have a Sequence)

Sheepherding was a major occupation of the early Spanish settlers in New Mexico. Shepherds probably made up songs like *"Tengo, tengo, tengo"* to pass the time and to entertain one another.

Listen for the melodic sequence in this song. **Compare** this sequence to the melody pattern in *"Thula, thula, ngoana,"* on the previous page. How is it different? How is it the same?

Now **sing** or **play** the new sequence. To continue the sequence, **create** an additional two lines for the song. (You can end your melody by making the last note *do*.)

CD 9–35

TENGO, TENGO, TENGO
(I Have Three Sheep)

English Words by Julie Scott

Folk Song from New Mexico

1. Ten - go, ten - go, ten - go, y tú no tie - nes na - da;
2. U - na me da le - che, y o - tra me da la - na;
1. I have some-thing splen - did! And you have, you have noth - ing!
2. One sheep gives me sweet milk, An - oth - er gives me wool; __

Ten - go tres o - ve - jas, a - llá en la ca - ña - da.
Yo - tra man - te - qui - lla, ¡Ay! Pa - ra la se - ma - na.
I have three fine sheep, and they're graz - ing in the gul - ly.
That one gives me but - ter, Oh! It will last a week. __

Accompany the Sequence

Play the accompaniment below as others **sing** *"Tengo, tengo, tengo."*
To help you get ready, follow these steps.

- Sing the bass xylophone part, using pitch syllables and then
  letter names. Then play it.

- Tap or clap the woodblock part, using rhythm syllables. Then play it.

- Play the glockenspiel part, first by itself and then with the other parts.

Soprano and Alto Glockenspiels

Bass Xylophone

Show What You Know!

Here is another melodic sequence, but some of the notes are missing! The
first pattern of the melodic sequence is shown. It has only three notes.
The sequence continues three more times. **Identify** the missing notes.
Then **play** the entire sequence on a xylophone or keyboard instrument.

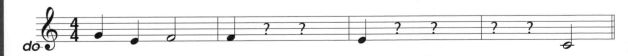

A Slovak Melody

Slovak culture has a long history of folk songs and dances. Find a sequence in this Slovak melody. Look for lines that have a similar shape. Does the sequence move upward or downward? **Sing** "Tancovačka" and point to the sequences.

CD 9–39

Tancovačka
(Dancing)

Slovak Folk Song

VERSE

Tan - cuj, tan - cuj, vy - krú - caj, vy - krú - caj,
Come and dance, turn light - ly, turn light - ly A -

Len mi pie - cku ne - zrú - caj, ne - zrú - caj.
round the camp - fire burn - ing so bright - ly. The

Do - brá pie - cka na zi - mu, na zi - mu,
snow falls fast and cold is the weath - er. Come

Ked' ne - má - me pe - ri - nu, pe - ri - nu.
dance, come dance, we'll ___ all turn to - geth - er.

Practice *fa* and *ti*

Sing the first four lines of *"Tancovačka"* again, this time using pitch syllables.

Move to show the melodic contour of *"Tancovačka."* Use a repeated movement to go with the melodic sequence in the first four lines. Use different movements for the last four lines of the song.

KEYBOARD CLASSICS

The harpsichord is one of the oldest keyboard instruments. Harpsichords were popular in the 1600s and 1700s.

Although the harpsichord looks similar to a piano, it sounds much different. When you press a key on a harpsichord, the string inside is plucked by a quill. Originally, harpsichord quills were feathers. Today quills are made of leather or plastic.

Listen to the harpsichord in *Gigue* by Bach.

CD 10–1
Gigue

**from *French Suite No. 5*
by Johann Sebastian Bach**

See page 113 for another *gigue* by Bach, played on violin.

▶
The Latin inscription on this harpsichord reads, "Without knowledge, art is nothing."

Pipes Galore

Organ pipes can be small and thin, or long and thick. They are made of wood or metal. Pipe organs can have hundreds or even thousands of pipes. The different pipe shapes and sizes produce different sounds when air is blown through them.

Listen to this famous composition for organ. Notice how the timbre changes as the air moves through the different pipes of the organ.

CD 10–2

Toccata in D Minor

by Johann Sebastian Bach

This organ selection was written in 1708. It is frequently performed today and is one of Bach's most famous works.

M·U·S·I·C   M·A·K·E·R·S

Johann Sebastian Bach

Johann Sebastian Bach (1685–1750) was a German composer of the Baroque era (1600–1750). Among the first instruments he learned to play were the violin and organ. During his lifetime, Bach was famous for his ability to improvise on the organ. He was employed by the nobility of several cities in Germany as an organist, choir director, teacher, and composer. Bach wrote church, orchestra, keyboard, vocal, and choral music.

Piano and Forte

The first pianos were called *pianoforte* because the performer could make both soft *(piano)* and loud *(forte)* sounds by touching the keys in different ways. When the player presses a piano key, a hammer inside the instrument strikes one or more strings. Striking harder makes a louder sound.

The first *pianofortes* were made around 1700. By 1825, the piano looked and sounded similar to the pianos we know today. **Listen** to these piano pieces.

CD 10–3
Waltz in D-flat ("Minute" Waltz)

by Frederic Chopin

This piece has the nickname "Minute" Waltz because it is played in a very fast tempo. However, it usually takes longer than one minute to play.

CD 10–4
Prelude in A Major

by Frederic Chopin
as performed by Vladimir Ashkenazy

Chopin (1810–1849) was an acclaimed pianist during his lifetime and is considered one of the greatest composers for the instrument.

▲ *Pianoforte Cantata* (1835)

M·U·S·I·C M·A·K·E·R·S

Vladimir Ashkenazy

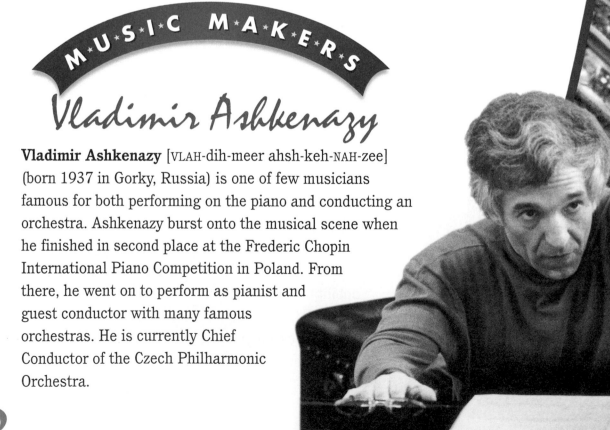

Vladimir Ashkenazy [VLAH-dih-meer ahsh-keh-NAH-zee] (born 1937 in Gorky, Russia) is one of few musicians famous for both performing on the piano and conducting an orchestra. Ashkenazy burst onto the musical scene when he finished in second place at the Frederic Chopin International Piano Competition in Poland. From there, he went on to perform as pianist and guest conductor with many famous orchestras. He is currently Chief Conductor of the Czech Philharmonic Orchestra.

234

The Newest Keyboards

Electronic music was created in the 20th century. The best-known electronic instrument is the synthesizer. It might look like a keyboard, but it can mimic the sounds of all types of instruments, as well as produce completely new sounds. **Listen** to this synthesizer version of *Close Encounters of the Third Kind.*

 CD 10–5

Close Encounters of the Third Kind

by John Williams

This music comes from the movie soundtrack. The main theme features the pattern *re, mi, do,* low *do,* and low *so.*

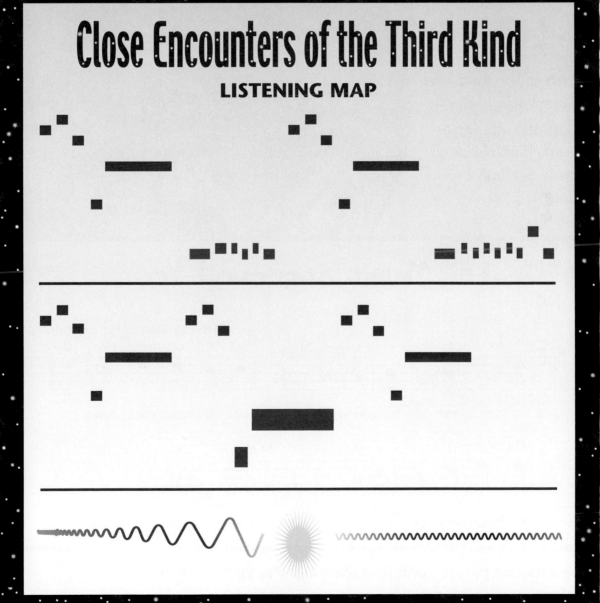

Close Encounters of the Third Kind
LISTENING MAP

Round and Round

A melody performed alone has a thin musical texture. A melody performed with an accompaniment has a thicker musical texture.

When a melody is performed as a round, harmony is created and the musical texture changes from thin to thicker.

Silently read the words of "Let Music Surround You" as you **listen** to the song.

Sing "Let Music Surround You" in unison and then as a round. Stand in a circle to let the music surround you as you sing.

CD 10–6

Let Music Surround You

Words and Music by Fran Smartt Addicott

I A   G   A   G   II A   G   A   G

Let   mus-ic   sur-round you,   let   it   warm your   heart.

III A   G   A   G   IV A   G   A

Those who sing   in   har-mo-ny,   ne-ver __ grow a - part.

Create a motion for each phrase of the song. **Perform** the motions as you **sing** in unison and in harmony.

236

A Symphony Goes Round

Now **listen** to an orchestra perform the melody below as part of a symphony.

CD 10–8

Symphony No. 1, Movement 3

by Gustav Mahler

The melody in this movement is a minor-key variation on the familiar round "*Frère Jacques.*"

Mahler changed the texture in his symphony by presenting the melody as a round. To make the texture even thicker, he added an ostinato and a countermelody. **Play** the ostinato below.

Listen to the countermelody. What instruments play the ostinato and countermelody?

Creating Textures

With a group of friends, **create** your own arrangement using the melodies above. Will you play in unison, or as a round? How will the texture change? Will you start with ostinatos or the melody?

Harmony Moves Me

If the energy of
this song doesn't get you
moving, the message of the words will!

Listen to the Isley Brothers perform *Twist and Shout*. Do the "twist" as you **move** to the song.

CD 10–9
Twist and Shout

**by Phil Medley and Bert Russell
as performed by the Isley Brothers**

This song has been recorded by many artists
such as the Beatles and Ike and Tina Turner.

The Isley Brothers ▶

238

Play Your Own Harmony

Practice the ostinato pattern below on any melody instrument.

(8 times with verse)   *(4 times with interlude)*

Listen to *Twist and Shout* again. To add harmony, **play** the ostinato shown above. The notes of this ostinato are the lowest notes of the chords used in *Twist and Shout*.

M·U·S·I·C M·A·K·E·R·S
The Isley Brothers

The **Isley Brothers** began their career as a gospel singing group in the early 1960s. They crossed over to doo-wop and recorded hit songs like *Shout* and *Twist and Shout*. Due to frustration with record companies of the time, the Isley Brothers formed their own record label, T-Neck Records, and began recording a new sound with a young Jimi Hendrix. The Isley Brothers have since recorded with Motown and gone back to their own label. They are known for their originality and for laying the groundwork for rock, funk, and rap music.

▼ Teens dancing the twist in the 1960s

Chords Galore

Here's a hint to help you figure out what this song is all about. Just remember a *keel* is a kind of boat, and *weel* is a Scottish word for "well."

CD 10–10

The Keel Row

Folk Song from Northumbria

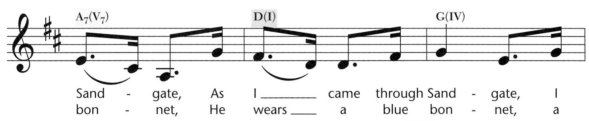

VERSE

D(I) G(IV) D(I)

1. As I _____ came through Sand - gate, through Sand - gate, through
2. "He wears __ a blue bon - net, blue bon - net, blue

A₇(V₇) D(I) G(IV)

Sand - gate, As I _____ came through Sand - gate, I
bon - net, He wears ___ a blue bon - net, a

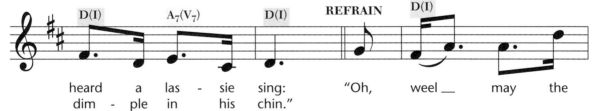

D(I) A₇(V₇) D(I) **REFRAIN** D(I)

heard a las - sie sing: "Oh, weel __ may the
dim - ple in his chin."

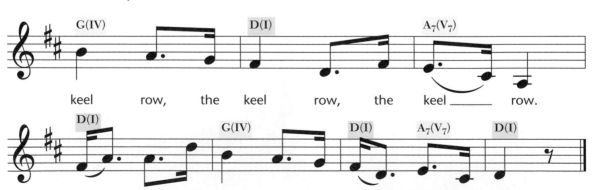

G(IV) D(I) A₇(V₇)

keel row, the keel row, the keel _____ row.

D(I) G(IV) D(I) A₇(V₇) D(I)

Weel _ may the keel row that my __ lad - die's in."

240

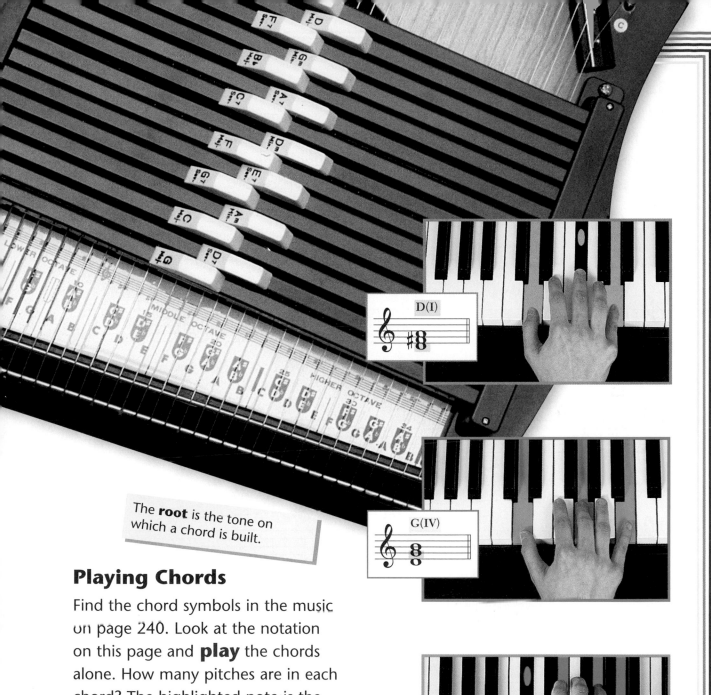

The **root** is the tone on which a chord is built.

Playing Chords

Find the chord symbols in the music on page 240. Look at the notation on this page and **play** the chords alone. How many pitches are in each chord? The highlighted note is the **root** of the chord. Now follow the song notation and play the chords as others **sing** "The Keel Row."

Tune In

An average Scottish keel boat was about sixty feet long, ten feet wide, and four feet deep. The boats were propelled by long poles. Twelve to twenty men, including oarsmen and a pilot, were needed to push the boat up river.

Same Chords, New Song

"*El borrego*" comes from the musical heritage of *Los californios*—Mexican ranchers who lived in California territory in the early 1800s. **Listen** to the song as you follow the chord symbols in the music. Then **compare** the chords to those in "The Keel Row," on page 240.

compare the chords to those in "The Keel Row," on page 240.

CD 10–12

English Words by Julie Scott

El borrego
(The Lamb)

Folk Song from Mexico

A

Se - ño - ra,   su   bo - rre - gui - to,   me   quie -
Se - ño - ra,   your   lit - tle   lamb wants   to   take

re   lle - var ___ al   rí - o,   y   yo   le   di - go   que
me   down   to   the   cold   riv - er,   but   I   must   tell   the   lamb,

no,   por - que   me   mue - ro   de ___ frí - o.
"No!"   be - cause   the   cold   wa - ter   makes _ me   shiv - er.

B *Faster*

Sa - le   la   lin - da,   sa - le   la   fe - a,   y el   bo - rre -
Out goes   the   beau - ty,   brim - ming with   laugh - ter,   Out goes   the

gui - to   con   su   za - le - a.   To - pe   que   to - pe,
lamb,   who's   frol - ick - ing   af - ter.   Bump in - to   her,   then

to - pe   con   e - lla.   To - pe   que   to - pe,   to - pe   con   él.
bump in - to   him.   Then bump in - to   her,   then bump in - to   him.

242

◄ Mission San Luis Rey, founded in 1798, is the largest of all California missions. It once maintained a herd of livestock that included more than 50,000 cattle and sheep.

Mallets and Maracas

Play this accompaniment during the **B** section of "*El borrego.*"

SINGING in PARTS

Gold was discovered in California in 1848. By 1849, thousands of Americans rushed to California to seek their fortunes. Some, like "Sweet Betsy from Pike," traveled in covered wagons to get there. The trip was long and hard. **Sing** "Sweet Betsy from Pike" and find out what happened on the way.

CD 10–16
MIDI 17

SWEET BETSY FROM PIKE

Folk Song from the United States
Adapted and Arranged by Lillian Wiedman

A VERSE C   G₇   C

do

1. Oh, don't you re - mem - ber sweet Bet - sy from Pike?
2. One ev' - ning quite ear - ly they camped on the Platte,
3. They soon reached the de - sert where Bet - sy gave out.

C   D₇   G

She crossed the wide prai - ries with her hus - band, Ike,
'Twas near by the road on a green shad - y flat.
And down on the sand she lay roll - ing a - bout.

Am   Em   F   C

With two yoke of ox - en, an old yel - low dog,
Poor Bet - sy, quite tired, ___ lay down for re - pose,
While Ike, in great tears, ___ looked on in sur - prise:

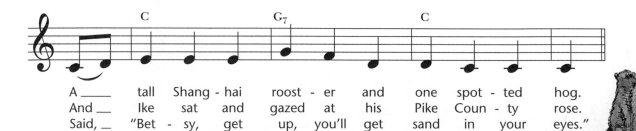

C   G₇   C

A ___ tall Shang - hai roost - er and one spot - ted hog.
And ___ Ike sat and gazed at his Pike Coun - ty rose.
Said, ___ "Bet - sy, get up, you'll get sand in your eyes."

REFRAIN

B Too - ra - lee, _____ too - ra - lay, _____

Too - ra - lee, too - ra - lay,

Sing-ing too - ra - lee, too - ra - lee, too - ra - lee ay.

4. The rooster ran off and the oxen all died,
   The last piece of bacon that morning was fried.
   Poor Ike got discouraged and Betsy got mad,
   The dog wagged his tail and looked awfully sad. *Refrain*

5. The alkali desert was burning and hot,
   And Ike, he decided to leave on the spot:
   "My dear old Pike County, I'll go back to you."
   Said Betsy, "You'll go by yourself if you do." *Refrain*

6. They swam the wide rivers, they crossed the tall peaks,
   They camped out on prairies for weeks and for weeks,
   Fought hunger and rattlers and big storms of dust,
   Determined to reach California or bust. *Refrain*

Two-Part Harmony

Identify the refrain of "Sweet Betsy from Pike."
Sing the melody first, and then learn the harmony
part. **Perform** both parts together.

Review, Assess,

What Do You Know?

Match the terms below with their definitions.

1. accent

a melody started at different times

2. theme and variations

a melody pattern repeated at a higher or lower pitch level

3. melodic sequence

stress on certain notes

4. round

a melody repeated with changes

What Do You Hear? 6

 CD 10–18

Listen to the following examples of keyboard music. Point to the name of the instrument you hear in each example.

1. piano   harpsichord   organ   synthesizer

2. piano   harpsichord   organ   synthesizer

3. piano   harpsichord   organ   synthesizer

4. piano   harpsichord   organ   synthesizer

Piano ▲

Harpsichord ▲

Organ ▲

Synthesizer ▲

Perform, Create

What You Can Do

Move to Variations

Listen to *Russian Sailors' Dance,* on page 224, and perform the body percussion pattern. Create your own body percussion part for *Russian Sailors' Dance* and perform it for the class.

Perform with Accents

Sing "*El rancho grande,*" on page 215. Decide where to add accents and then perform them as you sing.

Create with Rhythms

Sing "Dry Bones Come Skipping," on page 218. Perform small steady-beat movements to accompany the **A** sections and different steady-beat movements with the **B** section. Using the rhythms in the song, create a rhythm ostinato. Perform the ostinato on nonpitched percussion instruments as you sing the song.

Move with Sequences

Sing "*Tancovačka,*" on page 230. Perform hand movements to show the contour of the melodic sequences in the verse.

Sing in Rounds

Sing "Let Music Surround You," on page 236, as a round. Always sing with good vocal quality.

PATHS TO
Making
Music

Song of the City

"Theme from New York, New York" was written for a movie *New York, New York*. Read the words to this song. Create a story about someone from a small town who really wants to live in the big city. What are some reasons a person might want to live in a big city?

CD 10–22

Theme from New York, New York

Words by Fred Ebb

Music by John Kander

Start spread-in' the news, I'm leav-ing to - day,

I wan - na be a part _ of it New York, New York. _

GOING PLACES U.S.A.

Begin a musical trip around the United States. Start on the east coast with "Theme from New York, New York" and travel to the west coast with "California, Here I Come."

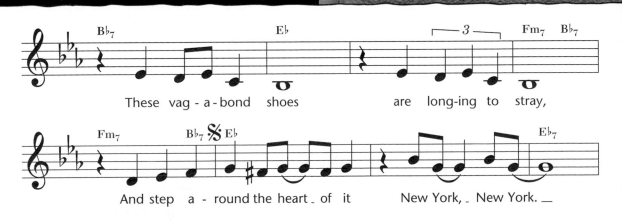

These vag-a-bond shoes are long-ing to stray,

And step a-round the heart of it New York, New York.

Ride the Wave
SING A SHANTY

We'll start our trip with whale watching in the Atlantic. Of course, on board you may have to work a little, and working on a ship can be really hard. Imagine being on board for weeks, or even years! How would you pass the time, raise your spirits, or lighten your work? You might sing a sea shanty. From about 1493 to 1928, this is what most sailors did.

Sing "Blow, Ye Winds." How do the tones in the color boxes move? Now sing "Rio Grande" on page 256 and **identify** steps, leaps, and repeated notes in the song.

CD 10–25

Blow, Ye Winds

Folk Song from the United States

VERSE

1. 'Tis   ad - ver - tised in   Bos - ton, New York, and   Buf - fa - lo,
2. They   send you to New   Bed - ford, that   fa - mous whal - ing   port,
3. It's   now we're out to   sea, my boys, the   wind be - gins to   blow,
4. The   skip - per's on the   quar - ter - deck a - squint - ing   at the   sails,

Five   hun - dred brave A - mer - i - cans,   a - whal - ing for   to   go. ___
And   give you   to some   land sharks ___   to   board and fit you   out. ___
One   half the watch is   sick on deck and the oth - er   half be - low. ___
When   up   a - loft the   look - out sights a   school ___ of ___   whales. ___

REFRAIN

Sing - ing, "Blow,   ye winds in the morn - ing, And   blow, ye winds, high - O!

Clear   a - way your   run - ning gear, And   blow,   ye winds, high - O!"

5. "Now clear away the boats, my boys,
   and after him we'll trail,
But if you get too near to him,
   he'll kick you with his tail!"   *Refrain*

6. Now we've got him turned up,
   we tow him alongside;
We over with our blubber hooks
   and rob him of his hide.   *Refrain*

7. Next comes the stowing down, my boys;
   'twill take both night and day,
And you'll all have fifty cents apiece
   when you collect your pay.   *Refrain*

Rio Grande

Shanty from the United States

VERSE

Solo D   A₇   D

1. Oh say, were you ev – er in Ri – o Grande?
2. A jol – ly good ship and a jol – ly good crew,
3. The an – chor's a – weigh and the sails they are set,
4. Good – bye ___ to Sal – ly and Sar – ah and Sue,

Chorus D   *Solo* G   D

A – way ___ for Ri – o!

It's there that the riv – er runs
A jol – ly good mate and a
The gals that we're leav – ing we'll
To all who are list'–ning, it's

A₇   D   *Chorus* D   A₇   D

down gold – en sand,
jol – ly good crew,   We are bound for Ri – o Grande! ___
nev – er for – get,
good – bye to you,

REFRAIN

Chorus D

And a – way ___ for Ri – o!   A – way ___ for Ri – o!

Solo G   D   A₇   D   *Chorus* D   A₇   D

So fare _ ye well _ my bon-ny young girl, We are bound for Ri – o Grande! _

Tune In

Hunting whales for oil was a main occupation of sailors. Voyages could last up to three years. Many sailors were injured or killed by a whale's tail.

Tales of the Sea

Sailors also told tales to pass the time. These tales were often about natural disasters they encountered. Many times they used their imagination to make their own tales more enjoyable. Listen to the recording of one such tale.

CD 10–30

The Sea Wolf

by Violet McDougal

The fishermen say, when your catch is done
And you're sculling in with the tide,
You must take great care that the Sea Wolf's share
Is tossed to him overside.
They say that the Sea Wolf rides by day
Unseen on the crested waves,
And the sea mists rise from his cold green eyes
When he comes from his salt sea caves.
The fishermen say, when it storms at night
And the great seas bellow and roar,
That the Sea Wolf rides on the plunging tides,
And you hear his howl at the door.
And you must throw open your door at once,
And fling your catch to the waves,
Till he drags his share to his cold sea lair,
Straight down to his salt sea caves.
Then the storm will pass and the still stars shine,
In peace—so the fishermen say—
But the Sea Wolf waits by the cold Sea Gates
For the dawn of another day.

Sailing to the Gulf

The sea shanty "'Round the Bay of Mexico" was probably sung in ports throughout the Gulf of Mexico. **Listen** to the song as you follow the music. Then **compare** the form to that of "Rio Grande," on page 256. In what way are the two songs similar?

Sing "'Round the Bay of Mexico." Take turns being the leader (*Solo*) and the ship's crew (*Chorus*).

CD 10–31

'Round the Bay of Mexico

Traditional Shanty
Collected by Stan Hugill

Solo
D   Chorus   G   D

1. Heave a-way, my bul-ly boys,   'Way-ay, heave a-way!
2. Heave a-way, and a-round goes she,
3. Heave a-round and with a will,
4. Heave a-way, for she's trimmed tight,

Solo
G   D   Em   A₇   Chorus D   G A₇ D

Heave a-way, why don't you make some noise, boys? 'Round the Bay of Mex-i-co!
Six for you and sev-en for ____ me, ____
If she don't go she will stay there still, ____
Bend your backs if you want to sleep to-night, __

258

Arts Connection

▲ *The Port of Galveston* by Julius Stockfleth
(1857–1935). Sailing ships and tugboats are shown
navigating this busy Texas Gulf Coast seaport in the
late 19th century.

Form a Chorus

Perform these accompaniments during the chorus
phrases of "'Round the Bay of Mexico."

Tune In

Shanties were sung as crews raised and lowered the ship's sails, which could weigh up to 2,500 pounds. The crew would rest as the leader sang, and then haul the sails during the chorus.

Chorus (part 1)

Heave a - way, heave a - way!

Chorus (part 2)

Heave a - way, heave a-way!

Chorus (part 3)

Heave a-way, heave a - way!

The Celtic Connection

▲ Celtic basket

Celtic music comes from what is now Ireland, Scotland, Wales, France, and Spain. When people from these areas came to the United States, they brought their music with them. "How Can I Keep from Singing?" is one of those songs.

Listen to the song. In this melody, there are two different repeated rhythm patterns. Find and **play** these two patterns.

1.    2.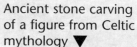

How many times do you hear pattern 1 in the first four measures? While listening to "How Can I Keep from Singing?" tap pattern 1 and snap pattern 2.

Play this recorder part while others **sing** the song.

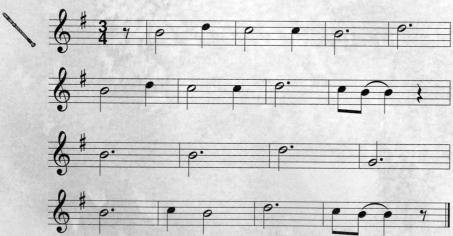

Ancient stone carving of a figure from Celtic mythology ▼

Listen to this contemporary version of the song.

 CD 10–35

How Can I Keep from Singing?

Celtic Folk Song
as performed by Alfreda Gerald and the Taliesin Orchestra

This recording of "How Can I Keep from Singing?" features the *uilleann* pipes, a favorite instrument in Scotland and Ireland.

How Can I Keep from Singing?

CD 10–33

Celtic Folk Song

1. My life flows on   in end - less song,   a - bove earth's lam - en -
2. What though the tem - pest 'round me roars,   I know the truth, it
3. When ty - rants trem - ble, sick with fear,   And hear their death knells

ta - tion. __   I hear the real,   though far - off song   that
liv - eth. __   What though the dark - ness 'round me close,   songs
ring - ing. __   When friends re - joice   both far and near,   how

hails a new   cre - a - tion. __   Through all the tu - mult
in the night   it giv - eth. __   No storm can shake my
can I keep   from sing - ing? __   In pris - on cell and

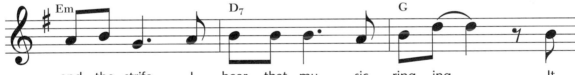

and the strife   I hear that mu - sic   ring - ing. __   It
in - most calm   while to that rock   I'm cling - ing. __   Since
dun - geon vile   our thoughts to them   are wing - ing. __   When

sounds an ech - o ____ in my soul,   how
love is lord of ____ heaven and earth,   how
friends by shame are ____ un - de - filed,   how

can I keep   from sing - ing? ____
can I keep   from sing - ing? ____
can I keep   from sing - ing? ____

GET THAT PIONEER SPIRIT

The pioneer spirit has long been a source of pride for all Americans. Those who settled long ago and the most recent settlers to arrive on our shores are all pioneers. How do we keep our pioneer spirit alive? One really great way is to sing about it.

CD 11–1

THE GLENDY BURKE

Words and Music by Stephen Foster

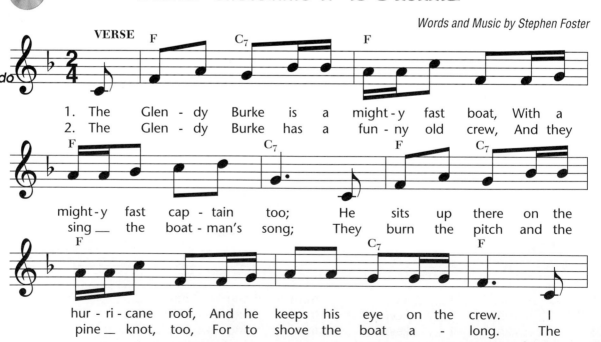

1. The Glen-dy Burke is a might-y fast boat, With a
2. The Glen-dy Burke has a fun-ny old crew, And they

might-y fast cap-tain too; He sits up there on the
sing __ the boat-man's song; They burn the pitch and the

hur-ri-cane roof, And he keeps his eye on the crew. I
pine __ knot, too, For to shove the boat a - long. The

Preparing for Pioneer Singing

Read the following examples using rhythm syllables. Then clap the rhythm patterns.

1.

2.

Sing "The Glendy Burke." Which pattern above can you **identify** in the song?

can't stay here, for the work's too hard, I'm __ bound to leave this town; I'll
smoke goes up and the en - gine roars, And the wheel goes round and round; So

take my duds and tote 'em on my back, When the Glen - dy Burke comes down.
fare ye well, for I'll take a lit - tle ride, When the Glen - dy Burke comes down.

REFRAIN

Ho! for Lou' - si - an - a! I'm bound to leave this town, I'll

take my duds and tote 'em on my back, When the Glen - dy Burke comes down.

Reading Challenges

Count and **identify** the *do-re-mi* and the *mi-re-do* patterns in "Oh, Susanna." Sing only the *do-re-mi* patterns and "think" the rest of the song.

Take this challenge. **Sing** all of "Oh, Susanna" using pitch syllables.

OH, SUSANNA

Words and Music by Stephen Foster

CD 11–3

1. I ___ came from Al - a - ba - ma With my ban - jo on my knee,
2. I ___ had a dream the oth - er night, When ev - 'ry - thing was still,

I'm ___ going to Loui - si - an - a, My ___ true love for to see;
I ___ thought I saw Su - san - na A - com - ing down the hill.

It ___ rained all night the day I left, The weath - er it was dry;
The _ buck-wheat cake was in her mouth, The tear was in her eye.

The _ sun so hot I froze to death; Su - san - na, don't you cry.
Says _ I, "I'm com - ing from the South, Su - san - na, don't you cry."

REFRAIN

Oh, Su - san - na, Oh, don't you cry for me,

I've __ come from Al - a - ba - ma With my ban - jo on my knee.

Pioneer Dancing

Move to the song "Oh, Susanna" or "The Glendy Burke" by following these dance movements.

Verse

Refrain

▲ Girls take 8 steps in and 8 steps back while boys clap. Switch the movements.

▲ Partners link right arms and circle to the right. Link left arms and circle to the left.

Visit **Take It to the Net** at *www.sfsuccessnet.com* to learn more about Stephen Foster and his music.

What's in a Song?

"Follow the Drinkin' Gourd" was a song with a secret message for enslaved African Americans in the 1800s. The words *drinkin' gourd* were code for "The Big Dipper." Escaping slaves followed the stars in the constellation to find their way north to freedom. People who formed the "Underground Railroad" took big risks by providing secret hiding places along the way.

 CD 11–5

Follow the Drinkin' Gourd

Song of the Underground Railroad

REFRAIN

Am   Em   Am

Fol - low ____ the drink - in' gourd. ___ Fol - low ____ the

Em   G   D

drink - in' gourd. ___ For the old man is a - wait - ing for to

Em   Bm   Em   Bm   Em   *Fine*

car - ry you to free-dom If you fol - low the drink - in' gourd.

Vocal Timbres

Listen to "Follow the Drinkin' Gourd."
Who is singing—men, women, children?
Do you hear a chorus or a solo voice? Is this song
accompanied? If you hear instruments, **identify** them.
Musicians refer to differences in sound as timbre.

Choose an instrument and **play** this accompaniment
while others **sing** "Follow the Drinkin' Gourd."

REFRAIN   Soprano and Alto Xylophones

Alto Xylophone

Bass Xylophone

VERSE   Em   Am

1. When the sun comes up and the first quail calls, _ Fol - low ____ the
2. Now the river-bank will make a ____ mighty good road; _ Dead trees ____ will

Em   G   D

drink - in' gourd. _   For the   old man   is   a - wait - ing   for   to
show you   the   way. __   And the   left ____ foot,   peg - foot,

Em   Bm   Em   Bm   Em   *D.C. al Fine*

car - ry you to free-dom If you   fol - low   the   drink - in'   gourd.
trav - el - in'   on, __ Just you   fol - low   the   drink - in'   gourd.

Listen to "Wade in the Water." How is the timbre in this song different from what you heard in "Follow the Drinkin' Gourd"? **Sing** both songs either with a group or as a soloist. How can you vary the timbre of each song as it is being performed?

CD 11–7
MIDI 18

Wade in the Water

African American Spiritual

REFRAIN

Wade _____ in the wa - ter, ___ wade _____ in the

wa - ter child - ren. Wade _____ in the wa - ter, ___

God's gon - na trou - ble the wa - ter. _____

VERSE

1. Now Jor - dan's wa - ter is chil - ly and cold, _____
2. Now Jor - dan's wa - ter is deep _ and wide, _____
3. If you _ get there _ be - fore _ I do, _____

God's gon - na trou - ble the wa - ter. _____

It chills _ the bod - y, but not _ the soul, _____
Meet _ my moth - er on _ the oth - er side,
Tell all _ my friends _ I'm com - ing too. _____

God's gon - na trou - ble the wa - ter. _____

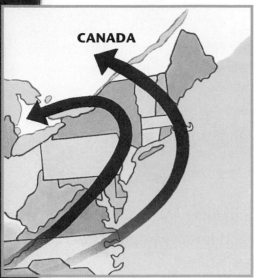

CANADA

▲ Routes of the Underground Railroad.

An Important Song— An Important Person

Harriet Tubman was born a slave around 1820 in Maryland. In 1849, she escaped to freedom in Philadelphia by way of the Underground Railroad. After experiencing freedom, she knew that she must free other slaves. Harriet Tubman made numerous trips south to lead about 300 people to freedom. It is said that she often sang "Wade in the Water" to send a message of hope to the people she helped.

CD 11–9

Harriet Tubman

by Eloise Greenfield

Harriet Tubman didn't take no stuff
Wasn't scared of nothing neither
Didn't come in this world to be no slave
And wasn't going to stay one either.

"Farewell!" she said to her friends one night
She was mighty sad to leave 'em
But she ran away that dark, hot night
Ran looking for her freedom.

She ran to the woods and ran through the woods
With the slave catchers right behind her
And she kept on going till she got to the North
Where mean men couldn't find her.

Nineteen times she went back South
To get three hundred others
She ran for her freedom nineteen times
To save black sisters and brothers.

Harriet Tubman didn't take no stuff
Wasn't scared of nothing neither
Didn't come in this world to be no slave
And didn't stay one either.

And didn't stay one either.

Meter Matters

Here's a riddle: What has three to twelve instruments (violins, trumpets, guitars, harps), plays terrific music, and is really popular in Mexico and the southwestern part of the United States?

. . . A *mariachi* band!

Listen to *"Cielito lindo"* and "Streets of Laredo." Both songs are in meter in 3. **Compare** and **describe** the tempo of each song.

CD 11–10
MIDI 19

Cielito lindo

English Words by Alice Firgau   *Folk Song from Mexico*

1. De   la   sie - rra   mo - re - na,   Cie - li - to
1. From   the   dark, ____ dis - tant   moun-tain,   Cie - li - to

lin - do,   vie - nen   ba - jan - do, _____
lin - do,   I _____ see   de - scend - ing, _____

Un   par   de o - ji - tos   ne - gros,   Cie - li - to
Your dark eyes ____ flash - ing   bright - ly,   Cie - li - to

lin - do,   de _____ con - tra - ban - do. _____
lin - do,   love's ____ mes - sage   send - ing. _____

REFRAIN

B♭   E♭   F₇

Ay,   ay,   ay,   ay! _____ Can - ta y no
Ay,   ay,   ay,   ay! _____ Sing,   sing with

B♭   F₇

llo - res. _____ Por - que   can - tan - do se a - le - gran, Cie -
glad - ness. _____ For   in   those hearts that are sing - ing, Cie -

F₇   B♭   1.   2. *To next Refrain*

- li - to   lin - do,   los co - ra - zo - nes. _____ _____
- li - to   lin - do,   there is no   sad - ness. ____ ____

REFRAIN

B♭   E♭   F₇

Ay,   ay,   ay,   ay! _____ Can - ta y no
Ay,   ay,   ay,   ay! _____ Sing,   sing with

B♭   F₇

llo - res. _____ Por - que   can - tan - do se a - le - gran, Cie -
glad - ness. _____ For   in   those hearts that are sing - ing, Cie -

F₇   F₇   B♭

- li - to   lin - do,   los co - ra - zo - nes. _____
- li - to   lin - do,   there is no   sad - ness. _____

2. *Ese lunar que tienes, Cielito lindo,*
   Junto a la boca,
   No se lo des a nadie, Cielito lindo,
   que a mi me toca. Refrain

2. For your kisses, my lovely *Cielito lindo,*
   My heart is aching,
   And when I can't be near you, *Cielito lindo,*
   my heart is breaking. *Refrain*

Streets of Laredo

Cowboy Song from the United States

1. As I _____ walked out in the streets of La - re - do,
2. "I see by your out - fit that you are a cow - boy,"
3. "Now once in the sad - dle I used to ride hand - some,

As I walked out in La - re - do one day,
These words he said as I bold - ly walked by;
'A handsome young cow - boy' is what they would say,

I spied a young cow - boy wrapped up in white lin - en,
"Come lis - ten to me and I'll tell my sad sto - ry
I'd ride in - to town and go down to the card - house,

Wrapped up in white lin - en and cold as the clay.
I'm shot in the chest and I'm sure I will die."
But I'm shot in the chest and I'm dy - ing to - day."

4. "Go run to the spring for a cup of cold water,
   To cool down my fever," the young cowboy said.
   But when I returned, his poor soul had departed,
   And I wept when I saw the young cowboy was dead.

5. We'll beat the drum slowly and play the fife lowly,
   We'll play the dead march as we bear him along.
   We'll go to the graveyard and lay the sod o'er him;
   He was a young cowboy, but he had done wrong.

Creating Accompaniments for Cowboy Songs

Perform the following rhythms. Then **create** a four-measure ostinato for "Streets of Laredo" to play on temple blocks while you sing the song.

Listen to *El siquisirí*, a folk song from Mexico. **Identify** the meter.

CD 11–16
El siquisirí

Traditional Music from Mexico as performed by Xocoyotzin Herrera

This recording uses the harp and other string instruments.

MIDI Use sequencing software to open the song file for "Streets of Laredo." Play the file at fast and slow tempos.

"Driving" to KANSAS

"Streets of Laredo," in the previous lesson, is a good example of a **ballad**. A *corrido* is a type of ballad from Mexico.

A **ballad** is a song that tells a story.

The adventurous story told in "*Corrido de Kansas*" involves a group of *vaqueros* (Mexican cowboys) on a cattle drive from Texas to Kansas. During a cattle drive, cowboys could encounter many dangers — including violent weather and wild animals. Before you **sing** "*Corrido de Kansas*," read the lyrics to discover one more danger the *vaqueros* faced.

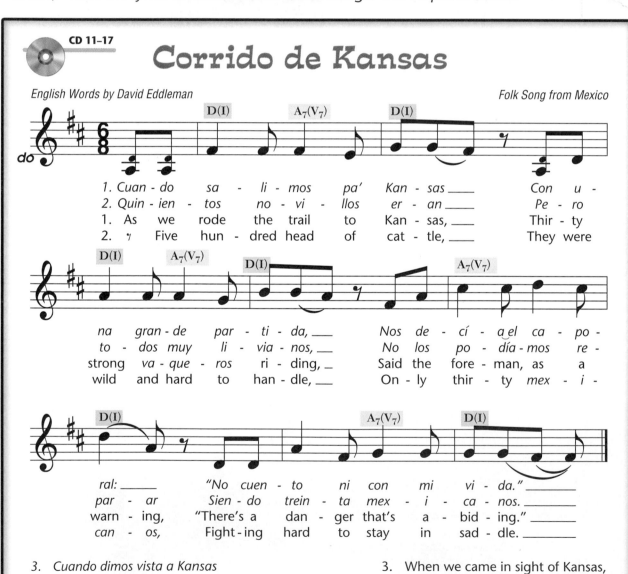

CD 11–17

Corrido de Kansas

English Words by David Eddleman

Folk Song from Mexico

1. Cuan - do sa - li - mos pa' Kan - sas ___ Con u -
2. Quin - ien - tos no - vi - llos er - an ___ Pe - ro
1. As we rode the trail to Kan - sas, ___ Thir - ty
2. Five hun - dred head of cat - tle, ___ They were

na gran - de par - ti - da, ___ Nos de - cí - a el ca - po -
to - dos muy li - via - nos, ___ No los po - día - mos re -
strong va - que - ros ri - ding, _ Said the fore - man, as a
wild and hard to han - dle, ___ On - ly thir - ty mex - i -

ral: ___ "No cuen - to ni con mi vi - da." ___
par - ar Sien - do trein - ta mex - i - ca - nos. ___
warn - ing, "There's a dan - ger that's a - bid - ing." ___
can - os, Fight - ing hard to stay in sad - dle. ___

3. Cuando dimos vista a Kansas
   Era puritito correr,
   Eran los caminos largos,
   Y pensaba yo en volver.

3. When we came in sight of Kansas,
   A stampede broke out a-churning,
   Down the dusty trail a-winding,
   And I thought about returning.

274

Corrido Chords

"*Corrido de Kansas*" uses just two chords for the accompaniment:

• The D (I) chord, which is based on **do**.

• The A$_7$ (V$_7$) chord, which is based on **so**.

Play the two chord patterns below to accompany the song. How are they different? In which pattern are the last two measures the same as the first two?

▼ Nineteenth-century cattle trail map

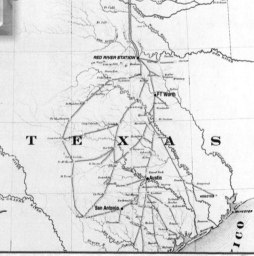

Arts Connection

▲ *California Vaqueros* by James Walker (1818–1889). *Vaqueros* were riding horses and herding cattle long before American cowboys of the Old West. This rich heritage introduced into the English language such words as *corral*, *rodeo*, *stampede*, and — from the word *vaquero* — *buckaroo*.

Element: RHYTHM | **Skill: PLAYING** | **Connection: STYLE**

Take a Road Trip

As we continue our journey, let's take a detour down Route 66. You may have heard of this famous highway that ran from Chicago to California. Many jazz artists have performed the song "Route 66" using their own vocal style.

HISTORIC
ROUTE
66

CD 11–21

Route 66

s, l, t, @r ma m f s

Swing Style

Words and Music by Bobby Troup

If you ev-er plan to mo-tor west, ___

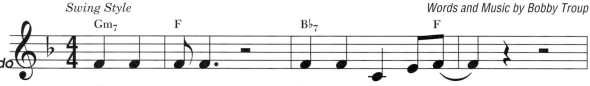

trav-el my ___ way, _ take the high - way _ that's the best. _

Get your kicks on Route ___ Six - ty - six! ___

It winds from Chi-ca - go to L. A., ___

more than two thou-sand miles _ all ___ the way. _

Swing Rhythms

Listen to "Route 66." Are the rhythms of the melody performed exactly as they are notated?

Get your kicks on Route ___ Six - ty - six! ___

Now you go thru Saint Loo - ey and Jop - lin, Mis-sour - i and

O - kla - ho - ma Cit - y is might - y pret - ty; You'll see ___

___ Am - a - ril - lo; ___ Gal-lup, New Mex - i - co; ___ Flag -

- staff, Ar - i - zo - na; Don't ___ for - get Wi - no - na, King-

- man, Bar - stow, San ___ Ber - nar - di - no. Won't you ___

Let's Swing!

In swing style, eighth notes are performed unevenly. The first eighth note of each beat is a little longer than normal. The second eighth note of each beat is a little shorter.

Imitate the swing style you hear on the recording of "Route 66." **Listen** especially to the way the eighth notes on the words *Oklahoma City is might–* are performed in swing style.

Bb7   F
_____ get hip _____ to this time - ly tip, _____

D7 Fm   G7   C7   F
When you make _ that Cal - i - for - nia trip, _

D7 Fm   G7   C7   F
get your kicks   on   Route _ Six - ty - six! _

D7 *p* Fm   G7   C7   F
Get your kicks   on   Route _ Six - ty - six! _

M·U·S·I·C M·A·K·E·R·S

Harry James

Jazz trumpeter **Harry James** (1916–1983) led one of the most successful big bands of the 1930s and 40s. James was an admirer of jazz legend Louis Armstrong. But it was the jazz clarinetist Benny Goodman who gave James his first big break when, in 1937, he made him a leading member of the famous Goodman band. James soon became known for his rich tone, wide range, and exciting playing.

HISTORIC ROUTE 66

Swing Band

This rendition of "Route 66" is performed by a jazz "big band." **Listen** to the performance and **describe** what you hear.

 CD 11–24
Route 66

**by Bobby Troup
as performed by Harry James and
His Orchestra**

As a child, James played trumpet in his father's circus band.

Visit **Take It to the Net** at *www.sfsuccessnet.com* to learn more about jazz.

Give Me Five

How many notes are in a scale? Eight is a correct answer, but not the only correct one. There are many different scales with various numbers of notes. The pentatonic scale has only five notes.

Sing the pentatonic song "Pastures of Plenty."

CD 11–25

Pastures of Plenty

Words and Music by Woody Guthrie

1. It's   a might-y hard row that my poor hands has hoed. ___ My
2. I ___ worked in your or-chards of pea-ches and prunes; ___
3. Green ___ pas-tures of plen-ty from dry de-sert ground, ___ From the
4. It's ___ al-ways we ram-bled, that riv-er and I; ___ All a-

poor feet has trav-eled a hot dust-y road. ___
Slept on the ground ___ in the light of the moon. ___ On the
Grand Cou-lee Dam ___ where the wa-ters run down. ___ Ev-ery
long your green val-ley I will work 'till I die. ___ My ___

Out of your Dust ___ Bowl and west-ward we rolled, And your
edge of the ci - ty you'll see us and then, We ___
state in the Un - ion us mi-grants has been, We'll ___
land I'll de-fend ___ with my life if it be, 'Cause my

des-erts was hot and your moun-tains _____ was cold. _____
come with the dust and we're gone with _____ the wind. _____
work in this fight, and we'll fight 'till _____ we win. _____
pas-tures of plen-ty must al-ways _____ be free. _____

Pentatonic Pastures

Listen to Woody Guthrie's "Pastures of Plenty." This song uses the pitches *do, re, mi, so,* and *la.* The tonal center (resting place) is *la.*

la   do   re   mi   so

Play this accompaniment as others **sing** "Pastures of Plenty."

Alto Glockenspiel

Bass Xylophone

MUSIC MAKERS

Woody Guthrie

Woody Guthrie (1912–1967) was named after President Woodrow Wilson. At a very young age, he loved making music. By the end of his life, he had written more than 1,000 songs! Many of his songs are about his love for America and social issues of the times. "Pastures of Plenty" is about the migrant workers and the troubles they faced during the Dust Bowl. Woody Guthrie was a great American folk singer, guitarist, and composer. Many people were influenced by Guthrie—Bruce Springsteen, Joan Baez, Bob Dylan, and Guthrie's son, Arlo Guthrie.

THE BEAT GOES ON...

How do you know you are alive? One good answer is that you have a pulse. Music has a pulse, called the beat.

The song "I Walk in Beauty" has a very steady pulse, like a heartbeat. It speaks of the Navajo belief of an inner beauty called *hozho.*

Sing "I Walk in Beauty" and lightly tap the pulse on your chest.

CD 12–1

I WALK IN BEAUTY

Words and Music by Arliene Nofchissey Williams (Navajo)

He ne - ya - na, he ya he ya _ na, He ne - ya - na,

1.

2.

he ya hi yo _____ he ya hi yo _____ he ya hi yo. I

yearn for beau - ty, yes I do, yes I do; I learn of ___ beau - ty,

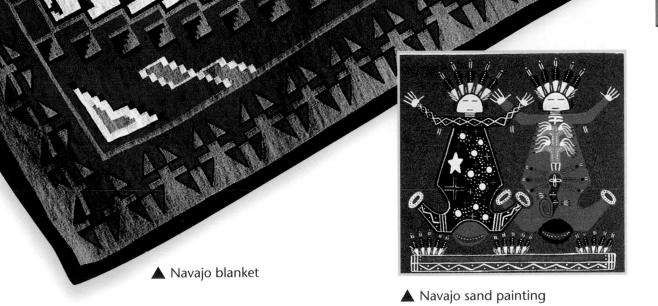

▲ Navajo blanket

▲ Navajo sand painting

yes I do, you know I do; I beam with beau - ty, just for you and on - ly you, *he*

ya, ____ he ya hi yo. He ne - ya - na, he ya he ya - na,

He ne - ya - na, he ya hi yo ____ he ya hi yo.

A Changing Meter—A Steady Beat

Look at the notation for "Farewell to the Warriors" and **sing** the song. Notice that the meter changes, but the beat stays the same.

 CD 12–3

FAREWELL TO THE WARRIORS

As sung by Mrs. Charles Mee, about 1908

Native American Song of the Chippewa

Um - be a - ni - ma - djag wa - su - gi - di -

zha - min, ya wi a ya wi ___ a

ya ya ___ wi a ya wi a _____

The People and Their Songs

The song "Farewell to the Warriors" is a Chippewa song. The Chippewas live near the Great Lakes. After the Revolutionary War, some Chippewas (more commonly called Ojibways) moved to land they were given on the Grand River in Ontario, Canada.

"I Walk in Beauty" was composed by Navajo singer/songwriter Arliene Nofchissey Williams. The Navajos are from the southwest region of the United States.

Find the areas of the Chippewa and Navajo Nations on a map.

Navajo Nation
Chippewa Nation

M·U·S·I·C M·A·K·E·R·S

J. Bryan Burton

J. Bryan Burton (born 1948) is a music educator of Choctaw and European descent. His interest in Native Americans has led him to learn about many Native American singers and dancers and about their history and culture. Dr. Burton teaches at West Chester University in West Chester, Pennsylvania. He is the author of a collection of songs. His book *Moving Within the Circle* is about the history of various Native American people, their customs, and their music.

Listen as J. Bryan Burton talks about his work.

CD 12–6
Interview with J. Bryan Burton

Tune In

There are many Native American instruments such as drums, rattles, and flutes. The Apache play a string instrument called *Tsii' edo a'tl* (the wood that sings). Many of the Eastern Woodland tribes, such as the Chippewa, play drums filled with water!

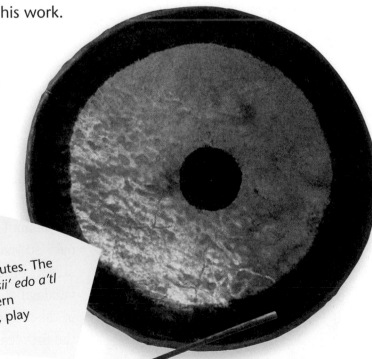

▲ Chippewa drum and stick

CALIFORNIA, HERE WE COME!

Ever since the Gold Rush in 1849, people have come to California. "Go West" became a common phrase among easterners seeking to make their fortunes. The song "California, Here I Come" captures the spirit of California as a land of opportunity. Al Jolson wrote the song in 1923.

Listen to and then **sing** "California, Here I Come." When the same melodic phrase repeats but starts on a different pitch level, we call it a melodic sequence. How many melodic sequences can you **identify** in this song?

MUSIC MAKERS

Al Jolson

Al Jolson (1886–1950) was an entertainer for over 40 years. He started his career dancing on street corners. Eventually, he worked in a circus, vaudeville, on the radio, in recording studios, and in the movies (his 1927 film, *The Jazz Singer,* was the first feature talking picture). Al Jolson was known as the "World's Greatest Entertainer."

CD 12–7

CALIFORNIA, HERE I COME

Words and Music by Al Jolson,
Bud Desylva, and Joseph Meyer

Cal - i - for - nia, here I come. ___

Right back where I start - ed from. ___

Where bow - ers of flow - ers bloom in the spring. ___

Each morn - ing at dawn - ing bird - ies sing and ev - 'ry - thing. A

sun - kissed miss said, "Don't be late." ___

That's why I can hard - ly wait. ___

O - pen up that Gold - en Gate. ___ Cal - i -

for - nia, here I come! ___

United We Sing

The United States is made up of people from all over the world. Many American folk songs were influenced by the musical styles of the settlers in the area. **Sing** "Cotton-Eye Joe." Then **listen** to how it is performed in another style.

Cotton-Eye Joe

CD 12–9

Folk Song from Tennessee

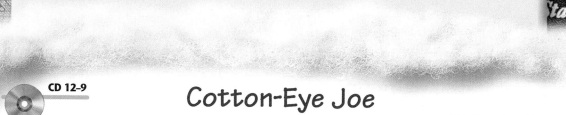

1. Where did you come from? Where did you go?

Where did you come from, Cot-ton-Eye ___ Joe?

2. I've come for to see you,
   I've come for to sing,
   I've come for to bring you
   A song and a ring.

3. When did you leave here?
   Where did you go?
   When you coming back here,
   Cotton-Eye Joe?

4. Left here last winter,
   I've wandered through the year.
   Seen people dyin',
   Seen them with their fear.

5. I've been to the cities,
   Buildings cracking down,
   Seen the people calling,
   Falling to the ground.

6. I'll come back tomorrow,
   If I can find a ride,
   Or I'll sail in the breezes,
   Blowin' on the tide.

7. Well, when you do come back here,
   Look what I have brung,
   A meadow to be run in,
   A song to be sung.

8. Where did you come from?
   Where did you go?
   Where did you come from,
   Cotton-Eye Joe?

Bring Your Passport

A passport identifies you when you travel abroad. The type of music you like is your musical passport. Let's take a trip around the world and learn about people and their cultures through their music.

Dancing to *Cotton-Eye Joe*

"Cotton-Eye Joe" is a traditional folk melody that became very popular in dances in the Southwestern United States. Do the dance movements as you **listen** to this country bluegrass version of *Cotton-Eye Joe.*

1. Cross

2. Kick

Bluegrass Listening

Listen to Alison Krauss and the Union Station Band play some country bluegrass music. As you listen, ask yourself these questions: What instrument is featured? What is the meter? How would you dance to this music?

CD 12–13
Dusty Miller

Traditional Fiddle Tune
as performed by Alison Krauss and the Union Station Band

M·U·S·I·C M·A·K·E·R·S

Alison Krauss

Alison Krauss (born 1971) began learning music by taking classical violin lessons. She first played in a classical style. However, at the age of eight, she decided that she liked playing the country-fiddle style more. In 1983 when she was 12 years old, she won the Illinois State Fiddle Championship. Two years later, Krauss signed her first record contract. In 1990 she received her first of five Grammy awards. Her backup band is called Union Station and features a banjo, bass, guitar, and Dobro® (a type of acoustic guitar). In 1993 she joined the cast of the Grand Ole Opry, making her the youngest cast member.

Russian Music

A Tree with Many Branches

Let's take a musical trip to Russia. Russia is located on the continent of Asia. A small part of Russia is located in Europe.

Listen to *"Ai, Dunaiï moy."* Can you hum the melody of this Russian folk song? Would you recognize the melody if you heard it again?

St. Basil's Cathedral ▶
in Moscow

Folk Melodies in Classical Music

Listen to *1812 Overture*. Raise your hand when you hear the melody of *"Ai, Dunaiĭ moy."*

CD 12–18
1812 Overture

by Piotr Tchaikovsky

Tchaikovsky's [chai-KOF-skee] *1812 Overture* was written to celebrate Russia's victory over France. In some performances, actual cannons are used in the orchestra!

◀ Fabergé egg (1911) depicting Czar Nicholas II of Russia

CD 12–14

Ai, Dunaiĭ moy
(Ah, My Merry Dunaii)

Folk Song from Russia

U vo - rot, vo - rot, vo - rot, Da u vo - rot ba -
At their __ fa - ther's gate, they stand, They're gath - ered round, a

tyush - ki - nykh. __ Ai, Du - naiĭ moy, Du - naiĭ, __ Ai, ve - syo -
hap - py __ band. _ Oh, My __ dear Du - naii, __ Oh, my mer -

liy Du - naiĭ! __ Ra - zgu - lya - li - sya re - bya - ta,
ry Du - naii! __ Mer - ry lads are loud - ly __ sing - ing,

Ras - po - te - shi - lis. __ Ai, Du - naiĭ
Laugh - ing voices hap - pi - ly ring - ing. Oh, my __

moy, Du - naiĭ, __ Ai, ve - syo - liy Du - naiĭ! __
dear Du - naii, __ Oh, my mer - ry Du - naii! __

Russian Tribute to a Tree

The birch tree is often found in the vast forests of Russia. **Listen** to *"Beriozka,"* a tribute to the tree. As you listen, **move** to show the melodic contour.

CD 12–19

Beriozka
(The Birch Tree)

Folk Song from Russia

1. Во по - ле бе - рё - зынь - ка сто - я - ла,
1. See the love - ly birch in the mead - ow,
2. Oh, my lit - tle tree, I need branch - es,
3. From an - oth - er branch I will make now,
4. When I play my new bal - a - lai - ka,

Во по - ле куд - ря - ва - я сто - я - ла.
Curl - y leaves all danc - ing when the wind blows.
For three sil - ver flutes I need three branch - es.
I will make a tin - gling bal - a - lai - ka.
I will think of you, my love - ly birch tree.

Лю - ли, лю - ли, сто - я - ла,
Loo - lee - loo, when the wind blows,
Loo - lee - loo, three _____ branch - es,
Loo - lee - loo, bal - a - lai - ka,
Loo - lee - loo, love - ly birch tree,

Лю - ли, лю - ли, сто - я - ла.
Loo - lee - loo, when the wind blows.
Loo - lee - loo, three _____ branch - es.
Loo - lee - loo, bal - a - lai - ka.
Loo - lee - loo, love - ly birch tree.

Piotr Ilyich Tchaikovsky

Piotr Tchaikovsky (1840–1893) was born in Russia. He started music lessons when he was five years old. During his lifetime, not everyone appreciated his music. Of course this worried him, but he continued to compose. When the famous Carnegie Hall in New York City opened in 1891, he was invited to participate in the opening ceremonies. Tchaikovsky wrote many compositions with sweeping melodies. One of his best known works is *The Nutcracker*.

Listen for the melody of *"Beriozka"* in this symphony by Tchaikovsky.

CD 12–23
Symphony No. 4, Movement 4

by Piotr Tchaikovsky
Tchaikovsky labeled this movement *Allegro con fuoco*—"fast and with fire."

To hear an example of a *balalaika,* refer to page 466 in the Sound Bank.

◄ One of the many things made from the birch tree in Russia is the national instrument, the *balalaika* [bah-lah-LIE-kah].

Visit **Take It to the Net** at *www.sfsuccessnet.com* to learn more about Piotr Tchaikovsky.

Bring Your Passport

The Irish Harper

Welcome to Ireland, its people, and its music! One of the first instruments used in playing the music of Ireland was the harp. When you **listen** to the recording of "The Bard of Armagh," you will hear the harp and another ancient instrument. **Identify** the instrument. Why do you think these instruments were among the first created?

CD 12–24

The Bard of Armagh

Words attributed to Thomas Campbell   *Folk Tune from Ireland*

1. Oh! List to the tale of a poor Irish harper,
2. At wake or at fair I would twirl my shillelagh,

And scorn not the strings in his old with-er'd ___ hand;
And trip through a jig with my shoes bound with ___ straw;

But re-mem-ber those fin-gers could ___ once move much sharp-er,
And ___ all the ___ pret-ty maid-ens from ___ vil-lage and val-ley,

To wa-ken the ech-oes of his dear na-tive land.
Love the bold Phel-im Bra-dy, the ___ bard of Ar-magh.

The Timbre of Irish Music

Listen to the instruments in these musical selections from Ireland. Remember, each instrument has its own timbre.

CD 12–26

MacAllistrum's March–Mairseail Alasdroim

**Traditional Irish March
as performed by the Chieftains with the Belfast Harp Orchestra**

This music was written to honor Alistar MacAllistrum, a Celtic [KEL-tik] hero.

CD 12–27

Crowley's Reel

**Traditional Irish Reel
as performed by James Galway**

A reel is a folk dance performed in pairs, with couples facing one another.

▲ Irish harp

MUSIC MAKERS

James Galway

James Galway (born 1939), one of the world's greatest flute players, is from Belfast, Ireland. Galway has played with symphony orchestras, jazz artists, and groups like the Chieftains. He enjoys playing many different styles of music from all over the world. He has many flutes. One is made of gold!

Irish Music in America

Irish melodies have found their way around the world and into the United States. Notice the similarities between "The Bard of Armagh" (page 296) and "Streets of Laredo" (page 272).

Listen to another example of Irish dance music and **identify** the instruments.

CD 12–28
Crowley's/Jackson's

Traditional Irish Melody
as performed by Eileen Ivers, John Doyle, and Tommy Hayes

Eileen Ivers is a performer with *Riverdance*, a stage production that showcases traditional Irish dance.

▲ Eileen Ivers

Tune In

Lord of the Dance has featured a variety of performers, including Irish folk dancers, solo singers, a flute soloist, and a fiddle duet.

▲ *Lord of the Dance* performers

Listen and Look

Listen to the instrumental and vocal timbres used in *Dúlamán*.

CD 12–29
Dúlamán

**Traditional Irish Song
as performed by Altan**

The word *dúlamán* means seaweed.

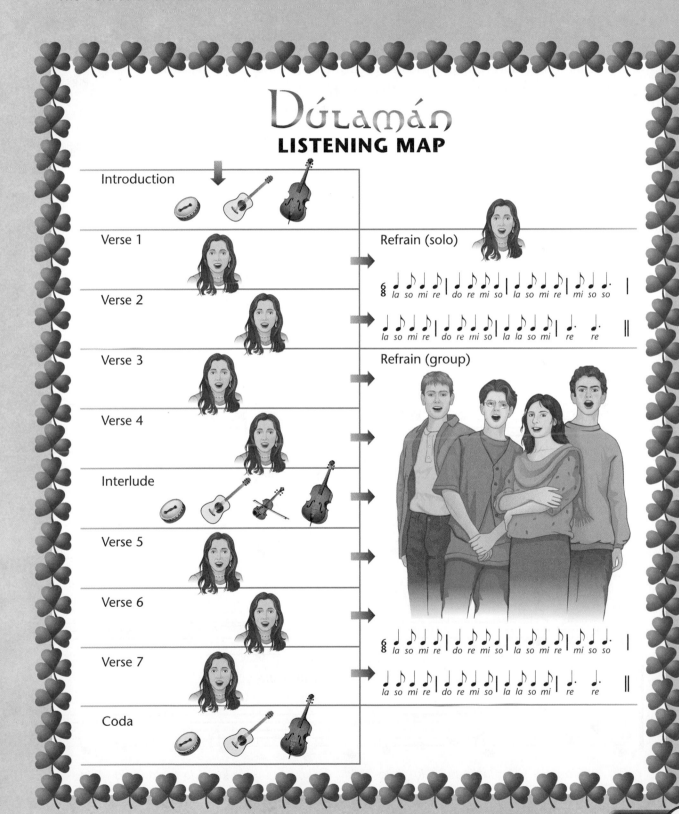

SONG OF SOUTH AFRICA

Africa has many different peoples and countries. "*Tina singu*" is from South Africa, a country located at the southern tip of the continent. The song is often sung at sporting events. **Sing** "*Tina singu*."

CD 12–30

TINA SINGU

Folk Song from South Africa

Introduction (first time only)
Leader

Ti - na sing - u   le - lu - vu - tae - o.   Wat-sha, wat-sha, wat-sha,
We burn with the   fire __ of life, __ oh,

Leader   *Group*

Ti - na,   Ti - na sing - u   le - lu - vu - tae - o.
We burn,   we burn with the   fire __ of life, __ oh,

1. F   2. F *Part 2*

Wat - sha,   wat - sha,   wat - sha,   wat - sha,   la - la - la - la - la -

Wat - sha, _____   wat - sha, _____

la,   la - la - la - la - la - la,   la - la - la - la - la -

Playing and Singing Parts

Play the steady beat of *"Tina singu"* on a drum. Then play the rhythm of the melody. How are they the same? How are they different? Choose one of these rhythm patterns to accompany the song.

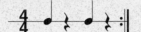  

CD-ROM Use the Melody and Rhythm Maker in *Making Music* to create an accompaniment for *"Tina singu."*

1 — wat - sha,   wat - sha,   wat - sha. _____

2 — la,   la - la - la - la - la - la,   la - la - la - la - la -

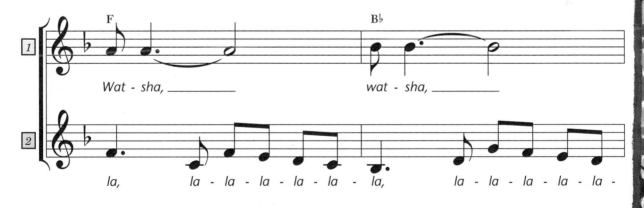

1 — Wat - sha, _____   wat - sha, _____

2 — la,   la - la - la - la - la - la,   la - la - la - la - la -

1 — wat - sha,   wat - sha,   wat - sha.

2 — la,   la - la - la - la - la - la.

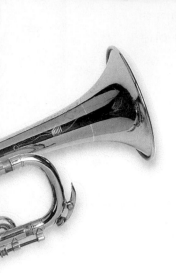

Music Flows in Mexico

¡Olé! The people of Mexico have a rich musical heritage. **Sing** "La raspa," a popular Mexican *mariachi* tune. The letters will help you **identify** the form.

CD 13–1
MIDI 21

La raspa

English Words by Kim Williams

Folk Song from Mexico

A G   D₇

La ras - pa yo bai - lé   al de - re - cho y al re - vés.
The ras - pa I will dance,   as for-ward and back I go.

D₇   G

Si quie - res tú bai - lar,   em - pie-za a mo - ver los pies.
So if you want to dance,   be - gin with your heel and toe.

B G   D₇   G

Brin - ca, brin - ca, brin - ca tam-bién,   mue - ve, mue - ve mu-cho los pies.
Al - ways mov - ing, mov-ing your feet,   back and forth now jump to the beat.

G   D₇   G

Que la ras - pa vas a bai - lar   al de - re - cho y al re - vés.
This is how the dance we will do,   laugh-ing, laugh-ing all the way through.

Listen to this example of a *mariachi* band.

CD 13–6
El mariachi

Traditional *Mariachi* from Mexico

Mariachi comes from a Coca Indian word meaning "musician."

A G D₇

Si quie - res tú bai - lar la ras - pa co - mo yo,
So if you want to dance the ras-pa the way I do,

D₇ G

Me tie - nes que se - guir al de - re - cho y al re - vés.
Be - gin to move your feet, and you will be danc - ing, too.

C *Instrumental* C G D₇ G

C G D₇ G

A G D₇

La ras - pa yo bai - lé al de - re - cho y al re - vés.
The ras - pa I will dance, as for-ward and back I go.

D₇ G

Si quie - res tú bai - lar, em - pie-za a mo - ver los pies.
So if you want to dance, be - gin with your heel and toe.

Bring Your Passport

Unit 8 303

Arts Connection

▲ *Dance in Tehuantepec* (1928) by Diego Rivera. Mexican artist Diego Rivera (1866–1957) is sometimes called "the artist of the people." He created large paintings called murals, showing the lives of everyday people.

A Poem of the People

Read this poem. Notice how the words paint a picture. What do you think this poem means?

Toltec Poem from Ancient Mexico
Translated by Toni de Gerez

Like the feathers
of the quetzal bird
my song is beautiful
Now look!
My song is bending over the earth
My song is born
in the house of butterflies

▲ Mayan pottery with *quetzal* birds

Doing the Dance

Move to show rondo form as you **sing** *"La raspa."*

A
▲ Do the hop step.

B
▲ Take 4 side steps, then reverse.

C
▲ Hook arms with your partner, then spin.

Rowing in VENEZUELA

The South American country of Venezuela is a land of many beautiful bodies of water. The largest lake, Lake Maracaibo, is in the northwestern part of the country. "*Bogando a la luz del sol*" describes a calm scene of someone gently rowing across such a lake at sunrise.

Listen to the melody of the song.

CD 13–7

Bogando a la luz del sol
(Rowing Toward the Sunlight)

English Words by David Eddleman

Folk Song from Venezuela

So-plan las bri-sas de la _____ ma-ña-na, Ri-zan-do el la-go mur-
Soft-ly the breez-es of morn-ing are sigh-ing, The whisp'r-ing wa-ters are

mu-ra-dor, _____ Y por o-rien-te su faz a-
gent-ly stirred; _____ The sun-light dawn-ing from East is

so-ma Cual ra-ro in-cen-dio la luz del sol.
show-ing, Its face a-glow-ing, a rare de-light.

Y por o-rien-te su faz a-so-ma
The sun-light dawn-ing from East is show-ing,

Cual ra-ro in-cen-dio la luz del sol.
Its face a-glow-ing, a rare de-light.

Choose a Melody

Sing the countermelody below while others sing the melody of "*Bogando a la luz del sol.*" The countermelody adds harmony. **Describe** how this affects the texture of the song.

Are you familiar with Venice, the city in Italy that is entirely surrounded by water? When the first European explorers came to what is now Venezuela, they chose the name because the country reminded them of Venice. *Venezuela* means "Little Venice."

Countermelody

So - plan las bri - sas de la ma - ña - na, _____
Soft - ly the breez - es of morn - ing are sigh - ing, _____

Y por o - rien - te su faz a - so - ma.
The sun - light dawn - ing, dawn - ing from East is show - ing.

Y por o - rien - te su faz a - so - ma
The sun - light dawn - ing from East is show - ing,

Cual ra - ro in - cen - dio la luz del sol.
Its face a - glow - ing, a rare de - light.

▼ Rafael Aparicio performing on the Venezuelan harp

Listen to this example of a *joropo* [hoh-ROH-poh], a lively dance-song, from the same Llanera plains region as "*Bogando a la luz del sol.*" Both songs feature the Venezuelan harp.

CD 13–12

Carnaval Llanero

Traditional Joropo from Venezuela as performed by Rafael Angel Aparicio y los Hermanos Aparicios

The ancestor of the Venezuelan harp was the Spanish harp, an instrument similar to the older Arabic harp. North African Arabic culture was an important influence in Spain, beginning in the Middle Ages.

Cherry Blossom Time

In Japan one of the loveliest sights is the cherry blossoms in spring. For more than 1,000 years, the Japanese have been celebrating the cherry blossom ceremony! "*Sakura*" is a song about the beauty of the cherry blossoms.

CD 13–13
MIDI 22

Sakura

English Words by Lorene Hoyt

Folk Song from Japan
Modern Arrangement by Henry Burnett

```
      Sa - ku - ra,    Sa - ku - ra,    Ya - yo - i    no
1.    Sa - ku - ra,    Sa - ku - ra,    Cher - ry   blos - soms
2.    Sa - ku - ra,    Sa - ku - ra,    Blos - soms   wav - ing
```

```
so - ra ___ wa,    Mi - wa - ta - su   ka - gi - ri,
ev - 'ry - where.  Clouds of   glo - ry   fill   the ___ sky,
in    the ___ breeze.  Yo - shi - no,   the   cher - ry ___ land,
```

```
Ka - su - mi ka  ku - mo - ka,   Ni - o - i  zo   i - zu - ru;
Mist of beau - ty   in   the _ air,  Love - ly   col - ors   float - ing _ by,
Tat - su - ta,  the   ma - ple _ trees,  Ka - ra - sa - ki,   pine   tree _ grand,
```

```
i - za - ya,   i - za - ya   Mi _ ni   yu - kan. ___
Sa - ku - ra,   Sa - ku - ra,  Let _ all   come _ sing - ing.
Sa - ku - ra,   Sa - ku - ra,  Let _ all   come _ sing - ing.
```

Blossoms in Bloom

Listen to the recording of "*Sakura.*" The song is accompanied by a Japanese string instrument, the *koto.* **Describe** the dynamics, phrasing, and mood expressed by the performers on the recording. **Sing** "*Sakura*" with expression. **Play** the following ostinato on the drum to accompany "*Sakura.*"

Play this countermelody for recorder to accompany *"Sakura."*

House of Spring

by Muso Soseki
Translated by W.S. Merwin and Soiku Shigematsu

Hundreds of open flowers
    all come from
       the one branch
Look
    all their colors
       appear in my garden
I open the clattering gate
    and in the wind
       I see
the spring sunlight
    already it has reached
       worlds without number

MIDI Play each of the first three *koto* tracks in the MIDI song file for *"Sakura."* Play the patterns on glockenspiel or keyboards.

Bring Your Passport

Unit 8   309

Travel to India

India is a large country with many different geographical regions. India has jungles, forests, large rivers, lakes, oceans, grasslands, and part of the highest mountain range in the world—the Himalayas!

Listen to the Hindu chant *"Shri Ram, jai Ram."* The instrument you hear is called the *sitar.* This Indian instrument has a long neck and metal strings.

"Shri Ram, jai Ram" is sung by a leader and a group. When you think you know the melody, **sing** along with the group.

To hear another example of the *sitar,* turn to the Sound Bank on page 470.

MUSIC MAKERS

Anoushka Shankar

Anoushka Shankar (born 1981) is one of the world's recognized master sitar players. Like her father, Ravi, she is a master of improvisation and an excellent performer. She studied with her father and made her professional debut at age thirteen.

Shri Ram, jai Ram

Hindu Chant

Leader   **Group**

Shri Ram, jai Ram, jai jai Ram, Shri Ram, jai Ram, jai jai Ram,

Leader   **Group**

Shri Ram, jai Ram, jai jai Ram, Shri Ram, jai Ram, jai jai Ram,

Leader   **Group**   1.

Shri Ram, jai Ram, jai jai Ram, __ Shri Ram, jai Ram, jai jai Ram __

2.   **Leader**

jai Ram, jai jai Ram, __ Shri Ram, jai Ram, jai jai Ram,

Group   **All**

Shri Ram, jai Ram, jai jai Ram. Shan - ti, Shan - ti, Shan - ti.

Listen to *Charukeshi* and **identify** the sound of the *sitar* and the *tabla* drums. **Describe** their timbre.

CD 13–19
Charukeshi

Raga from India
as performed by Anoushka Shankar

A *raga* is a special series of notes and patterns. Hundreds of different *ragas* are used in classical Indian music.

Visit **Take It to the Net** at *www.sfsuccessnet.com* to learn more about Ravi and Anoushka Shankar.

Bring Your Passport

Play a Chinese Treasure

China is a huge country with the largest population in the world.

"*Feng yang hua gu*" is a Chinese folk song about vendors selling their wares. Name some of the things being sold in this song.

Sing "*Feng yang hua gu*," then **play** these parts to accompany the song.

Alto Xylophone

312

CD 13–20

Feng yang hwa gu

(Feng Yang Song)

Folk Song from China

VERSE

Zuo __ shou __ luo,   *you __ shou __ gu,*   *Shou na zhe*
1. Sing the *Feng Yang* Song;   Sing it loud and long.   Clash cym - bals,
2. Gifts for you have I,   Kites that swoop and fly;   Small trin - kets,

luo __ gu   *lai __ chang __ ge!*   *Bie di _____ ge er __*
beat the drum,   Strike the met - al gong!   We are the ven - dors who
man - y toys,   All of you may buy.   Pa - per of gold shin - ing,

wo ye bu hui chang,   *Zhi hui __ chang _ ge*   *Feng _ Yang _ ge.*
trav - el all day long,   Call-ing our wares _ to the   Feng _ Yang _ Song.
Bam-boo smooth and strong,   Call-ing the clear, _ ringing toy - man's _ song.

REFRAIN

Feng la, _____ feng __ yang __ ge __ er _____ lai,
Feng yang, feng yang, beat the gong, _ strike the clap - pers well.

Der lang dang piao yi piao,   *Der lang dang piao yi piao,*   *Der piao*
Clash cym - bals, *byah yah yang,*   Clash cym-bals, *byah yah yang!*   *Brrr dong!*

der piao! Der piao der piao piao ye der piao piao piao yi piao!
Brrr dong! Brrr dong yah feng yang, feng yang, Brrr, __ beat the drum!

Chinese Timbres

"*Xiao*" is another Chinese folk melody.
What is this song about?

Listen to "*Xiao*" and then **describe** the timbre
of the featured instruments.

CD 13–24
MIDI 23

Xiao (Bamboo Flute)

Folk Song from China

Yi   geng   zi _____ zhu   zhi _____ miao _____ miao;
From   the   pur - ple,   straight _ bam - boo;

Sung   yu   bao   bao   zuo   guan   xiao. _____
I   have   made   a   flute   for   you. _____

Xiao   er   dui   zheng   kou   Kou   er   dui   zheng   xiao;
Take   the   bam - boo   flute,   Put   it   to   your   lips,

Xiao   zhong   chui ____ chu   shi ____ xin ____ diao;
Play   a   new ____ and   lilt - ing ____ song.

Xiao   bao ___ bao   Yi   di   yi   di   xue   hui   liao, _____
My   lit - tle   one,   Play   a   new and   lilt - ing   song, _____

Xiao   bao ___ bao   Yi   di   yi   di   xue   hui   liao. _____
My   lit - tle   one,   Play   a   new and   lilt - ing   song. _____

314

▲ Since 1984, Music from China has been sharing both old and new music with American audiences. The performers in the group play instruments invented hundreds to thousands of years ago.

Pipa ▶

Erhu ▼

Listen to this musical picture of a bird.

Sheng ▶

CD 13–28

Birds in the Forest

by Yi Jianquan
as performed by Music from China

This selection features traditional Chinese instruments. The sound of the bird is played on the *gao-hu*, a relative of the *erhu*.

Video Library See the video *From Mao to Mozart* for more information on Chinese music.

Israeli Song and Dance

Israel has become one of the most prosperous and modern countries in the Middle East.

The **repeat signs** ‖: and :‖ tell the performer to perform all the music between the signs twice.

"*Yibane amenu*" is an Israeli song sung as a round. **Sing** the song and follow the **repeat signs**.

CD 13–29

Yibane amenu

Round from Israel

Yi - ba - ne a - me - nu b - 'ar - tse - nu;
In our land we shall re - build our na - tion.

B - 'ar - tse - nu, yi - ba - ne,
Build our na - tion in our land,

Yi - ba - ne,   Yi - ba - ne.   Yi - ba - ne.
In our land,   In our land.   In our land.

Accompaniment Parts

Choose a rhythm instrument and **play** this part to accompany
"*Yibane amenu.*"

Create your own melody ostinato using these notes:

CD 13–33
Ve' David y'fey enayiam

by M. Shelem

Ve' David y'fey enayiam is one of the oldest and most
popular Israeli dances.

Move to the Steady Beat

This Israeli dance includes steps that give
everyone a chance to dance with a
different partner.

▼ View of Jerusalem

A Flight to the Caribbean

Caribbean is the name given to a large collection of islands located off the coasts of Central and South America.

Listen to the recording "Wings of a Dove," a Caribbean song from the West Indies. The melody pattern in the color boxes below is called a melodic sequence.

CD 13–35

Wings of a Dove

Folk Song from the West Indies

If I had the wings of a dove, If I had the wings of a

dove, I would fly, fly a - way,

Fly _____ a - way _____ and be _____ at rest.

Fine

B G   D   A₇

Since I have no wings,   Since I have no wings,   Since I have no wings, how can I

D   G   D

fly? _____   Since I have no wings,   Since I have no wings,

E₇   A₇   *D.C. al Fine*

Since I have no wings, I'm gon-na   sing,   sing,   sing,   sing.

Play the Caribbean Way

Play the part below on cowbell, drum, claves, or maracas.

Listen to this music from the Caribbean country of Dominica.

CD 13–37

Mwen boyko samba

Traditional *Samba* from Dominica

This selection is played on steel drums. Like Trinidad and other Caribbean countries, Dominica has a strong tradition of steel drumming.

Reggae Is All Right

Let's continue our tour of the Caribbean with a visit to the island of Jamaica. **Sing** "Three Little Birds," by the Jamaican musician Bob Marley. Using the letters **A** and **B**, **describe** the form of the song. How does the form compare to that of "Wings of a Dove" in the previous lesson?

"Three Little Birds" is an example of reggae [REH-gay] music — a style that combines the sound of American pop music with African-based Jamaican instruments and rhythm patterns. Reggae often uses short ostinatos played on keyboard, electric guitar, bass, and drums.

MUSIC MAKERS

Bob Marley

Robert Nesta (Bob) Marley (1945–1981) was born in Jamaica. He grew up playing music and made his first recording at age 16. Soon after, Marley and several of his musician friends formed a band called the Wailers. It was this group that made reggae music known all over the world.

Much of Bob Marley's music is about social issues, such as unity and peace. In 1978 he was awarded the Peace Medal of the Third World from the United Nations.

Three Little Birds

Words and Music by Bob Marley

REFRAIN **A** 𝄋 D

Don't wor - ry a - bout a thing,

G / D

'cause ev-'ry lit-tle thing gon-na be all right.

D

Sing-in' don't wor - ry a - bout a thing,

D G D *Fine*

'cause ev-'ry lit-tle thing gon-na be all right.

VERSE **B** D / A

Rise up this morn-ing, smile with the ris - ing sun.

A Bm G

Three lit - tle birds sit by my door-step,

G D A

Sing-in' sweet songs of mel-o-dies pure and true,

A G D *D. S. al Fine*

Sing-in': "This is my mes-sage to you-hoo-hoo." Sing-in' don't

Revisiting a Dream

"When I was a little boy, I had the same dream over and over again. I would push my tongue against the roof of my mouth, close my eyes, and before I knew it, I'd be floating around in the clouds. I got older and grown up. No matter how hard I pushed my tongue, I couldn't get back to that cloud place. Maybe when I get to be a real old man, I'll have that dream again, because someone told me that real old people and real young people often have the same dreams. I hope so!"

Tomie dePaola, children's book author

Chasing a Dream

Hopes and dreams are very important. As you sing the songs in this unit, think of your hopes and dreams.

Sharing a Song

Some people dream about living in communities where people care for and help each other. Other people dream about their goals and ambitions. **Sing** "Love Can Build a Bridge." Imagine what we could do by sharing and working together.

CD 14–3

Love Can Build a Bridge

Words and Music by Paul Overstreet, Naomi Judd, and John Jarvis

VERSE *mp*

1. I'd glad-ly walk a-cross the des-ert with no shoes up-on my feet to
whis-per love so loud-ly, ev-'ry heart would un-der-stand that

share with you the last bite of bread I had to eat. I would
love and on-ly love can join the tribes of man. I would

swim out to save you in your sea of bro-ken dreams. When
give my heart de-si-res so that you might see. The

all your hopes are sink - ing, let me show you what love means.
first step is to re-a-lize that it all be-gins with you and me.

REFRAIN *mf*

Love can build a bridge be-tween your heart and mine.

Love can build a bridge, don't you think it's time? Don't you think it's time?

1.

2.

7

2. I would

When we stand to - geth - er, ___ it's our fin - est hour. _ We can do _

an - y - thing, _ an - y - thing, _ keep be - liev - in' in the pow - er.

_ Don't you think _ it's time? Love and on - ly

love, love and on - ly love.

Moving to the Sounds of a Dream

Find the refrain of "Love Can Build a Bridge." Look for repeated words and music. **Create** your own movements to show the meaning of the lyrics of the refrain. **Move** each time the refrain occurs.

Sing FOR FREEDOM

In the 1960s, "We Shall Overcome" was sung by people seeking civil rights in the United States. **Perform** the last two lines of the song using rhythm syllables. Then **sing** this famous freedom song.

CD 14–5

WE SHALL OVERCOME

New Words and Arrangement by
Zilphia Horton, Frank Hamilton, Guy Carawan, and Pete Seeger

Freedom Song from the United States

1. We shall o - ver - come, _____ We shall o - ver - come, _____
2. We'll walk hand in hand, _____ We'll walk hand in hand, _____
3. We are not a - fraid, _____ We are not a - fraid, _____

We shall o - ver - come some - day; _____
We'll walk hand in hand some - day; _____
We are not a - fraid to - day; _____

Oh, _____ deep in my heart I do be - lieve,

(last time)

We shall o - ver - come some day. _____

4. We shall broth-ers be, . . .   5. Truth shall make us free, . . .

What Kind of Land?

For most people, freedom means independence, equality, and justice. **Listen** to *What Kind of Land?*, a song that questions the founding of the United States as a free nation while it held some of its people in slavery.

"What kind of land is this gon' be?

Freedom built on slavery.

How will it stand in time?"

CD 14–7
What Kind of Land?

by Bernice Johnson Reagon

Bernice Johnson Reagon and her daughter Toshi performed *What Kind of Land?* for the PBS television documentary *Africans in America*.

▼ Bernice Johnson Reagon

Hope Keeps Dreams Alive

Sometimes it takes work and patience to make a dream come true. Hope keeps us focused on our dreams. **Listen** to "Love Will Guide Us," a song of hope.

◀ These workers are building homes with Habitat for Humanity.

CD 14–8

Love Will Guide Us

Words by Sally Rogers

Traditional Melody

Refrain Love will ____ guide us, peace ____ has
1. If you ____ can - not sing ____ like

tried ____ us. Hope in - side ____
an - gels, If you ____ can -

us ____ will lead the way, On the ____
not ____ speak be - fore thou - sands, You can ____

Time Signature Review

Identify the time signature at the beginning of "Love Will Guide Us." How many beats are in each measure? Tap the steady beat as you **listen** and **sing** along. **Create** a movement that shows the number of beats in each measure.

Sally Rogers, a folk musician, performs traditional children's songs. She lives in Connecticut and performs throughout the United States. She has sung on radio shows such as *A Prairie Home Companion.* Rogers plays banjo, guitar, and dulcimer. She says, "When we sing together, we can't help but know we are not alone in both our work and our play."

road _____ from _____ greed ___ to giv - ing.
give _____ from _____ deep ___ with - in _____ you.

Love will ___ guide _____ us _____
You can ___ change _____ the _____

through the dark _____ night. *(to Verses)*
world with your _____ love. *(to Refrain)*

2. You are like no other being.
   What you can give, no other can give,
   To the future of our precious children.
   To the future of the world where we live.
   (to Refrain)

3. Hear the song of peace within you.
   Heed the song of peace in your heart.
   Spring's new beginning shall lead to the harvest.
   Love will guide us on our way.
   (to Refrain)

During the Great Depression in the 1930s, many people lost their jobs. Some people became hoboes, traveling from place to place in railroad cars looking for work. "Big Rock Candy Mountain" is a famous hobo song— a song of hope for better times.

CD 14–10

BIG ROCK CANDY MOUNTAIN

Traditional

VERSE

C   F   C

1. In the Big Rock Can-dy Moun-tain, There's a land that's fair and bright,
2. In the Big Rock Can-dy Moun-tain, Where the ho-bo nev-er begs,

F   C   F   G7

Where the hand-outs grow on bush-es, And you sleep out ev-'ry night;
And the bull-dogs all are tooth-less, And the hens lay soft-boiled eggs;

C   F   C

Where the box-cars all are emp-ty, And the sun shines ev-'ry day,
All the trees are full of ap-ples, And the barns are full of hay,

F   C   F   C   F   C

Oh, I'm bound to go where there is-n't an-y snow, Where the rain does-n't fall,
There's a lake of stew and ___ so-da pop, _ too, You can paddle all a-round

Rock Candy Rhythms

"Big Rock Candy Mountain" has two sections—a verse and a refrain. Find measures with exactly the same rhythm in both verse and refrain. As you **sing** the song, **move** in one way during the verse and in a different way during the refrain.

Tune In

Did you know that there is a place called Rock Candy Mountain in Utah, near the town of Marysvale?

and the wind does-n't blow, In the Big Rock Can - dy Moun-tain.
in a big ca - noe, In the Big Rock Can - dy Moun-tain.

REFRAIN

Oh, the buzz - in' of the bees in the syc - a - more trees

'Round the so - da wa - ter foun - tain, Where the lem-on-ade springs

and the blue - bird sings in the Big Rock Can - dy Moun - tain.

Chasing a Dream

Home Is Where the Heart Is

Pete Seeger, one of America's favorite folk singers, lived in the Hudson River Valley as a child. "Sailing Down My Golden River" is a song about the river, his home, and family.

CD 14–12

Sailing Down My Golden River

Words and Music by Pete Seeger

1. Sail - ing down my gol - den riv - er, _____
2. Sun and wa - ter, old life giv - ers, _____
3. Sun - light glanc - ing on the wa - ter, _____
4. Life to raise my sons and daugh - ters, ___

Sun and wa - ter _____ all my own,
I'll have them where ___ 'ere I roam,
Life and death are _____ all my own,
Gold - en spar - kles _____ in the foam,

And I was nev - er a - lone.
And I was not far from home.
And I was nev - er a - lone.
And I was not far from home.

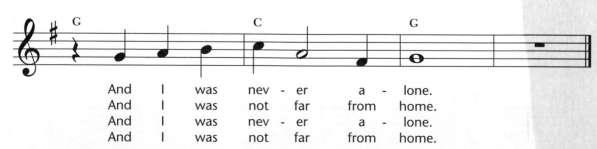

Dreaming About Home

People share their dreams of home in many ways. Musicians write songs, dancers move, and poets write. Think about what makes your home special. Write a poem or story, **compose** a song, or create a dance that tells something about your home.

Playing Melody Instruments

Identify the notes below by letter name. Then **play** the parts to accompany "Sailing Down My Golden River."

Recorder

Xylophone

Pete Seeger and other members of the Seeger family have collected and recorded American folk songs. **Listen** to this example.

CD 14–14

She'll Be Coming 'Round the Mountain When She Comes

American Folk Song
as performed by Peggy and Mike Seeger

This selection features banjo and guitar.

Pathway to the Stars

The words of "*Niu lang zhi nü*" come from a Chinese legend. In the legend, a cowherd and a weaving maid are represented by two stars in the sky—Altair and Vega. On July 7th of each year, the Milky Way stretches between the two stars. This is the only day of the year the cowherd and the weaving maid can meet. The rest of the year, they can only dream of each other.

Singing Stars

Vega, the weaving maid in the Chinese legend, is a very bright star in the constellation Lyra. Altair, the cowherd in the Chinese legend, is a star in the constellation Aquila.

Sing this folk song from China, *"Niu lang zhi nü."*
Listen to the timbres of Chinese instruments in the recording.

CD 14–15
MIDI 24

Niu lang zhi nü
(The Cowherd and the Weaving Maid)

English Words by Mary Shamrock   *Folk Song from China*

迢 ___ 迢 ___ 牵 牛 星 皎 ___ 皎 ___
1. Tiau ___ tiau ___ chien niu hsing, jiau ___ jiau ___
1. High a - bove, the cow - herd star, weav - ing maid, so

河 汉 女 织 ___ 织 握 素 手
hě han nü hsien ___ hsien ien su shou
bright, so far. Grace - ful hands, soft and white,

扎 扎 弄 机 杼 盈 盈
zha zha nong ji zhu ing ing
weav - ing through each night. Shin - ing

一 水 间 脉 ___ 脉 ___ 不 得 语
i hsuei jien mu - o mu - o bu de ü
far a - part, weep - ing with a si - lent heart.

2. Zhong zhru bu cheng zhang,
   chi ti lei zhru ü
   ne han ching chie chien
   hsiang chü fu ji hsü
   ing ing i hsuei jien
   muo muo bu de ü

2. They must wait throughout the day
   for the moon to light the way.
   Each alone, through the years
   freely flow the tears.
   Shining far apart,
   weeping with a silent heart.

Guiding Stars

Read aloud these Chinese poems about home, family, and friends. Think of ways to **move** as each poem is read. **Create** an instrumental accompaniment to show the meaning and feeling of the poem.

Quiet Night

by Li Bai

A moonbeam on my bed
Or frost on the ground?
I look up at the full moon,
I look down and think of home.

NEWS OF HOME

by Wang Wei

You've just come from my old hometown.
You must have some news of home.
The day you left, was the plum tree
By my window in bloom yet?

Traveler's Song

by Meng Jai

My loving mother, thread in hand,
Mended the coat I have on now.
Stitch by stitch, just before I left home,
Thinking that I might be gone a long time.
How can a blade of young grass
Ever repay the warmth of spring sun?

Music from China

As you follow the listening map below, **listen** for the timbre of the *sheng*.

CD 14–19
Bumper Harvest Celebration

by Lu Zaiyi and Xu Caoming
as performed by the Shanghai National Music Orchestra

The *sheng*, a native instrument of China, is a type of mouth organ.

Bumper Harvest Celebration
LISTENING MAP

Lost and Found

As settlers moved across the American frontier, they often sang songs about people and places they left behind. **Sing** "My Bonnie Lies Over the Ocean."

How many ties can you find in this song? Which phrases have exactly the same rhythm?

CD 14–20

My Bonnie Lies Over the Ocean

Folk Song from the United States

VERSE

1. My Bon - nie lies o - ver the o - cean, _____
2. Last night as I lay on my pil - low, _____
3. Oh, blow ye winds o - ver the o - cean, _____
4. The winds have blown o - ver the o - cean, _____

My Bon - nie lies o - ver the sea; _____
Last night as I lay on my bed; _____
Oh, blow ye winds o - ver the sea; _____
The winds have blown o - ver the sea; _____

My Bon - nie lies o - ver the o - cean, _____
Last night as I lay on my pil - low, _____
Oh, blow ye winds o - ver the o - cean, _____
The winds have blown o - ver the o - cean, _____

Oh, bring back my Bon - nie to me. _____
I dreamt that my Bon - nie was dead. _____
And bring back my Bon - nie to me. _____
And brought back my Bon - nie to me. _____

REFRAIN

Bring back, bring back,

bring back my Bon - nie to me, to me;

Bring back, bring back, oh,

bring back my Bon - nie to me. _____

Almost the Same Song

A parody is a comical imitation of a song or story. Here is a parody of "My Bonnie Lies Over the Ocean." The words are different, but the melody is the same. **Sing** this parody. Then write your own.

Cowboy's Dream

Anonymous Parody

Last night as I lay on the prairie,
And looked at the stars in the sky,
I wondered if ever a cowboy,
Could drift to that sweet by and by.

Roll on, roll on,
Roll on, little dogies, roll on, roll on.
Roll on, roll on,
Roll on, little dogies, roll on.

The Original Forty-Niners

Gold was discovered in California in 1848. By 1849, thousands of people traveled to this state, dreaming of gold. They were called "forty-niners."

The trip to California was hard and took a long time. The forty-niners had to cross the prairie in wagons. Others sailed from the east coast of the United States around the tip of South America to reach California. They were willing to do all of this to find gold!

Play an accompaniment for "Clementine" using an Autoharp. Find the G and D_7 chords, then strum as you **sing.** Do the verse and refrain have the same chord pattern?

▲ Panning for gold

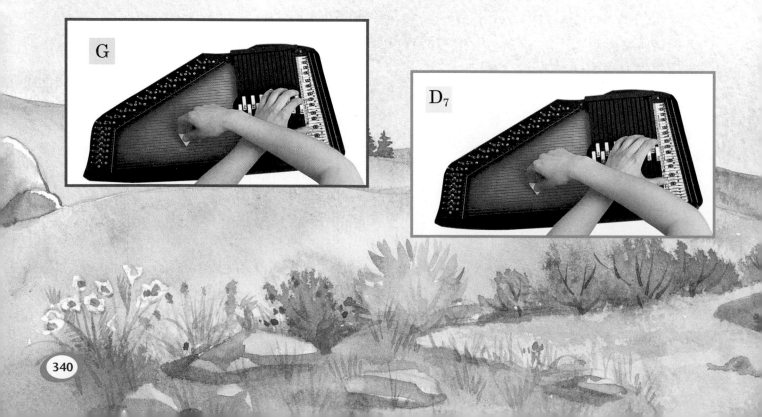

G

D_7

Songs About Life

The forty-niners made up songs about their experiences. Many of their songs were about the hard work of mining and the rough conditions of living in California. **Sing** "Clementine," a song about the gold rush years.

Clementine

Folk Song from the United States

1. In a cav-ern by a can-yon, Ex-ca-vat-ing for a mine,
2. Light she was and like a feath-er, And her shoes were num-ber nine,

Dwelt a min-er, for-ty-nin-er, And his daugh-ter, Clem-en-tine.
Her-ring box-es with-out top-ses, San-dals were for Clem-en-tine.

Oh, my dar-lin', oh, my dar-lin', Oh, my dar-lin' Clem-en-tine,

You are lost and gone for-ev-er, Dread-ful sor-ry, Clem-en-tine.

3. Drove she ducklings to the water
   Every morning just at nine;
   Struck her foot against a splinter,
   Fell into the foaming brine.   *Refrain*

4. Rosy lips above the water
   Blowing bubbles mighty fine;
   But, alas! I was no swimmer,
   So I lost my Clementine.   *Refrain*

The miners seeking their fortunes were called prospectors. When a large deposit of gold was found, it was called the mother lode.

Back at the Ranch

Some of the forty-niners found gold in the California hills, while some never reached California at all. Eventually, many became farmers, lumberjacks, or ranchers. Having a successful ranch became a new dream. **Listen** to *Saturday Night Waltz* and follow the map of the melody.

CD 15–3
Saturday Night Waltz

from *Rodeo*
by Aaron Copland

In 1942, Aaron Copland wrote music for a ballet called *Rodeo*. The ballet is about life on a ranch. It includes a Saturday night dance scene.

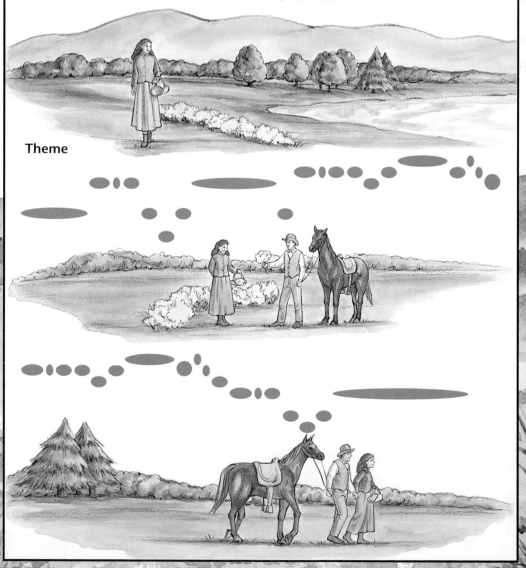

SATURDAY NIGHT WALTZ
LISTENING MAP

Theme

MUSIC MAKERS

Aaron Copland

American composer **Aaron Copland** (1900–1990) wrote some of the best-loved and most familiar orchestra music of the 20th century. He developed a distinctly American style by using jazz rhythms and folk melodies in his orchestral music. He wrote two ballets about the American West—*Billy the Kid* and *Rodeo*. He also wrote music based on the poems of Emily Dickinson and a composition about Abraham Lincoln called *Lincoln Portrait*.

Dance with Partners

Learn to do a square dance, one of the kinds of dances done at a hoedown. Choose your partner and get ready to **move**!

CD 15 4
Forked Deer/Fisher's Hornpipe

**Traditional Tune
as performed by Karen Mueller**

This recording features Autoharp, fiddle, and bass—traditional hoedown instruments.

Chasing a Dream

An Appleseed Song

Johnny Appleseed was a legendary American figure who had a dream about a world filled with apple trees, where people would never be hungry. **Sing** this song about Johnny Appleseed.

USPS. Displayed with permission.

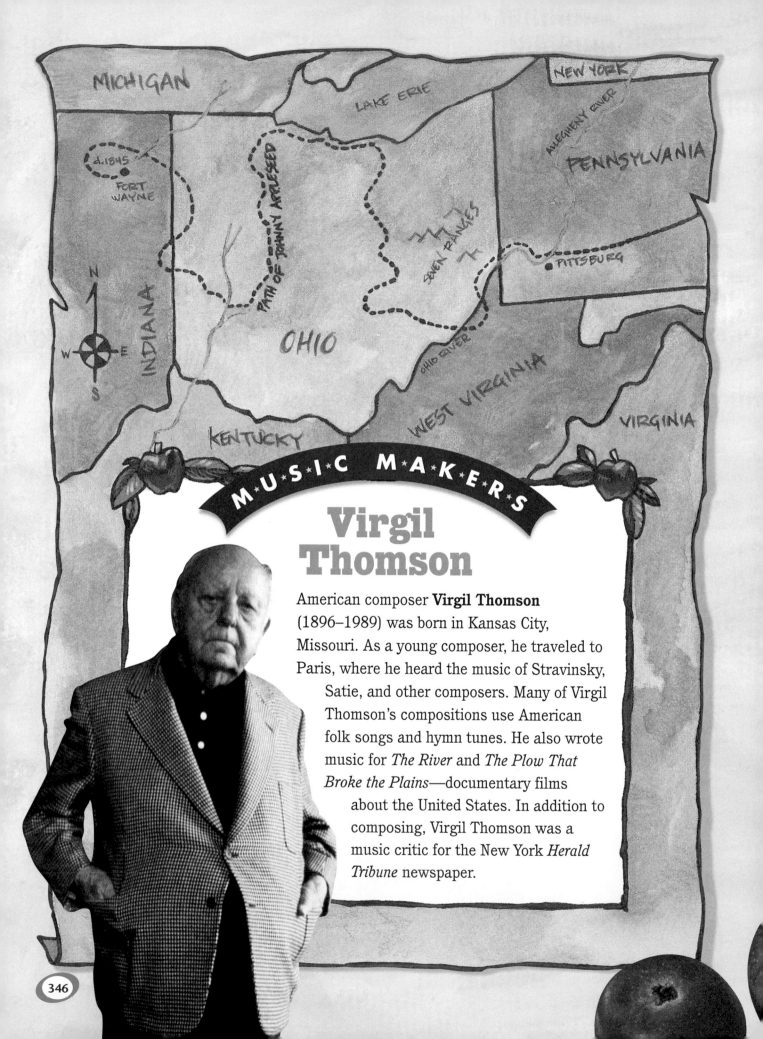

MUSIC MAKERS

Virgil Thomson

American composer **Virgil Thomson** (1896–1989) was born in Kansas City, Missouri. As a young composer, he traveled to Paris, where he heard the music of Stravinsky, Satie, and other composers. Many of Virgil Thomson's compositions use American folk songs and hymn tunes. He also wrote music for *The River* and *The Plow That Broke the Plains*—documentary films about the United States. In addition to composing, Virgil Thomson was a music critic for the New York *Herald Tribune* newspaper.

Form and Timbre

Johnny Appleseed walked hundreds of miles to make his dream come true. Follow the listening map below and **identify** the form of *Walking Song*.

CD 15–9
Walking Song

from *Acadian Songs*
by Virgil Thomson

This selection features clarinet, flute, violin, trumpet, and oboe.

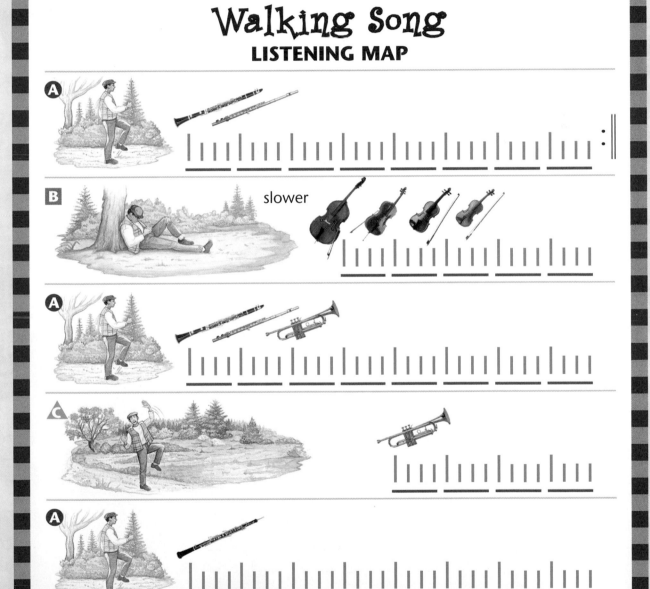

Walking Song
LISTENING MAP

A

B   slower

A

C

A

Chasing a Dream

Peace AND HARMONY

Peace is the dream of people all over the world. Learning to live together with respect and dignity can help make the dream of peace come true. **Sing** "Peace Round" in unison. Then, sing it as a round or with ostinatos to create harmony. How can you be a peacemaker in your school or community?

CD 15–10

Peace Round

Words by Jean Ritchie

Traditional

I What a good-ly thing, II if the chil-dren of the world

III could live to-geth - er IV in _____ peace.

▲ On May 25, 1986, over five million Americans participated in Hands Across America. At a designated time, participants across sixteen states joined hands to raise money for hungry and homeless people.

Sing for Peace

Below are two ostinatos from "Peace Round." Look up words for peace in different languages and **sing** them as ostinatos. Choose the one you like best, and add the ostinato to your performance of "Peace Round."

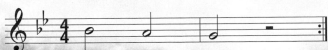

Move for Peace

Move to the half-note beat as you **sing** "Peace Round." Then **perform** a movement round.

Listen to this interview with Jean Ritchie, who wrote the words of "Peace Round."

CD 15–12

 Interview with Jean Ritchie

M·U·S·I·C M·A·K·E·R·S

Jean Ritchie

Jean Ritchie (born 1922) is one of the most famous folk musicians in the United States. During the 1960s and 1970s, she introduced thousands of people to the folk songs of Kentucky. Some of the music she performed and recorded was passed down from her Irish, English, and Scottish ancestors. Before Jean Ritchie began performing, few people were familiar with the mountain dulcimer. Because of her music, people began to play the instrument again. In 1998, Jean Ritchie won the Folk Alliance Lifetime Achievement Award.

Earth Speaks

Read this poem and think about
what you heard Earth say today.

Prayer for Earth

by Myra Cohn Livingston

Last night
an owl
called from the hill.
Coyotes howled.
A deer stood still
nibbling at bushes far away.
The moon shone silver.
Let this stay.

Today
two noisy crows
flew by,
their shadows pasted to the sky.
The sun broke out
through the clouds of gray.
An iris opened.
Let this stay.

Earth, Sea, and Sky

Earth is a home for everyone. It sustains us, providing all that we need to live. Its beauty and wonder inspire our hearts and minds. We are learning that it is also our responsibility to protect our precious Earth.

We Sail Together

The song *"Somos el barco"* is about our connection with the world around us.
Sing this song and think of how you are connected to the world.

CD 15–13

Somos el barco
(We Are the Boat)

Words and Music by Lorre Wyatt

REFRAIN

So-mos el bar - co ___ So-mos el mar

yo na - ve - go en ti Tu na - ve - gas en mí

We are the boat, we are the sea.

I sail in you, you sail in me.

1. The stream sings _ it to the riv - er, ___ The

riv - er sings _ it to the sea. The sea sings it

to the boat _ that car - ries you _ and me. ___ So-mos el

2.–4.

2. The boat we are ___ sail - ing in ___ was
3. With our hopes we ____ raise the sails ___ to
4. The voy - age has been ___ long and hard ___ and

built by man - y ____ hands. The sea we are
face the wind once ___ more. With our hearts ____ we
yet we're sail - ing ___ still. With a song to help us

sail - ing on _____ touch-es ev - 'ry sand. ___
chart the wa - ters ___ nev - er sailed be - fore. ___ So-mos el
pull to - geth - er ___ if we on - ly will. ___

D.S. al Fine

Play a Countermelody

Perform this recorder part during the refrain of *"Somos el barco."*

Countermelody Refrain

Our Planet

How would you describe our planet? You could use facts such as "the planet Earth is a sphere and revolves around the sun." You could use feelings like "our planet is very beautiful and exciting." Maybe you would use both.

Read this poem. Does the author use facts, feelings, or both to describe our planet?

Written in March

by William Wordsworth

The cock is crowing,
The stream is flowing,
The small birds twitter,
The green field sleeps in the sun;
The oldest and youngest
Are at work with the strongest;
The cattle are grazing,
Their heads never raising;
There are forty feeding like one!
Like an army defeated
The snow hath retreated,
And now doth fare ill
On the top of the bare hill;
The ploughboy is whooping—anon—anon;
There's joy in the mountains;
There's life in the fountains;
Small clouds are sailing,
Blue sky prevailing;
The rain is over and gone!

Often a composer will use only a few lines from a text to create a song. What lines from this poem would you use?

Sing "This Pretty Planet." Is this a song with facts, feelings, or both?

This Pretty Planet

CD 15–16

Words and Music by John Forster and Tom Chapin

This pret-ty plan-et spin-ning through space. You're a gar-den. You're a har-bor. You're a ho-ly place.

Gold-en sun go-ing down.

Gen-tle blue gi-ant. spin us a-round.

All through the night

Safe till the morn-ing light.

The Beautiful Earth

What feelings about Earth are expressed in this song?

Read this song using rhythm syllables. Now use pitch syllables and hand signs to **read** measures 9 and 10.

For the Beauty of the Earth

CD 15–18

Words by Folliott S. Pierpoint

Music by Conrad Kocher

1. For the beau-ty of the earth, For the beau-ty of the skies,
2. For the beau-ty of each hour Of the day and of the night,
3. For the joy of ear and eye, For the heart and mind's de-light,
4. For the joy of hu-man love, Broth-er, sis-ter, par-ent, child,

For the love which from our birth, O-ver and a-round us lies.
Hill and vale and tree and flower, Sun and moon and stars of light.
For the mys-tic har-mo-ny Link-ing sense to sound and sight.
Friends on earth and friends a-bove, For all gen-tle thoughts and mild.

Lord of all, to Thee we raise This our hymn of grate-ful praise.

Name the Continents

The largest land masses on Earth are called continents. Here's a great way to remember them!

Read "The Continents" using rhythm syllables. Then **perform** it as a **canon**.

A **canon** is a musical form in which the parts imitate each other. One part begins, or leads, and the other parts follow.

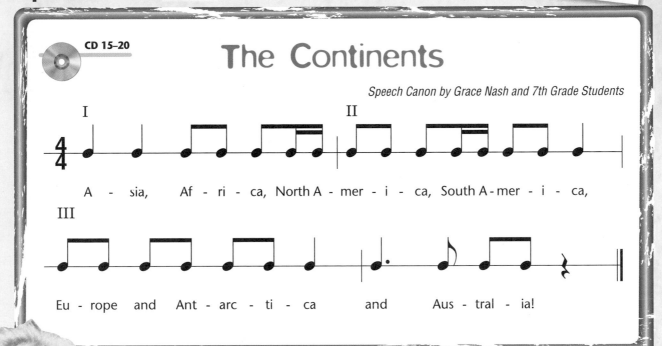

CD 15–20

The Continents

Speech Canon by Grace Nash and 7th Grade Students

I

A - sia, Af - ri - ca, North A - mer - i - ca, South A - mer - i - ca,

III

Eu - rope and Ant - arc - ti - ca and Aus - tral - ia!

OUR PLANET— Our Home

We are all together on planet Earth, spinning through space. The Earth is our home and our protector, so we all must take care of it. This Cherokee song puts these ideas into music. **Sing** the melody, and then the harmony part. Then, sing both parts together.

CD 15–22

The Earth Is Our Mother

Cherokee Song
Arranged by Barbara Sletto

1.,3. The Earth ___ is our Moth - er, we must take care of her. The
2. Her sa - cred ground we walk u - pon with ev - ery step we take. Her

Earth ___ is our Moth - er, we must take care of her.
sa - cred ground we walk up - on with ev - ery step we take.

Hey ___ yan - na, ho ___ yan - na, hey ___ yan yan.

Hey ___ yan - na, ho ___ yan - na hey ___ yan yan.

Protecting Earth

In the twentieth century, the United States government formed the Environmental Protection Agency (EPA) to protect our planet from damage caused by humans. For centuries, Native American traditions have considered Earth's resources to be precious, to be cared for rather than recklessly consumed. This poem by Chief Dan George expresses this sentiment.

And My Heart Soars

by Chief Dan George

The beauty of the trees,
The softness of the air,
The fragrance of the grass,
    speaks to me.

The summit of the mountain,
The thunder of the sky,
The rhythm of the sea,
    speaks to me.

The faintness of the stars,
The freshness of the morning,
The dew drop on the flower,
    speaks to me.

The strength of fire,
The taste of salmon,
The trail of the sun,

And the life that never goes away,
    They speak to me.

And my heart soars.

Water, Water Everywhere

"Singin' in the Rain" is a song from the movie *Singin' in the Rain*. In this scene, Gene Kelly is singing about being happy and in love, despite the rain and cloudy skies.

As you **sing** the song, think about times you were happy even when skies were gray.

CD 15–26

Singin' in the Rain

Words by Arthur Freed

Music by Nacio Herb Brown

I'm sing - in' in the rain, just sing - in' in the rain. What a glo - ri-ous feel - ing, I'm hap - py a - gain! I'm laugh - ing at clouds so dark up a - bove. The sun's ___ in my heart ___ and I'm read - y for

Experiment with Sound

Create an introduction to this song using percussion instruments to sound like a rainstorm. Start with distant rolls of thunder on the drums. As the thunder gets louder, add lightning by using an instrument such as the slapstick. Gradually make the sound of raindrops by using light finger taps on a hand drum or desktop. Have the raindrops get louder and faster. At the end, add a *coda* by gradually having the rain come to a stop. Then find a way to **create** a rainbow.

▲ Gene Kelly

love. Let the storm - y clouds chase ev - 'ry - one ____ from the

place. Come on ____ with the rain, I've a smile ____ on my

face! I'll walk down the lane with a hap - py re -

frain and sing - in', _ just sing - in' in ____ the rain!

When It Rains, It POURS

"The Wheel of the Water" is a song about a natural process. Read the text of the song and name the process.

CD 16–1

The Wheel of the Water

Words and Music by John Forster and Tom Chapin

The wheel of the wa-ter go 'round and 'round, And the

wheel of the wa-ter go 'round. And the

Wa-ter flow down, down, trick-le, trick-le down,

Down to the o - cean, trick-le, trick-le down.

A Piece of the Cake

This song is layered, just like a layer cake! It has five different voice parts, one on top of the other. When the song is put together, all five parts are sung at the same time. Practice each voice part separately. **Sing** the song by adding one voice part at a time.

Voice 3

C   G7

See the va-pors rise.   See them cloud the skies.

Voice 4

C   G7

Clouds rain down.   Thun-der and light-ning sound.

Voice 5

C   G7

Springs bub-ble, bub-ble up.   Springs bub-ble, bub-ble up.

Icing on the Cake

Create movements for each layer of "The Wheel of the Water" and make your movements express the text. How many sets of movements do you need? **Listen** to the song and **perform** your movements.

Our Cake Is Baked

Now it's time to put our piece together. To perform our creation we need five different voice groups and five different movement groups.

Now with all the layers we've created, **perform** the song. Good luck!

Arts Connection

▲ *Wooded Landscape* (1851) by Jean François Millet

Back to Nature

In the 1700s and early 1800s, many Europeans felt they had moved too far away from nature. As a result, the Pastoral Movement developed in the arts. During this time, many artists created works to express their feelings about nature.

Listen for the storm in this music by Ludwig van Beethoven. He composed this music to describe his love of nature.

CD 16–3

Symphony No. 6, Movement 4

by Ludwig van Beethoven

This symphony, subtitled "Pastorale," was first published in 1809.

Why Is There Day and Night?

Long, long ago before people had developed the science of astronomy, the Hmong people had their own system for explaining the stars, the sun, the moon, and other natural events. This is the ancient Hmong story of how day and night might have come to pass.

CD 16–4

Nruab hnub thiab hmo ntuj

"Why Is There Day and Night?"
Hmong Folk Tale

Listen to the story. Then using the script, "Vocal Part," "Daytime Music," and "Nighttime Music," **create** a musical play. **Compare** the melodic contour of the musical parts.

Long ago, there were nine suns and nine moons. When it was night, it was nighttime for a very long time. When it was day, it was daytime for a very long time. However, the people of the world worked very hard and still did not have enough food to eat, and they were angry.

Arts Connection

▲ *Paj ntaub* story-telling quilt (1999) by May Chao Lor. The Hmong people use quilts to document folklore and history.

So the people made a crossbow and went to shoot the suns. But the suns and moons would not come out. They were very afraid and were not willing to come out. The people asked what kind of animal could go and call the suns and the moons to come out.

The people asked a bull to call out the suns and moons. A bull came out huffing, puffing, and snorting. "Come out!" he shouted. But the suns and moons would not come out.

Then the people asked a tiger to try. A tiger came out growling and roaring. "Come out!" he shouted. But the suns and moons would not come out.

All instruments

Vocal Part

But the suns and moons would not come out!

Next the people asked a lee-nyu bird. The lee-nyu bird came out flapping, hooting, and squawking. "Come out!" she shouted. But the suns and moons would not come out.

Finally, the people asked the rooster to try. The rooster came out puffing up his chest very proudly, and started to crow.

Daytime Music

And then . . . the sun came out for a little while. And then . . . the moon came out for a little while. Since that time, there has been daytime and nighttime, so the people can work and have enough to eat. They have lived that way until now.

Nighttime Music

The Seasons

In what seasons do you begin and end the school year? This song is about the cycles of nature. **Sing** "Cycle Song of Life." Notice how the **descant** adds another layer to the texture.

A **descant** is a countermelody that decorates the main melody, often soaring above the melody of the song.

CD 16–6

Cycle Song of Life
(The River Song)

Words and Music by James Durst

1. The riv-er casts her murk-y eyes _toward heav-en, __
2. Just when it seems the night will last __ for-ev-er, __
3. To un-der-stand the laugh-ter of __ the spring-time, _

but nev-er stops to doubt that she must roll out to the sea.
the sun ap-pears to kiss a-wake the dark-ness in-to day.
you have to see the sum-mer melt a-way in-to the fall.

And the se-cret of what takes her to her si-lence _
And __ though his life is short, he makes the jour-ney __
But __ 'til you've known the end-less sleep of win-ter, __

goes with her to her death be-yond e-ter-ni-ty.
and knows deep in his heart that there's no oth-er way.
you'll nev-er hear the cy-cle song of life at all.

REFRAIN
Descant last time only

The riv-er just keeps flow-in' on and

And the riv-er just keeps flow-in' on and on. The

on. The sun keeps go-in' 'round,

sun keeps go-in' 'round to bring the dawn. And

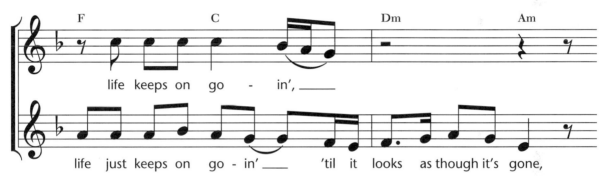

life keeps on go - in', _____

life just keeps on go-in' _____ 'til it looks as though it's gone,

repeat refrain last time

but it real-ly just keeps flow-in' on and on.

More of the Seasons

The Seasons by Antonio Vivaldi is a set of four concertos describing the seasons. **Listen** to this movement from *Spring.* What "special effects" did the composer use to create a musical image of this season?

CD 16–8

Spring, Movement 1

**from *The Four Seasons*
by Antonio Vivaldi**

This piece was written for small orchestra and solo violin.

Earth, Sea, and Sky

Unit 10 371

Seeing Stars

When the first star of the evening appears, make a wish. What did you wish for? In the song "Starlight, Star Bright," what does the composer wish for the world?

Look at the music for "Starlight, Star Bright." Do verses one and two have the same notation? Identify the form of the song. Then sing "Starlight, Star Bright."

MUSIC MAKERS

James Durst

James Durst is a composer, singer, and guitar player. Durst was born and raised in California. Now he spends his life traveling the world, bringing his music and the message of harmony and understanding to people everywhere. In each country he learns new songs. Recently he has started going into schools to work with students.

Starlight, Star Bright

Words and Music by James Durst

A C **REFRAIN** F C

do

Star - light, star bright, first star I

Gsus₄ G Am₇ Em F C

see to-night. I wish I may, I wish I might. _

C Dm₇ Gsus₄ G C Csus₄ C *Fine*

Have the wish I wish to - night.

B F **VERSE** G C F G

1. Shine __ on peo-ple of the earth; __ make us wor - thy
   Shine __ on chil-dren ev - 'ry - where; _ keep them safe and
2. Shine __ on an - i - mals and plants; _ il - lu - mi-nate their
   Lit - tle bea-con out in space; _ shine up - on the

Am₇ Em B♭ Dm₇ A♭

of our birth. Bright-en paths thru dark of night;
free from care. Feed their bod - ies, souls and minds;
life - long dance. Light the land, the sky, and sea;
hu - man race. Grant this hum - ble, hope - ful prayer;

Gsus₄ G₇ *D.C. after each verse*

that we might walk in truth and light.
that they might bless this world in kind.
and all that share life's mys - ter - y.
for peace to flour - ish ev - 'ry - where.

The Moving Moon

In this song, the words describe the Korean idea of what can be seen in the moon. What shapes have you discovered while gazing at the moon?

Sing "Sailboat in the Sky."

CD 16–11
MIDI 25

Sailboat in the Sky

English Words by Aura Kontra

Folk Song from Korea

푸 른 하 늘 은__ 하 수 하 얀 쪽 배 에
Pu reun ha nul eun - ha su ha yan jjok bae ae,
See the small white boat in the sky, sail - ing toward the west,

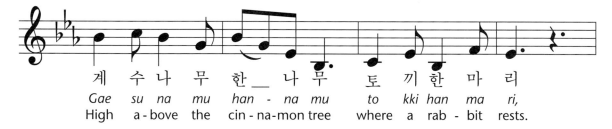

계 수 나 무 한__ 나 무 토 끼 한 마 리
Gae su na mu han - na mu to kki han ma ri,
High a - bove the cin - na-mon tree where a rab - bit rests.

돛 대 도 아 니 달 고 삿 대 도 없 이
Dot dae do ah ni dal go sat dae do up si,
With no sails or oars, it skims o'er the Mil - ky Way,

가 기 도 잘 도 간 다 서__ 쪽 나 라 로
Ga gi do jal do gahn da so - jjok na ra ro.
Float - ing a - mong the clouds as slow-ly it fades a - way.

Strong and Weak Beats

Sing the song again. Clap on the first beat of each measure and pat on the fourth beat of each measure.

Korean Hand Game

Below is a picture of a traditional Korean hand game often played while singing the song. The game is played quickly. To learn it, **move** slowly and then speed up.

The Planets

The planets in our solar system have long inspired people's imagination. The British composer Gustav Holst wrote an entire suite based on this subject. Listen to "Mars, the Bringer of War" from *The Planets*.

M·U·S·I·C M·A·K·E·R·S

Gustav Holst

Gustav Holst (1874–1934) was a musician, composer, and teacher. As a child he studied piano. Later, he went to the Royal College of Music in London and studied composition and trombone. As a teacher, Holst was known for encouraging beginners. He was a believer in learning music by "doing" music. Holst composed for both orchestra and wind bands. Perhaps his most famous work is *The Planets*.

Moving Through Space

Perform this rhythm game several times to learn the names of the planets. Each time, perform it at a slightly faster tempo.

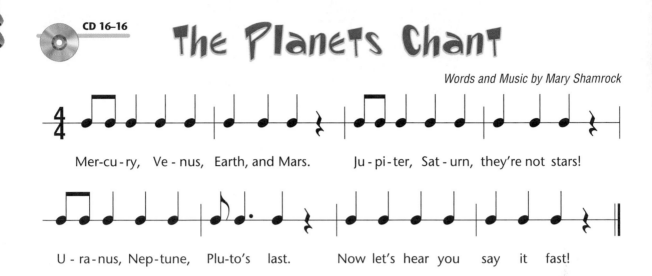

CD 16–16

The Planets Chant

Words and Music by Mary Shamrock

Mer-cu-ry, Ve - nus, Earth, and Mars.   Ju - pi-ter, Sat - urn, they're not stars!

U - ra-nus, Nep-tune, Plu-to's last.   Now let's hear you say it fast!

Pat thighs

Clap.

Clap right hands.

Clap.

Clap left hands

Clap.

Clap with partner.

Clap.

Listen again to Holst's compositon. If you had the chance, which planet would you visit first?

CD 16–15

Mars, the Bringer of War

from *The Planets, Suite for Large Orchestra*, Op. 32 by Gustav Holst

This selection is one of seven pieces in this suite. The other planets included in the entire work are Mercury, Venus, Jupiter, Saturn, Uranus, and Neptune.

We'll begin our choral adventure by singing the calypso song "Shake the Papaya Down."

CD 16–18
MIDI 26

Shake the Papaya Down

Calypso Song
Arranged by Ruth E. Dwyer and Judith M. Waller
Edited by Henry H. Leck

Ma - ma says no play; This is a work - day.
Sweet, sweet pa - pa - ya, Fruit of the Is - land,

Up with the bright sun; Get all the work done. If you will help me,
When all the work's done, Dance on the white sands. If you will help me,

Climb up the tall tree, Shake the pa - pa - ya down.
Climb up the tall tree, Shake the pa - pa - ya down.

Shake them down, _ Shake them down, _ Climb the tall _ tree, Shake them down. _

Shake them down, _ Shake them down, _ Shake the pa - pa - ya down.

Sing Out!

Welcome to the wonderful world of choral music. Experience the world around you in a way that can only happen when you sing.

1 Ma-ma says no play; This is a work-day. Up with the bright sun;

2 Shake them down, _ Shake them down, _ Climb the tall __ tree,

1 Get all the work done. If you will help me, Climb up the tall tree,

2 shake them down. _ Shake them down, _ Shake them down, _

1 Shake the pa - pa - ya down.

2 Shake the pa - pa - ya down.

43

1 Shake the pa - pa - ya down.

2 Shake the pa - pa - ya down.

3 Shake the pa - pa - ya down.

45 *cresc.*

1 Shake the pa - pa - ya down. Shake the pa - pa - ya

2 Shake the pa - pa - ya down. Shake the pa - pa - ya

3 Shake the pa - pa - ya down. Shake the pa - pa - ya

48 *a tempo*

1 down. _____

2 down. _____

3 down. _____

A Sequence of Seagulls

"Seagull, Seagull, Sit on the Shore" is really two songs in one. **Listen** to the recording. You may already know one or both of the partner melodies.

Speak the lyrics of the first two lines of the song. Which beginning letter sound is repeated the most? This device, used by poets and other writers, is called *alliteration* [uh-lih-ter-AY-shun]. (Verse 3 of "Paw-Paw Patch," on page 93, is a good example of alliteration that uses the P sound.)

Singing Tips

Follow these guidelines when you **sing** "Seagull, Seagull, Sit on the Shore":

• Place a little extra "weight" on beats 1 and 3 to underscore the S consonant and the rhythmic feel of the song.

• Be sure to sing *sit on*, not *si ton*; and *Santy Anna*, not *Santee-yana*.

Reading Music Tips

In music, a sequence occurs when a melody pattern is repeated, beginning each time on a pitch one step higher or lower. Look at measures 2–4 and measures 14–16 and **identify** whether each sequence moves up or down.

Knowing the Score

Listen to the recording as you follow the score. Then **describe** what happens

• In Voice 2 at measure 13.

• In Voice 1 and Voice 2 in measures 24–32.

The last line of the score (measures 33–36) is a type of *coda*—a short, final ending. **Describe** what happens to the rhythm of the melody in each voice part.

Seagull, Seagull, Sit on the Shore

Arranged by Susan Brumfield

Traditional

Sea-gull, sea-gull, sit on the shore, sit on the shore, sit on the shore.
Cap-tain, cap-tain, hoist up the sails, hoist up the sails, hoist up the sails.

Sea-gull, sea-gull, sit on the shore, and sail on, my San-ty An-na.
Cap-tain, cap-tain, hoist up the sails, and sail on, my San-ty An-na.

For my love is far a - way, far a - way, far a - way,

For my love is far a - way, 'cross the o - cean.

Blue hor - i - zon, head-ing for home, head-ing for home, head-ing for home.

'Cross the waves and back a - gain, back a - gain, back a - gain.

Blue hor - i - zon, head-ing for home, oh sail on, my San-ty An - na.

'Cross the waves and back a - gain, San - ty An-na.

Sail on, my San - ty An - na.

San - ty An - na.

Sing Out!

A Fiddlin' Folk Song

As Americans migrated westward from the original thirteen colonies, they took their music with them. Dancing was a favorite pastime, usually accompanied by fiddles or banjos. **Listen** for these and other instruments as they accompany the fiddle tune "Cindy."

▲ Fiddle and banjo players at Jackson's Ferry, Virginia

Singing Tips

For a crisp and energetic sound, clearly enunciate the beginning and final consonants of each word. **Sing** words such as *wish, hangin', sweet,* and *fine* with added emphasis and expression.

Reading Music Tips

Each phrase in section **A** begins with an eighth-note pick-up. Say "1 and 2 **and 1**" to emphasize the pick-up and the downbeat that follows. Next, say the words of each phrase in rhythm. Then **sing** the entire section.

Knowing the Score

"Cindy" has two sections—a verse and a refrain. Learn one of the countermelodies in the refrain and then **perform** it with the other voice parts. **Describe** how this affects the texture of the song.

CD 16–22
MIDI 28

Cindy

Folk Song from the Southern United States

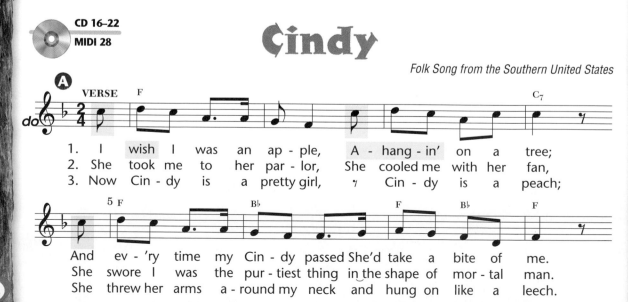

A VERSE

1. I wish I was an ap-ple, A-hang-in' on a tree;
2. She took me to her par-lor, She cooled me with her fan,
3. Now Cin-dy is a pretty girl, Cin-dy is a peach;

And ev-'ry time my Cin-dy passed She'd take a bite of me.
She swore I was the pur-tiest thing in the shape of mor-tal man.
She threw her arms a-round my neck and hung on like a leech.

You ought to see my Cin - dy, She lives a - way down South;
I wish I had a nee - dle, As fine as I could sew,
Well, Cin - dy had one blue eye, She al - so had one brown;

She is so sweet the hon - ey bees All swarm a - round her mouth.
I'd sew that gal to my coat - tail, And down the road I'd go.
One eye looked in the coun - try, 𝄌 The other one looked in town.

B **REFRAIN**
Countermelody 1

1 Get a-long home, _____ Get a-long home, _____

Countermelody 2

2 Get a-long home, dear Cin - dy, __ Home, sweet Cin - dy,

Melody

3 Get a-long home, Cin - dy, Cin - dy, Get a-long home, Cin - dy, Cin - dy,

1 Get a-long home. _____ I'll mar - ry you some day!

2 Get a-long home, my dear lit - tle girl, I'll mar - ry you some day!

3 Get a-long home, Cin - dy, Cin - dy, I'll mar - ry you some day!

Listen to another American country fiddle tune.

CD 16–25
Bonaparte's Retreat

Traditional Dance Tune
arranged and performed by Mark O'Connor

Mark O'Connor is a U.S. National Fiddle Champion.

◀ Mark O'Connor

Get It Together

"Lullaby and Dance" is a song with two very different sections. "Lullaby" is Cajun. The Cajuns are descendants of early French settlers in Nova Scotia and New Brunswick in Canada and later in Louisiana and Texas. "Dance" is based on a traditional American play-party song.

Arts Connection

◀ *Fiddling Sailor* by Christian Pierre, a contemporary Cajun American artist

Singing Tips

Sing the vowel *e* in words such as *sweep, dreams,* and *seems* with slightly rounded lips to avoid a wide vowel quality. When singing the word *away,* prolong the *a* vowel sound in *way* for four beats.

Reading Music Tips

Identify and **sing** the *do, mi,* and *so* pattern in measures 4–5. Find and sing all the other *do, mi,* and *so* patterns in "Lullaby and Dance."

Knowing the Score

Which voice part has the melody in measures 11–14 and in measures 22–25? Where do Voice 1 and Voice 2 sing the same rhythms and pitches together? To discover when the texture and harmony of this composition change, find the measures where Voice 1 has different rhythms and pitches from those found in Voice 2.

The proper *e* vowel mouth position ▶

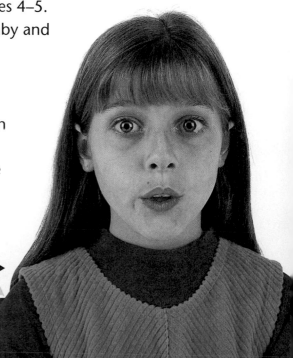

Lullaby and Dance

Traditional
Arranged by Ruth E. Dwyer

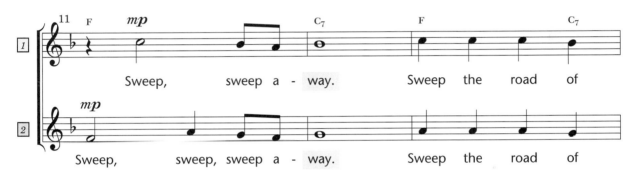

Sweep, sweep, sweep a - way.   Sweep the road of dreams. Peo-ple say   that in the

night,   The   tur-tle will   talk   it   seems.   The   tur-tle will   talk   it   seems.

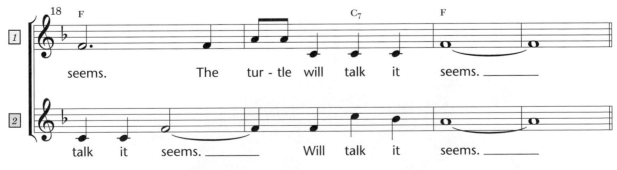

Sweep,   sweep a - way.   Sweep   the   road   of

Sweep,   sweep, sweep a - way.   Sweep   the   road   of

dreams. Peo-ple say   that in the night,   The   tur-tle will   talk   it

dreams. Peo-ple say ____ that in the night, ____   The   tur-tle will

seems.   The   tur - tle will talk   it   seems. _____

talk   it   seems. _____   Will   talk   it   seems. _____

1 / **2**

Come out to-night, Come out to-night, Come out to - night. _____

Come out to-night, Come out to-night, Come out to - night. _____

unison

Al - a - bam - a Gal, won't you come out to - night,

Come out to-night, Come out to - night. Al - a - bam - a Gal, won't you

come out to - night and dance by the light of the moon. The

moon shines bright the wind blows cool, I set my wag-on and un-hitched my mule.

Fid - dles tune a might bit high'r, Set your heels kick-in' 'round the fire.

Arts Connection

◄ *Horse and Rider* weather vane (1870). This is a classic example of 19th-century American folk art.

Measures 46–48:
- Part 1: Al-a-bam-a Gal, won't you come out to-night, Come out to-night,
- Part 2: Al-a-bam-a Gal, Come out to-night, Come out to-night,

Measures 49–50:
- Part 1: Come out to-night. Al-a-bam-a Gal, won't you
- Part 2: Come out to-night. Al-a-bam-a Gal,

Measures 51–53:
- Part 1: come out to-night and dance by the light of the moon. And
- Part 2: Come out to-night and dance by the light of the moon.

Measures 54–end:
- Part 1: dance by the light ____ dance by the light of the moon.
- Part 2: dance by the light of the moon.

Listen to an American Folk Tune

Here is another example of a folk tune from the southern United States.

Listen to *Jolie Blonde.*

CD 16–28
Jolie Blonde

**Cajun Folk Melody
as performed by the Hackberry Ramblers**

This song is a favorite at Cajun dances.

Singing Phrases

"Einini" is a Gaelic lullaby. Feel the rocking movement as you **sing** the song. Give the first note of each measure a little extra weight to create a swinging motion.

Singing Tips

This song uses many *e* and *a* vowels. They are similar and should be sung in almost the same way. Place the tip of your tongue against your lower teeth inside your mouth.

Reading Music Tips

Find *do* in the song and **identify** the key. Notice *mi*, *re*, and *do* are highlighted in the music. What is the first pitch syllable of the song? The composer suggests the song be sung *andante*, which means "walking tempo." The dynamic marking indicated is *mf*. Why were these expressions chosen?

Knowing the Score

On what beat of the measure does each phrase start? You already know the name for this. It is called an upbeat. How many upbeats are there in this song? Each upbeat in the song is the same note. Name the pitch.

View of Skellig and Puffin Islands, off the coast of Ireland

Einini

Gaelic Folk Song
Arranged by Cyndee Giebler

Andante

unison

mf

Ein - in - i, ein - in - i, cod - al -
ai - gi, cod - al - ai - gi, ein - in - i, ein - in - i, cod - al -
ai - gi, cod - al - ai - gi. Cod - al - ai - gi, cod - al - ai - gi, cois an
chlai amuigh, cois an chlai amuigh, cod - al - ai - gi, cod - al -
ai - gi, cois an chlai amuigh, cois an chlai amuigh.

Sing Out!

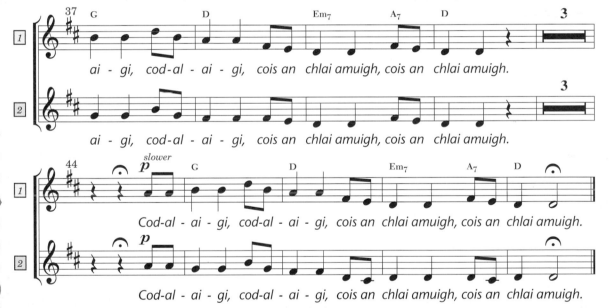

ai - gi, cod-al - ai - gi, cois an chlai amuigh, cois an chlai amuigh.

ai - gi, cod-al - ai - gi, cois an chlai amuigh, cois an chlai amuigh.

slower

Cod-al - ai - gi, cod-al - ai - gi, cois an chlai amuigh, cois an chlai amuigh.

Cod-al - ai - gi, cod-al - ai - gi, cois an chlai amuigh, cois an chlai amuigh.

Singing in Layers

"Little David, Play on Your Harp" is an African American spiritual.

Singing Tips

As you **sing** the words *play on your harp, hallelu,* make certain the *p* in the word *harp* is not connected to the *h* in *hallelu.*

Reading Music Tips

Practice speaking the syncopated rhythm pattern in the words *play on your.* Then practice the word *hallelu* with an accent on the *h.*

Knowing the Score

Find the words *Refrain, Verse,* and *ostinato.* What do these words mean? Is the melody ostinato sung with the verse or refrain?

CD 17–4
MIDI 31

Little David, Play on Your Harp

African American Spiritual
Arranged by Shirley McRae

REFRAIN

Lit - tle Da - vid, play on your harp, hal - le - lu, hal - le -
lu, Lit - tle Da - vid, play on your harp, hal - le - lu. _____

VERSE

1., 4. Lit - tle Da - vid was a shep - herd boy, he
2. Old ___ Dan - iel in the li - on's den, but
3. Lit - tle Da - vid was a might - y king, and

slew Go - li - ath and sang for joy.
he came out ___ all whole a - gain.
all the peo - ple came to sing.

14 *Refrain ostinato 1*

Play on your harp, ___ sing hal - le - lu.

19 *Refrain ostinato 2*

Play, play, sing hal - le - lu.

24 *Refrain ostinato 3*

Play on your harp, sing hal - le - lu - jah. ___

Listen for the melody as the Moses Hogan Chorale performs its version of *Little David, Play on Your Harp.* Then listen to Moses Hogan talk about his experiences in music. (In the photo below, he is in the first row, fourth from left.)

CD 17–6

Little David, Play on Your Harp

African American Spiritual as performed by the Moses Hogan Chorale
This version is performed *a cappella.*

Moses Hogan

Moses Hogan (1957–2003) was an accomplished pianist, conductor, and arranger. His awards included winning the Kosciuszko Foundation Chopin Competition. He was also the founder of the Moses Hogan Chorale, a group famous for its high quality choral performances.

CD 17–7

Interview with Moses Hogan

Two Melodies — One Song

Brazil is the largest South American country in both size and population, and the official language is Portuguese. *"Sambalele"* is a song that has two folk melodies that may be performed together. Melodies that can be performed in this way are called partner songs.

Singing Tips

Learn each melody of the song separately, then **sing** *"Sambalele."* Practice singing the song on the neutral syllable *pah,* accenting the initial consonant *p* for the rhythm pattern in measure 6.

Reading Music Tips

The rhythm of *"Sambalele"* is syncopated. Find this pattern in the song.

Practice this pattern before you **sing** the song. How many other rhythm patterns can you find in the song?

Carnaval celebration in Brazil ▶

Knowing the Score

What is the purpose of the five-measure rest at the beginning of the song? In which part of the song does the arranger create texture and harmony? Explain your answer.

Sambalele

English Words by Henry Leck

Folk Song from Brazil
Arranged by Henry Leck

CD 17–8
MIDI 32

Sam-ba - le - le ta do - en - te, tac - oa ca - be - ça que
Sam-ba - le - le is a fel - low, Who rare - ly gets to his

bra - da Sam-ba - le - le pre - ci - sa - va de u-mas de zoi - to lam-
pil - low, He spends his time loud - ly play - ing. No one can tell where he's

ba - das, Sam - ba - le - le ta do - en - te, tac - oa ca - be - ça, que
stay - ing, Sam - ba - le - le went out danc - ing, With his new cart he went

bra - da Sam - ba - le - le pre - ci - sa - va
pran - cing, then he ar - rived at the mar - ket,

de u-mas de zoi - to lam - ba - das, Sam - ba sam - ba
but he for - got how to park it. Sam - ba sam - ba

sam - ba - le - le Pi - sa - na ba - ra da sa - ia le - le!
sam - ba - le - le We wish your neigh-bors could tell where you stay.

26 F   Gm   C₇

Sam - ba   sam - ba   sam - ba - le - le!   Pi - sa - na   bar - ra   da
Sam - ba   sam - ba   sam - ba - le - le!   Of - ten   we   just   can - not

29 F   C₇   F   Gm

sa - ia   Ba - la - io   meu bem, Ba - la - io   sin - ha   ba -
find   you.   Ba - la - io   the brave, Ba - la - io   the fair   ba -

33 C₇   F   Gm

la - io   do   co - ra - ção   Mo - ça - que não tem ba - la - io   sin - ha   bo-taa
la - io whom we   a - dore.   I   know your dark hair and   pret-ty   dark eyes are the

37 C₇   F

cos - tu - ra   no   chão.   Ba - la - io   meu bem,   ba -
en - vy   of   us   all.   Ba - la - io   so   sweet   ba -

40 Gm   C₇   F

la - io   sin - ha   ba - la - io   do   co - ra - ção   Mo -
la - io   so   kind   ba - la - io   we   can't   ig - nore.   The

43 F   Gm   C₇

ça - que   não tem   ba - la - io   sin - ha   bo-taa   cos - tu - ra   no
beau-ty   you bring how   hap-py   you sing   we   all   want   to   see   you

1 chão! Ba - la - io meu bem, ba - la - io sin - ha, ba -
more. Ba - la - io so nice, ba - la - io pre - cise ba -

2 chão! Sam - ba - le - le ta do - en - te,
more. Sam - ba - le - le is a fel - low,

1 la - io do co - ra - ção Mo - ça - que não tem ba -
la - io you live next door. We hope that you stay, so

2 tac - ao ca - be - ça que bra - da! Sam - ba - le - le pre - ci -
who rare - ly gets to his pil - low, He spends his time loud - ly

Sound of the *Samba*

One of the most beloved kinds of music in Brazil is the *samba*. Every year a big celebration called *Carnaval* takes place. Many people parade through the streets singing and dancing to *samba* music.

Listen for the *samba* rhythms in this recording of *Bate-papo*.

CD 17–12

Bate-papo

***Batucada Street Samba* from Brazil
as performed by *Bateria Nota 10***

The *batucada samba* is the rhythmic foundation for *Carnaval*.

what's the score?

The beauty of nature is all around us. Read the words to "Circle 'Round the Moon." What do they mean? One challenge in reading music is to follow your part in a complete score. As you **listen** to "Circle 'Round the Moon," trace your part in the score.

Singing Tips

Learn the first phrase of "Circle 'Round the Moon." **Sing** this phrase wherever it appears in the song. Next, learn measures 13–15 and **sing** this phrase wherever it appears in the song. Now **sing** each phrase without taking a breath in the middle.

Reading Music Tips

Read measures 5–8 using pitch syllables. The melody often uses pitch syllables *do, mi,* and *so*. The melody also uses a ♪♪ ♪♪ rhythm pattern. Why does this rhythm pattern change to larger note values? How does this make the music feel?

Knowing the Score

The composer of "Circle 'Round the Moon" uses **word painting** to help create mood. An example of word painting appears in measure 13. Notice in the words *high above the trees,* the note for the word *high* is the highest note in the measure and the lowest note is for *trees.* How many other examples of word painting can you find?

Word painting is the positioning of pitch and rhythm patterns to resemble the meaning of words.

Circle 'Round the Moon
(From "Reflections of Youth")

Words and Music by
Mark Hierholzer

Cir-cle 'round the moon   in-vites me to stay out in the win-ter - time. _____

Crys-tals in the air   sug-gest that I pre-pare for the cold night air. _____

High a-bove the trees   you will make me see   that with such   a   sight

sheer de - light   is hid - den ev' - ry - where   for those who care to see. ___

___   Cav-erns down be-low   in - vite me to come down on the

slip - p'ry   rock. _____   I - ci - cles of stone   and

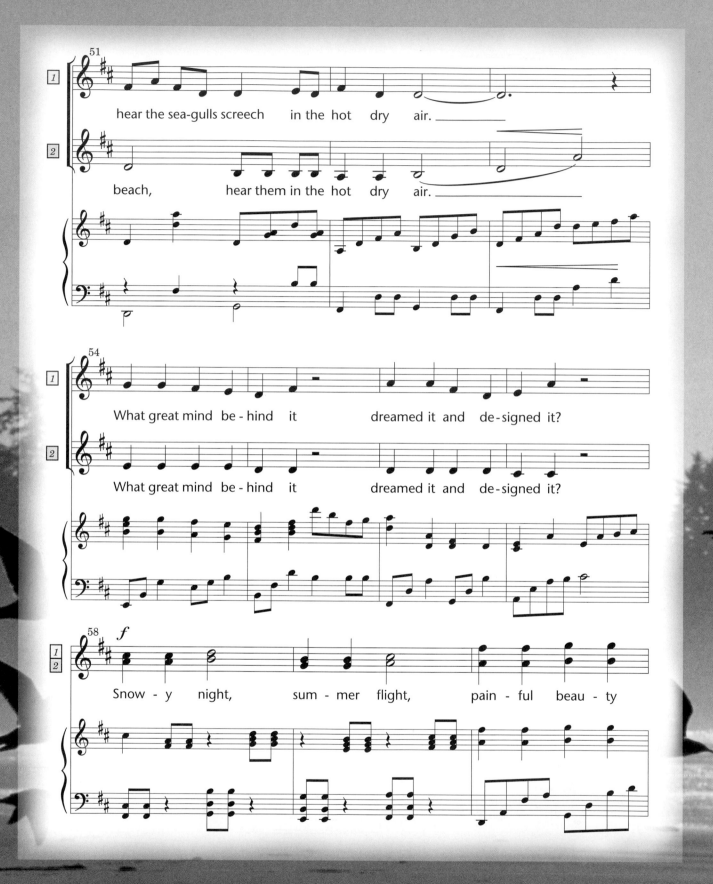

in my sight mak - ing me long for you._____

Music to My Ears

The words of "Circle 'Round the Moon" create a specific mood. This poem by James Whitcomb Riley also creates a specific mood. If you set "Extremes" to music, what dynamics would you choose? What tempo? What instruments might you choose for the accompaniment?

Extremes

by James Whitcomb Riley

A little boy once played so loud
That the thunder, up in a thundercloud,
Said, "Since I can't be heard, why, then
I'll never, never thunder again!"

And a little girl once kept so still
That she heard a fly on the sill
Whisper and say to a ladybird,
"She's the stillest child I ever heard."

Carols in Harmony

"A Merry Modal Christmas" is a collection of three European Christmas carols.

Singing Tips

Sing *"Pat-a-pan"* and *"La marche des rois"* on the neutral syllable *to* to create a pointed attack on each note. On "Coventry Carol," **sing** the melody on *loo* to create a *legato* feeling.

Reading Music Tips

For *"Pat-a-pan,"* **sing** low *la*-low *ti-do-re-mi* up the scale and *mi-re-do*-low *ti*-low *la* down. Perform the pattern slowly and quickly. Tap the rhythms in measures 46–49. This is a repeated rhythm pattern in *"La marche des rois."*

Knowing the Score

Identify the ostinato in *"Pat-a-pan."* Find the melody and harmony parts in "Coventry Carol" and *"La marche des rois."*

A Merry Modal Christmas

Words and Music by Bernard de la Monnoye (Pat-a-pan)
Carols from France and England
Arranged by Buryl Red

Pat-a-pan

mf

Prum, pum, pum!   Prum, pum,

mf

pum! *Guil - lo, prends ton tam - bou - rin, Toi prends ta flú - te, Ro -*
pum! Wil - lie, get your lit - tle drum, Ro - bin, bring your flute, and

mp

pum!   Prum, pum, pum!   Prum, pum,

bin; Au son de cés in - stru - ments, Tu - re - lu - re - lu, pat - a - pat - a -
come. Aren't they fun to play up - on? *Tu - re - lu - re - lu,* pat - a - pat - a -

pum!   Prum, pum, pum!   Prum, pum,

pan; Au son de cés in - stru - ments, Je di - rai No - ël gaie - ment.
pan; When you play your fife and drum, How can an - y - one be glum?

pum!   Prum, pum, pum!   Prum, pum, pum!

mp Coventry Carol

Lul - lay, Lul - lay,

p

Lul - lay, Lul - lay,

mp

Lul - lay, Thou lit - tle ti - ny Child,

By, by, lul - ly, lul - lay, lul - lay.

By, by, lul - ly, lul - lay; _____ Lul -

Lul - lay, Thou ti - ny Child,

lay, Thou lit - tle ti - ny Child,

By, by, lul - ly, lul - lay. _____

By, by, lul - ly, lul - lay. _____

2 *f La marche des rois*

Ce ma - tin, Ce ma - tin, Ce ma - tin, J'ai
This great day, This great day, This great day, I

ren - con - tré le train, De trois grands rois qui al - laient en - voy - a - ge _____
met up - on the way, The Kings of East as they came rid - ing proud - ly, _____

Ce ma - tin, j'ai ren - con - tré le train, De trois grands rois des - sus le
This great day, I met up - on the way, The Kings of East with all their

grand che - min. Tout char - gés d'or les sui - vant d'a - bord, De
fine ar - ray. The gifts of gold, frank - in - cense, and myrrh, Were

Join the Celebration

Some music just seems to be made for a celebration. *"La copa de la vida"* was sung by Ricky Martin for the 1998 World Cup in France. **Sing** the song and be part of the celebration.

CD 17–20

La copa de la vida (The Cup of Life)

Words and Music by Desmond Child and Robi Rosa

Do you real-ly want _ it? ____ Yeah! Do you real-ly want _

_____ it? ____ Yeah! Do you real-ly want _ it? ____ Yeah!

Go, go, go. Go, go, go. Al - lez, al - lez, al-lez. Al - lez, al - lez, al-lez.

414

Sing and celebrate

Music is an important part of our lives. We use music to celebrate special times.

Call Response   Call Response   C R C R Tutti   8

Go, go, go, go.   Go, go, go, go. Here we go, yeah!

VERSE *Solo*
Em   C   Em

1. The cup of life, this ___ is the one. ___   Now is the time, don't ___
2. *La vi-da es com - pe-ti-ción. ___*   *Hay que so-ñar, ser ___*

C   Em   C

___ ev-er stop.   Push it a-long, got - ta be strong. ___
___ *cam-pe-ón.*   *La co-pa es la ___ ben-di-ción, ___*

Push it a-long, right __ to the top. *Co - mo Cain y A - bel   es un par -*
la ga-na-rás,   go, __ go, __ go.   And when you feel the _ heat   the world is

ti - do __ cruel. _   *Tie - nes que pe - le - ar __   por un - a   es - tre -*
at your _ feet. _   No one   can hold you down _   if you real - ly   want _

- lla. ____   *Con - si - gue   con hon - or   la co - pa*
____ it. ____   Just steal your   des - ti - ny   right from the

del a - mor. _   *Pa - ra   so - bre - vi - vir __   y   lu - char por e -*
hands of __ fate. _   Reach for   the cup   of life _ 'cause your name is   on __

- lla. _   Lu - char por e - lla. __ Yeah!   Do you real - ly want _ it? __ Yeah!
____ it. ____   Do you real - ly   want _ it?

REFRAIN *Tutti*

Here   we   go.   *Al - lez, al - lez, al - lez.*   Go,   go,   go.   Al -
Uno,   dos,   tres,   o - lé, o - lé, o - lé.   *Un,   deux,   trois,*   Al -

lez, al - lez, al - lez. _____   To - night's the night   we're gon - na   cel - e - brate.   The
lez, al - lez, al - lez. _____

To Coda 2nd time ⊕

3

cup   of   life,   *al - lez, al - lez, al - lez. _____*

Every four years, the best soccer teams from around the world play in a month-long tournament called the World Cup. The first World Cup took place in 1930 and was won by Uruguay.

Coda

Call   Response   Call   Response   Call

Al - lez, al - lez, al - lez, al - lez. Al - lez, al - lez, al - lez, al - lez. Al -

Response   Tutti   1.   Call

lez, al - lez, al - lez, al - lez. Al - lez, al - lez, al - lez. _____   Al -

2.   Call   Response

lez, al-lez, al-lez. _____   Yeah!   Do you real-ly want _it? __   Yeah!

Yitzhak Rabin
▼ Nobel Peace Prize, 1994

SiNG in Peace

▲ Jane Addams
Nobel Peace Prize, 1931

This song from Israel could be from any country. The message is universal—peace in our world. Israel's Prime Minister, Yitzhak Rabin, was working for peace when he was assassinated. A copy of this song was found in his pocket.

Look at the song *"Shir l'shalom."* Notice the melodic rhythm is repeated many times. Clap the rhythm of the first phrase.

Now we're ready to sing the song.

CD 17–23

Shir l'shalom
(Hand in Hand–A Song for Peace)

Hebrew Words by Jacob Rotblitt
English Adaptation by Stanley Ralph Ross and Michael Isaacson

Music by Yair Rosenblum
Arranged by Michael Isaacson

do

1. Tnu la - she - mesh la - a - lot, la - bo - ker l' - ha -
2. Tnu la - she - mesh la - cha - dor mi - ba - 'ad la - pra -
1. Ev - 'ry day, the sun will rise and shine u - pon our __
2. As we gath - er side by side to plead for what we __

ir.   Ha - za - kah she - ba - tfi - lot ___ o -
chim.   Al ta - bi - tu l' - a - chor, __ ha -
land,   Urg - ing us to re - a - lize ___ we
need,   Throw a - way mis - ta - ken pride _ and

ta - nu lo tach __ zir.   Mi a - sher ku -
ni - chu la - hol - chim.   Su ey - na - yim
must walk hand - in - hand.   Peo - ple who were
peace will then suc - ceed. Broth - ers will em -

va ne - ro u - v' - a - far nit - man,
b' - tik - vah, lo de - rech ka - va - not.
once at war at last will un - der - stand,
brace a - gain and sis - ters will u - nite,

Be - chi mar lo ya - i - ro _____ lo
Shi - ru shir la - a - ha - vah, ___ v' -
It's a sign we can't ig - nore, ___ we
Ev - 'ry day we live in peace __ will

Sing and Celebrate

Unit 12 419

yach - zi - ro l' - chan.   Ish   o - ta - nu
lo la - mil - cha - mot.   Al   ta - gi - du
must walk hand - in - hand.   In   this world we
shine with rad - iant ___ light.   On - ly when we're

lo ya - shiv mi - bor tach - teet a -
yom ya - vo, ha vi - u et ha -
will sur - vive, give thanks to God a -
hand - in - hand can san - i - ty be ___

fel. Kan lo yo - i - lu lo shi - rey ha -
yom! Ki lo - cha - lom hu. U - v' - chol ha -
bove, be - cause we know the rea - son we are
near, let's strive to do our best to make sure

ni - tsa - chon ___ v' - lo shi - rey ha - lel.
ki - ka - rot ___ ha - ri - u l' - sha - lom!
all a - live, ___ is God's e - ter - nal ___ love.
war is banned _ and peace will con - quer ___ fear.

La' chen rak shi - ru shir l' - sha - lom, ___ al
And so we sing, sing, sing of a day ___ when

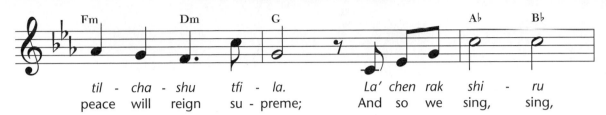

til - cha - shu   tfi - la.   La' chen rak   shi - ru
peace   will   reign   su - preme;   And   so   we   sing,   sing,

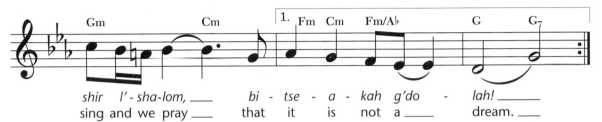

shir l' - sha-lom, ___   bi - tse - a - kah g'do - lah! _____
sing and we pray ___   that   it   is   not a ___   dream. ___

tse - a - kah g'do - lah! _____   g' - do - lah! _____
it   is   not a ___   dream, ___   Not   a   dream. _____

Mother Teresa ▶
Nobel Peace Prize,
1979

◀ Nelson Mandela
Nobel Peace Prize,
1993

Aung San Suu Kyi ▶
Nobel Peace Prize,
1991

Movin' and Groovin' Is a "Boo"tiful Thing

Originally a Celtic holiday, Halloween has come to mean costumes, trick or treating, and horror stories for children. *Little Shop of Horrors* was an Off-Broadway musical hit. It is about a flower shop employee and his plant, Audrey II, which is from outer space.

Sing "Little Shop of Horrors." Then choose an instrument and **play** the melody.

 CD 18–1

Little Shop of Horrors

Words by Howard Ashman

Music by Alan Menken

Lit - tle shop, _ lit - tle shop-pa hor - rors. Lit - tle shop, _ lit -

- tle shop-pa ter - ror. Call a cop. _ Lit - tle shop-pa hor - rors.

No, oh, oh, no - oh! ___ Lit - tle shop, _ lit -

- tle shop-pa hor - rors. Bob - sh'-bop, _ lit - tle shop-pa ter - ror.

Holiday Harmony

The shortest day of the year occurs on the winter solstice, December 21 or 22. In the northern parts of the world, snow, ice, and cold are associated with winter. This song paints a picture of a cold winter day. **Sing** the partner song "Winter Fantasy" and imagine the picture the song creates.

CD 18–3

Winter Fantasy

Words and Music by Jill Gallina

Snow-flakes fall - ing all o - ver town, slip - ping slid - ing
There's an i - cy chill in the air, tell - ing us that

ev - 'ry-bod - y rush - in' 'round.

win - ter's real - ly here. Oh!

I'm so glad that win - ter is here. Grab your sled and

let out a hap-py cheer be-cause it's snow-ing, blow-ing, all through the day.

Win - ter winds will sure - ly blow all your cares a - way.

Part II

Dash-ing thru the snow in a one-horse o-pen sleigh. O'er the fields we go

laugh-ing all the way. Bells on bob-tails ring, mak-ing spir-its bright. What

fun it is to laugh and sing a sleigh-ing song to-night. Oh!

Jin-gle bells, jin-gle bells, jin-gle all the way.

Oh, what fun it is to ride in a one-horse o-pen sleigh. ___

Jin-gle bells, jin-gle bells, jin-gle all the way.

Oh, what fun it is to ride in a one-horse o-pen sleigh.

A Cool Holiday Song

Many popular performers enjoy recording holiday music. **Listen** to this version of *Let It Snow! Let It Snow! Let It Snow!* by Harry Connick, Jr. Then **sing** your own version of the song.

CD 18–5

Let It Snow! Let It Snow! Let It Snow!

Words by Sammy Cahn

Music by Jule Styne

VERSE

The snow-man in the yard is fro-zen hard; He's a sor-ry sight to see,

If he had a brain he'd com-plain, Bet he wish-es he were me.

REFRAIN

Oh! the weath-er out-side is fright-ful, but the
It _____ does-n't show signs of stop-ping, and I

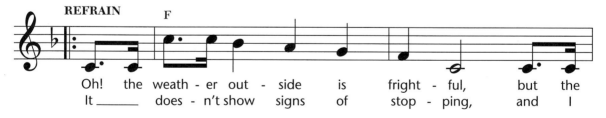

fire is so de-light-ful. And since we've no place to
brought some corn for pop-ping; The lights are turned way down

go, Let it snow! Let it snow! Let it snow!
low. Let it snow! Let it snow! Let it snow!

Harry Connick, Jr.

Harry Connick, Jr. (born 1967) has had a wonderful career in music and acting. Born in New Orleans, his musical style is rooted in New Orleans jazz. He started playing the piano at age three. Before Connick was 10 years old, he played with a professional jazz band and later with the New Orleans Symphony.

CD 18–7

Let It Snow! Let It Snow! Let It Snow!

by Jule Styne and Sammy Cahn
as performed by Harry Connick, Jr.

This recording features a jazz ensemble and an orchestra.

When we fi-nal-ly kiss good-night, how I'll hate go-ing out in the

storm! But if you'll real-ly hold me tight, all the way home I'll be warm. The

fire is slow-ly dy-ing, and, my dear, we're still good-bye-ing. But as

long as you love me so, Let it snow! Let it snow! Let it snow!

Sing and Celebrate

Harmony in Chanukah

Chanukah is a holiday observed by Jewish people. It is also called "The Festival of Lights." The eight days of Chanukah are celebrated by lighting candles on a *menorah*, exchanging gifts, and eating traditional foods such as *latkes* (potato pancakes). Families and friends also play games using a top called a *dreidel*.

Accompany the Chanukah song *"Ocho kandelikas"* on the guitar. Practice playing the E string and the B string on the guitar. Then follow the music on page 429 and **play** E or B as you sing the song.

▼ *Dreidel*

Singing in Ladino

When the Jews left Spain in 1492, they took with them a local Spanish language. It is called Judeo-Spanish or Ladino. This language is still known in many countries of the world where Jews have settled. **Sing** this Ladino song.

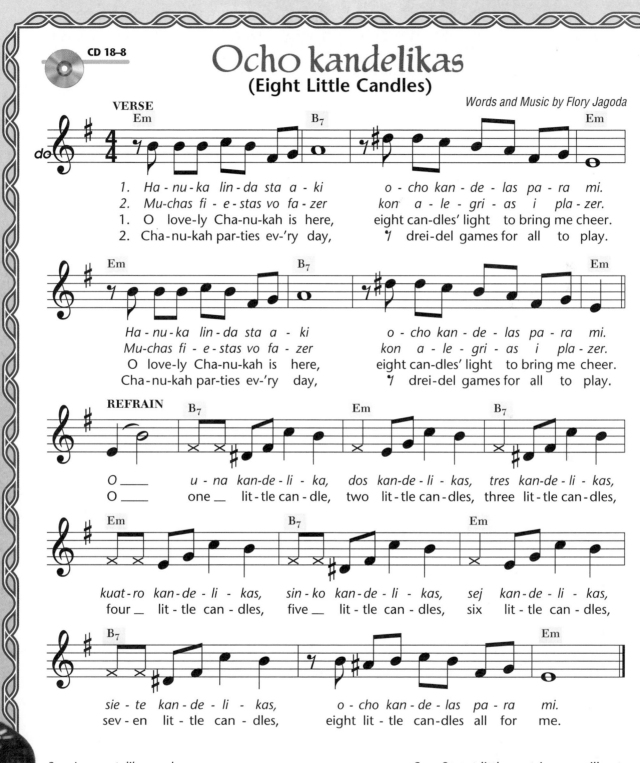

CD 18–8

Ocho kandelikas
(Eight Little Candles)

Words and Music by Flory Jagoda

VERSE

1. Ha - nu - ka lin - da sta a - ki   o - cho kan - de - las pa - ra mi.
2. Mu-chas fi - e - stas vo fa - zer   kon a - le - gri - as i pla - zer.
1. O love-ly Cha-nu-kah is here,   eight can-dles' light to bring me cheer.
2. Cha-nu-kah par-ties ev-'ry day,   drei-del games for all to play.

Ha - nu - ka lin - da sta a - ki   o - cho kan - de - las pa - ra mi.
Mu-chas fi - e - stas vo fa - zer   kon a - le - gri - as i pla - zer.
O love-ly Cha-nu-kah is here,   eight can-dles' light to bring me cheer.
Cha-nu-kah par-ties ev-'ry day,   drei-del games for all to play.

REFRAIN

O _____ u - na kan-de - li - ka, dos kan-de - li - kas, tres kan-de - li - kas,
O _____ one _ lit - tle can - dle, two lit-tle can - dles, three lit-tle can - dles,

kuat-ro kan-de - li - kas, sin-ko kan-de - li - kas, sej kan-de - li - kas,
four _ lit - tle can - dles, five _ lit - tle can - dles, six lit - tle can - dles,

sie - te kan - de - li - kas, o - cho kan - de - las pa - ra mi.
sev - en lit - tle can - dles, eight lit - tle can - dles all for me.

3. *Los pastelikos vo komer*
   kon almendrikas i la myel.
   Los pastelikos vo komer
   kon almendrikas i la myel.
   Refrain

3. Sweet little pastries we will eat,
   filled with almonds and honey.
   Sweet little pastries we will eat,
   filled with almonds and honey.
   Refrain

CHRISTMAS RHYTHMS

Christmas is a holiday celebrated by Christians all over the world. Christmas traditions differ from country to country. Although only one day is celebrated as Christmas Day, the Christmas season is actually twelve days.

Sing the song and notice the changes in meter.

CD 18–12 THE TWELVE DAYS OF CHRISTMAS

Christmas Song from England

On the first day of Christ-mas my true love gave to me, a

par - tridge _____ in a pear tree.

On the se-cond day of Christ-mas my true love gave to me,
third
fourth

four call - ing birds, three French _ hens, two tur - tle doves,

and a par - tridge _ in a pear tree.

On the fifth day of Christ-mas my true love gave to me,
sixth
seventh
eighth
ninth
tenth
eleventh
twelfth

8. *on to next ending* | 7. *on to next ending* | 6. *on to next ending*

twelve drum-mers drum-ming, eleven pip-ers pip-ing, ten lords a leap-ing,

5. *on to next ending* | 4. *on to next ending* | 3. *on to next ending*

nine la-dies danc-ing, eight maids a milk-ing, seven swans a swim-ming,

2. *on to next ending* | 1.

six geese a lay-ing, five gold-en rings, four _ call-ing birds,

three French hens, two _ tur-tle doves, and a par-tridge _ in a pear tree.

Listen to *Good King Wenceslas* [WEN-ses-lahs].
What story does this Christmas song tell?

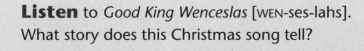

CD 18–14
Good King Wenceslas

**Traditional Carol
as performed by the Westminster Choir**

This traditional carol may have come from Bohemia, a
section of the former Czechoslovakia.

Nine-Day Celebration

In Mexico, Christmas is celebrated for nine days and is called *Las Posadas*. **Create** ostinatos in meter in 3 and meter in 2. **Perform** them while you sing *"Al quebrar la piñata."*

CD 18–15

AL QUEBRAR LA PIÑATA
(Piñata Song)

English Words by Verne Muñoz

Christmas Song from Mexico

En las no - ches de po - sa - das, _____
In the hap - py days of Christ - mas, _____

La pi - ña - ta_es lo me - jor; _____
Sounds of glad - ness fill the air; _____

La ni - ña más re - mil - ga - da _____
When it's time for the pi - ña - ta, _____

Se al - bo - ro - ta con ar - dor. _____
There's ex - cite - ment ev - 'ry - where. _____

Da - le, da - le, da - le, no pier - das el ti - no,
Take a stick and whack it, Be the one to crack it;

Que de la dis - tan - cia se pier - de el ca - mi - no.
Win pi - ña - ta's treas - ure, Can - dies for your pleas - ure.

A Seasonal Song

Listen to *Feliz Navidad,* a Christmas song in Spanish and English. **Create** an ostinato pattern to play while you listen.

CD 18–19
Feliz Navidad

written and performed by José Feliciano
Feliciano's arrangement of *Feliz Navidad* made the song popular across the United States.

KWANZAA
Hello and Goodbye

Kwanzaa is a Swahili word that means "first." The holiday, *Kwanzaa*, was created by Dr. Maulana Karenga to remind African Americans of their heritage. It is celebrated from December 26 through January 1.

Identify the phrases as you **listen** to "*Harambee*." **Sing** the song, and **perform** a slight *crescendo* at the beginning and a slight *decrescendo* at the end of each phrase.

©1997—USPS. Displayed with permission.

CD 18–20
MIDI 35

Harambee

Words and Music by James McBride

1. We gath-er for the Kwan-zaa hol-i-day this time each year _ With
2. ⅞ Sev-en dif-f'rent prin - ci-ples that help us learn to grow _ We
3. ⅞ Build-ing as a na - tion with our hon-or and our pride, _ We

rel - a - tives and friends from far and wide, __
cel - e - brate our faith and u - ni - ty, _____
learn to hon - or truth and show our love, __

Shar-ing in a peace-ful time of trust and love and song, _ With
Hop-ing that the best _ of all your wish-es do come true, _ We
Car-ing is a part _ of our re-spon-si-bil-i-ty. __ We

joy e - nough to last ___ the whole year long.
wish a hap - py Kwan - zaa to you.
want the world to live ___ in har - mo - ny.

REFRAIN

A Kwan-zaa hol - i - day ___ is a spe-cial hol - i - day, ___ A
Ha - ram - bee ___ means ___ hel - lo and good-bye, too, ___ A

1.

time to cel - e - brate ___ our his - to - ry.

2.

way of show - ing that ___ I care for you.

Celebrating
Kwanzaa ▶

Guide Our Hope

Singing brings people together during times of struggle. "We Shall Not Be Moved" is associated with the Civil Rights Movement in this country. This song reminds us of Dr. Martin Luther King's fight for the rights of African Americans.

Sing the song and then **play** it on a melody instrument.

▲ Martin Luther King, Jr. and his wife, Coretta, lead marchers in Selma, Alabama, in 1965.

CD 18–22

We Shall Not Be Moved

Traditional Freedom Song

1. We shall not, we shall not be
2. We're on our way to vic-tor - y, ____ we shall not be
3. Segre - ga-tion is __ our en-e - my, __ it must be re -

moved. ___ We shall not, we shall not be moved.
moved. We're on our way to vic-tor - y, ____ we shall not be moved.
moved. Segre - ga-tion is __ our en-e - my, __ it must be re-moved.

Just like a tree, that's plant - ed by the

wa - ter. We shall not be moved.

In 1963 Dr. King gave his famous "I Have a Dream" speech to a huge gathering in Washington, D.C. This event is called the March on Washington. ▶

CREATING LIVING TRADITIONS

▲ A Passover *seder*

During the eight days of Passover, Jews remember the freeing of Hebrew slaves in Egypt thousands of years ago. They celebrate by having traditional services called *seders* and reading from the *Haggadah*. Symbolic foods are eaten and traditional songs are sung. **Sing** "*Dayenu*," a traditional Passover song.

The Pyramids at Giza, Egypt

A Refrain to Remember

Analyze the form of this song. Which of these two sections is always sung with the same words? Which section has different words each time it is sung?

CD 19-1

Dayenu
(It Would Have Been Enough)

Jewish Passover Song

VERSE

1. I - lu ho - tzi, ho - tzi - a - nu, ho - tzi - a - nu mi - Mitz - ra - yim,
2. I - lu na - tan na - tan la - nu, na - tan la - nu et ha - Sha - bat,
1. Had he led us out of E - gypt, on - ly led us out of E - gypt,
2. Had he giv - en us the Sab - bath, on - ly giv - en us the Sab - bath,

ho - tzi - a - nu mi - Mitz - ra - yim, da - ye - nu.
na - tan la - nu et ha - Sha - bat, da - ye - nu.
Had he led us out of E - gypt, da - ye - nu.
Had he giv - en us the Sab - bath, da - ye - nu.

REFRAIN

Du - du - ye - nu, da da - ye - nu, da - da - ye - nu, da -

1. ye - nu, da - ye - nu, da - ye - nu.
2. ye - nu, da - ye - nu!

3. *Ilu natan natan lanu,*
   natan lanu et haTora,
   natan lanu et haTora, dayenu.
   Refrain

3. Had he given us the Tora,
   only given us the Tora,
   Had he given us the Tora, *dayenu.*
   Refrain

Sing and Celebrate

Heartbeat of a Nation

Patriotic songs are songs that express love of and loyalty to one's country. During war time, the armed forces defend our country and our freedom. Conduct "America" while others **sing** the song.

CD 19–5

America

Words by Samuel Francis Smith   *Traditional Melody*

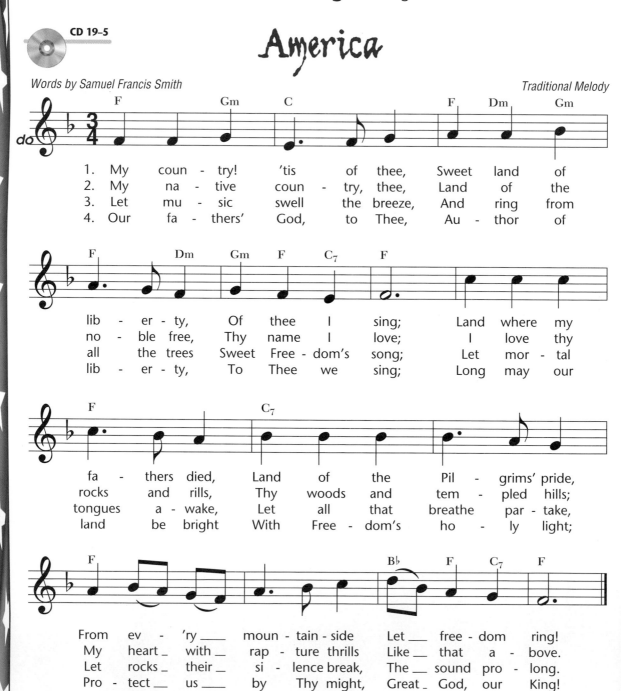

1. My coun - try! 'tis of thee, Sweet land of
2. My na - tive coun - try, thee, Land of the
3. Let mu - sic swell the breeze, And ring from
4. Our fa - thers' God, to Thee, Au - thor of

lib - er - ty, Of thee I sing; Land where my
no - ble free, Thy name I love; I love thy
all the trees Sweet Free - dom's song; Let mor - tal
lib - er - ty, To Thee we sing; Long may our

fa - thers died, Land of the Pil - grims' pride,
rocks and rills, Thy woods and tem - pled hills;
tongues a - wake, Let all that breathe par - take,
land be bright With Free - dom's ho - ly light;

From ev - 'ry ___ moun - tain - side Let ___ free - dom ring!
My heart _ with _ rap - ture thrills Like _ that a - bove.
Let rocks _ their _ si - lence break, The _ sound pro - long.
Pro - tect _ us ___ by Thy might, Great _ God, our King!

Our National Anthem

Sing "The Star-Spangled Banner" with pride. People stand to show respect for our country while they sing the National Anthem.

CD 19–7

The Star-Spangled Banner

Words by Francis Scott Key

Music by John Stafford Smith

Oh, __ say! can you see, by the dawn's ear - ly light, What so
stripes and bright stars, through the per - il - ous fight, O'er the

proud - ly we hailed at the twi - light's last gleam-ing, Whose broad
ram - parts we watched were so gal - lant - ly

stream-ing? And the rock - ets' red glare, the bombs burst - ing in

air, Gave proof through the night that our flag was still

there. Oh, say, does that __ Star - Span - gled Ban - ner __ yet __

wave __ O'er the land __ of the free and the home of the brave?

Reading Sequence 1, page 10

CD 1–9
MIDI 36

Rhythm: Reading

Use rhythm syllables to **read** and **perform** this two-part rhythm accompaniment for "Soldier, Soldier."

Reading Sequence 2, page 14

CD 1–21
MIDI 37

Rhythm: Reading and in Duple Meter

Use rhythm syllables to **read** and **perform** this rhythm accompaniment for *"Gakavik."*

Melody: Reading Steps, Skips, Repeated Pitches

For inner-hearing practice, **read** and **sing** this countermelody for "Gonna Ride Up in the Chariot." Use pitch syllables and hand signs.

Melody: Reading Pentatonic Patterns

Use pitch syllables and hand signs to **read** and **sing** this countermelody for *"Tsuki."*

Music Reading Practice

Reading Sequence 5, page 52

CD 3–4
MIDI 40

Rhythm: Reading with Ties

Use rhythm syllables to **read** and **perform** this two-part rhythm accompaniment for "Somebody's Knockin' at Your Door."

Reading Sequence 6, page 54

CD 3–11
MIDI 41

Rhythm: Reading ♪♩ ♪

Use rhythm syllables to **read** and **perform** this rhythm accompaniment for "Rock Island Line."

Melody: Reading *la,* and *so,*

Use pitch syllables and hand signs to **read** and **sing** this melody accompaniment for *"Hashewie."*

Fine

D.C. al Fine

Melody: Reading *do¹*

For inner-hearing practice, **read** and **sing** this countermelody for "Sourwood Mountain." Use pitch syllables and hand signs.

mi so so la so so do¹ so mi re do

do do do la, do mi so mi so do

do do do la, do mi so so la mi re do

Music Reading Practice

Reading Sequence 9, page 92

CD 4–38
MIDI 44

Rhythm: Reading ♩, ♫, ♬

Use rhythm syllables to **read** and **perform** this two-part
rhythm accompaniment for "Paw-Paw Patch."

Reading Sequence 10, page 98

CD 5–9
MIDI 45

Rhythm: Reading ♩, 𝄽, ♫, ♪♩ ♪ in Meter in 4

Use rhythm syllables to **read** and **perform** this rhythm
accompaniment for "Rise and Shine."

Melody: Reading *la₁* and *so₁*

Read and **sing** both written versions of this melody accompaniment for "Weevily Wheat." Use pitch syllables and hand signs.

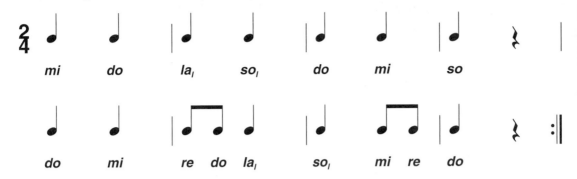

Melody: Reading *la* Pentatonic Patterns

Use pitch syllables and hand signs to **read** and **sing** this countermelody for "See the Children Playin'."

Music Reading Practice

Reading Sequence 13, page 134

CD 6–13
MIDI 48

Rhythm: Reading Upbeats

Use rhythm syllables to **read** and **perform** this rhythm accompaniment for "*Ochimbo.*"

Reading Sequence 14, page 138

CD 6–24
MIDI 49

Rhythm: Reading

Use rhythm syllables to **read** and **perform** this rhythm accompaniment for "Cumberland Gap."

Reading Sequence 15, page 144

CD 6–35
MIDI 50

Melody: Reading *do, re, mi, fa, so*

Use pitch syllables and hand signs to **read** and **sing** this melody accompaniment for *"Canción de cuna."*

 Reading Sequence 16, page 148

CD 7–3
MIDI 51

Melody: Reading *fa* in a New Key

Use pitch syllables and hand signs to **read** and **sing** this countermelody for *"Chairs to Mend."*

Music Reading Practice

Reading Sequence 17, page 176

CD 8–5
MIDI 52

Rhythm: Reading ♩. and ♪

Use rhythm syllables to **read** and **perform** this rhythm accompaniment for "*La Tarara.*"

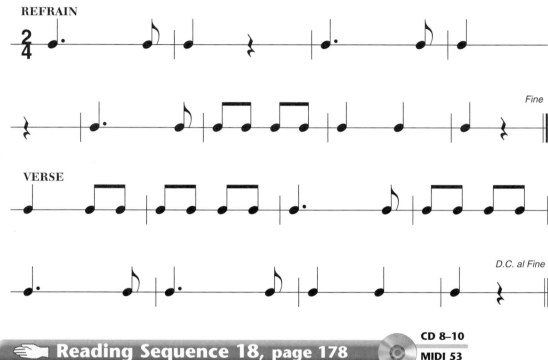

Reading Sequence 18, page 178

CD 8–10
MIDI 53

Rhythm: Reading ♪ and ♩.

Use rhythm syllables to **read** and **perform** this rhythm accompaniment for "Old House, Tear It Down!"

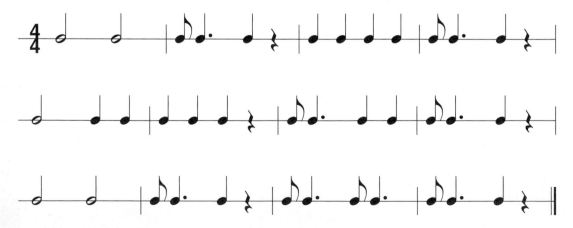

Melody: Reading *ti*

Read and **sing** both written versions of this countermelody for "Kookaburra." Use pitch syllables and hand signs.

Melody: Reading *ti* and the Major Scale

Use pitch syllables and hand signs to **read** and **sing** this melody accompaniment for "Missy-La, Massa-La."

Music Reading Practice

👉 **Reading Sequence 21, page 216**

CD 9–12
MIDI 56

Rhythm: Reading in Meter in 3

Use rhythm syllables to **read** and **perform** this counter-rhythm for "Oh, How Lovely Is the Evening."

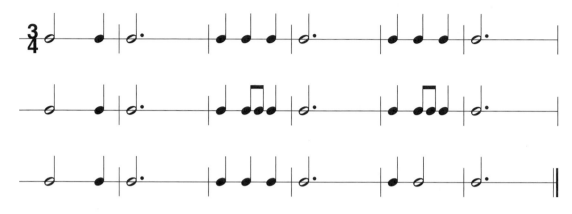

👉 **Reading Sequence 22, page 218**

CD 9–17
MIDI 57

Rhythm: Reading in Meter in 4

Use rhythm syllables to **read** and **perform** this counter-rhythm for "Dry Bones Come Skipping."

Reading Sequence 23, page 226

CD 9–31

MIDI 58

Melody: Reading a Melodic Sequence

Use pitch syllables and hand signs to **read** and **sing** this melody accompaniment for "*Thula, thula, ngoana.*"

Reading Sequence 24, page 230

CD 9–43

MIDI 59

Melody: Reading a Melodic Sequence

Use pitch syllables and hand signs to **read** and **sing** this melody accompaniment for "*Tancovačka.*"

Playing the Recorder

This section of your book will help you learn to **play** the soprano recorder, a small wind instrument.

Getting Ready

Extend your hand forward with palm upward. Pretend you have a small feather on your palm. Blow the "feather" gently so it moves across your palm without falling. This is all the air you need to produce a good sound.

Covering the Holes

Using your left hand, cover the holes shown in the picture. Be sure to press just hard enough so that the holes make a light mark on your fingers. Remove your hand to check that there is an outline of a circle on each finger.

Let's Play G and A

Put your hands back in position to play G. Cover the tip of the mouthpiece with your lips. Blow gently as you whisper *daah.* Practice playing G using a steady beat.

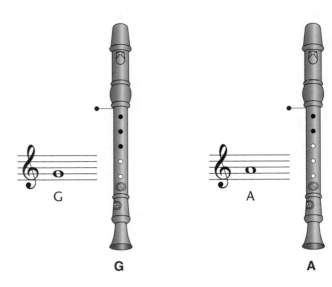

G

A

Counter this Melody

Play this countermelody throughout the first section of "Oh, Susanna" (page 264). **Create** a hand jive to perform as you **sing** the refrain.

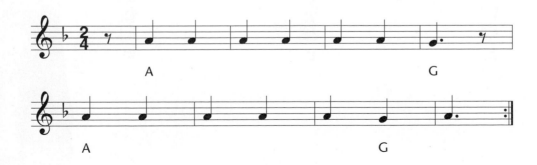

A   G

A   G

Adding B

Now you are ready to learn to play B. Cover the holes shown in the diagram. Before playing, predict if B will sound higher or lower than G or A. Here is a recorder part that you can **play** while others **sing** "Missy-La, Massa-La" on page 188. Make sure you observe the repeat signs at the end of each phrase.

B

G   A

Three New Notes

Here are three new notes. Cover the holes securely with your fingers arched and whisper *daah*.

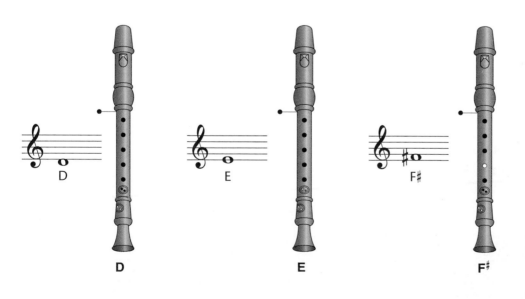

D   E   F♯

Now you are ready to **play** a countermelody to accompany the singing of "The Keel Row" on page 240. Does the countermelody have mostly leaps or steps?

"B-A-G" Songs Plus

Now that you can play G, A, B, D, and E, you will be able to **play** some of the songs in your book. Look at "See the Children Playin'," page 107; "Old House, Tear It Down," page 178; and "Love Will Guide Us," page 328. Practice individual phrases before playing the entire song.

Ready for High C and High D

Practice playing two new notes. Move your thumb slightly away from the hole when playing D.

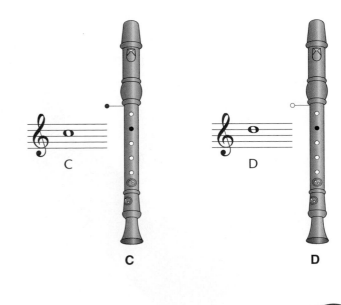

Going Up the Scale

The recorder part below for "Frog Music," on page 200, uses the first five notes of the G scale. Can you name these notes? After playing the recorder melody as written, **create** a new one. Keep the same melody but change the rhythm patterns. Before beginning, think of some patterns that can be used in place of quarter notes.

Pipes Around the World

Listen to these musical examples. Point to each instrument as you hear it being played.

CD 19–9

Pipes Around the World

Sound Montage

As you read the captions, study the pictures of these **aerophones** from around the world. Then **describe** how the size and shape of each instrument influences its sound.

Aerophones are instruments that produce sound by vibrating air.

Didgeridoo, a five-foot-long wooden instrument from Australia, is played by Aboriginals during various ceremonies and rituals. ▶

▲ *Shakuhachi*, an end-blown bamboo flute from Japan, can be found in various lengths, but most only have four finger holes and one thumb hole.

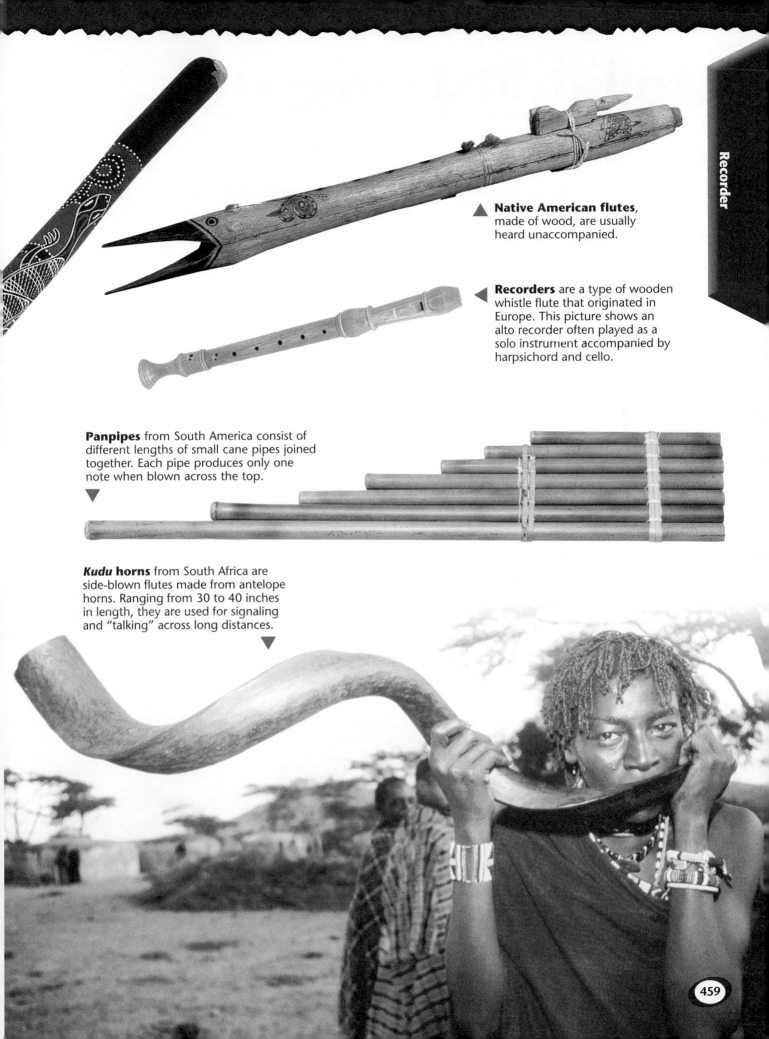

Native American flutes, made of wood, are usually heard unaccompanied.

Recorders are a type of wooden whistle flute that originated in Europe. This picture shows an alto recorder often played as a solo instrument accompanied by harpsichord and cello.

Panpipes from South America consist of different lengths of small cane pipes joined together. Each pipe produces only one note when blown across the top.

***Kudu* horns** from South Africa are side-blown flutes made from antelope horns. Ranging from 30 to 40 inches in length, they are used for signaling and "talking" across long distances.

Mallet Instruments

Playing Mallets

When using mallets to play instruments, follow these simple suggestions.

Holding the Mallets

Fold your fingers and thumbs around the mallet handle—the thumb should lie alongside the handle, but the pointer finger should not sit on top of the mallet. The backs of your hands should face the ceiling. Grip the handles on the hand grips, but not at the very end. (Smaller hands may need to grip further up toward the mallet head.) Elbows should hang easily at your sides. Avoid elbows that stick out to the side or hug the body.

Striking the Bars

Strike each bar at its center, not at either end. Let your mallet strike quickly and then bounce away. If you let the mallet stay on the bar, the sound is stopped.

Matching Mallets to Instruments

It is important to choose the appropriate mallet for each instrument to make its best sound.

For special effects, use hard wood mallets or mallet handles. Avoid anything that would damage the surface of the bars.

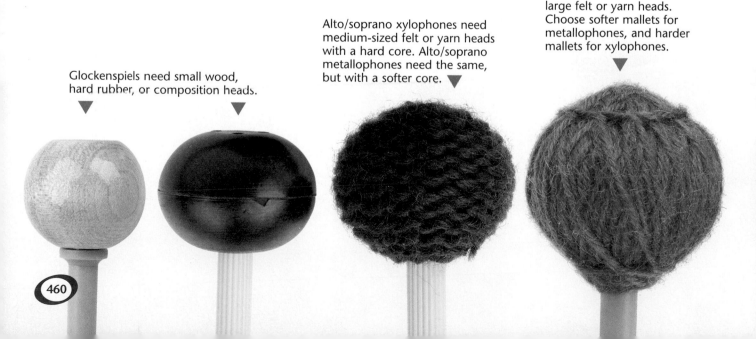

Glockenspiels need small wood, hard rubber, or composition heads. ▼

Alto/soprano xylophones need medium-sized felt or yarn heads with a hard core. Alto/soprano metallophones need the same, but with a softer core. ▼

Bass instruments need large felt or yarn heads. Choose softer mallets for metallophones, and harder mallets for xylophones. ▼

Playing Position

You may sit or stand while playing mallet instruments. This depends on the distance of the top of the instrument from the floor. Your body should stay straight with your arms placed easily in front of you to strike the bars.

Sit on the floor. ▶

Sit in a chair to play ▶
bass instruments.

◀ Stand

Sit in a chair. ▶

461

Playing the Guitar

Types of Guitars

There are three types of guitars—nylon-string classical, steel-string acoustic, and electric. Look at these photographs and learn the names of their parts.

tuning keys

nut

neck and fingerboard

fret

soundhole

pick-ups

tremelo arm

tone and volume controls

toggle switch

▲ Nylon-String Classical Guitar

▲ Steel-String Acoustic Guitar

▲ Electric Guitar

Tuning the Guitar

The strings on a guitar need to be tuned to certain pitches. It is also necessary to fine-tune and re-tune during long periods of performance. Follow these steps to tune the guitar.

- To get started quickly, you may ask your teacher to tune the guitar for you.
- Guitar strings are numbered 1, 2, 3, 4, 5, and 6, with string number 6 being the lowest (or largest).
- You can tune the guitar using the keys of the piano. The illustration at right shows what keys to use for tuning each guitar string.

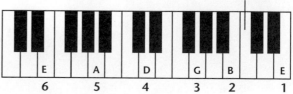

middle C

E   A   D   G   B   E
6   5   4   3   2   1

Getting Ready to Play

Follow these directions to learn how to **play** the guitar.

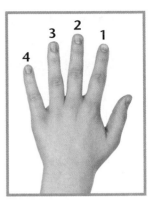

- The left-hand fingers press the strings on the frets to produce chords.
- The right-hand thumb brushes the strings in order to make the sound.
- Use the left-hand finger numbers when you read guitar chords.
- Always relax your body. The guitar neck should be slanted slightly upward.

Playing Your First Chords

Chords are indicated in most songs in this book. The chord names tell you which chords to play, and when to play them.

To play chords on the guitar

- Place the thumb of your left hand behind the neck.
- Keep your fingers arched as you reach around the neck to press the strings.
- Press the strings down onto the fingerboard.
- Keep your palm away from the neck.

Guitar Chords

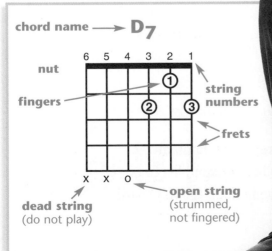

Playing the Keyboard

In this section of your book, we will learn to **play** keyboard instruments.

Sitting Position

For maximum support from your arms, shoulders, and back, sit slightly forward on the bench with your feet resting on the floor at all times. Your knees should be just under the front edge of the keyboard. You should feel a center of gravity, which will allow you to lean from side to side if necessary.

Hand Position

The best hand position is the shape of your hand as it hangs at your side. When you bring your hand up to the keyboard, curve your fingers at the middle joint and make your wrist parallel to the keyboard. You should feel "flexibility" in your elbows as they hang near your side. The elbow should follow through with the natural movement of your wrist.

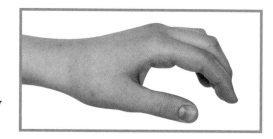

Finger Numbers

The fingers are numbered as pictured here.

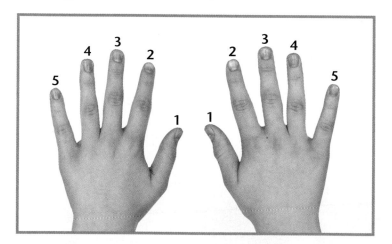

Fingerings for Melodies

How a melody moves determines the fingering on the keyboard. Look at the diagrams at the top of page 465. By translating the keyboard examples to one- and two-line staves, it is easy to see how right/left movement on the keyboard relates to up/down movement on the staff.

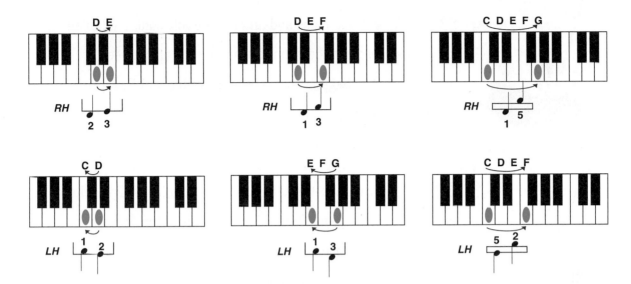

Three- and Five-Line Reading

Play these examples. Determine the fingering before you begin each one.

RH   Begin on G:

LH   Begin on C:

Playing from Treble and Bass Clefs

When playing keyboard music, read the music by following the upward and downward direction of the melody to determine if it moves by step, by leap, or if it stays on a repeated tone. You must also determine where to play the notes on the keyboard. Each note in printed music indicates one place, and only one place, where it can be played. **Play** the following examples in the treble and bass clefs.

Sound Bank

Bagpipes Drone pipes and an air reservoir contained in an animal skin bag are the main characteristics of this reed instrument. The bagpipe is common in Arabic and European countries. *Uillean* [ILL-uhn] refers to Irish bagpipes. CD 19–10

Balalaika [bah-lah-LIE-kah] A flat, triangular, long-necked instrument with a small sound hole on the front. It produces sound when any of the three metal strings are plucked. The *balalaika* is popular in Russian folk music and is a member of the lute family. CD 19–11

Bassoon A large, tube-shaped, woodwind instrument with a double-reed. Lower notes on the bassoon can be gruff or comical. Higher notes are softer, sweeter, and gentler sounding. CD 19–12

Cello A large, wooden string instrument. The player sits with the cello between his or her knees and reaches around the front to pluck or bow the strings. The cello has a low, rich-sounding voice. CD 19–13

Clarinet A wind instrument shaped like a cylinder. It is usually made of wood and has a reed in the mouthpiece. Low notes on the clarinet are soft and hollow. The middle and highest notes are open and bright. CD 19–14

Instrument Key: strings percussion woodwind brass keyboard

 **Conga** An Afro-Cuban drum with a long, barrel-shaped body. It comes in two sizes, the small *quinto* and the large *tumbador*. The conga is struck with the fingers and the palm of the hand. CD 19–15

Darabukah [dahr-ah-BOO-kah] An hour-glass-shaped drum common in the Middle East and northern Africa. CD 19–16

Didgeridoo [DIJ-er-ee-doo] This instrument from northern Australia is made from a termite-hollowed eucalyptus branch after its outer bark is removed. It is a straight natural trumpet that is end-blown. CD 19–17

Dulcimer A sound box made of wood, with strings across it. The strings are usually plucked. CD 19–18

Dundun **Drums** [DOON-doon] Most of these double-headed drums from West Africa have an hour-glass shape with the ends covered with goatskin drumheads that are fastened together with cords stretched down the length of the drum. Pressing the cords tightens the drumheads, producing sharp, high sounds. Relaxing the pressure on the cords lowers the pitch of the sound produced. CD 19–19

Erhu [EHR-hoo] A Chinese string instrument played with a bow. CD 19–20

◄ **Flute** A metal instrument shaped like a pipe. The player holds the flute sideways and blows across an open mouthpiece. The flute's voice is pure, clear, and sweet. Its low notes are the same ones children sing, but it can also play very high. CD 19–21

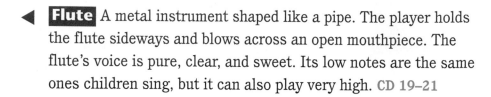

◄ **French Horn** A medium-sized instrument made of coiled brass tubing. At one end is a large bell. The player holds the horn on his or her lap and keeps one hand inside the bell. The sound of the horn is very mellow. CD 19–22

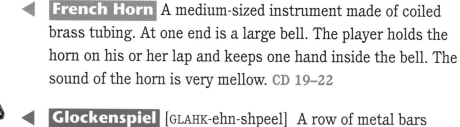

◄ **Glockenspiel** [GLAHK-ehn-shpeel] A row of metal bars mounted on a wooden frame and struck with mallets. It produces high-pitched bell-like sounds. CD 19–23

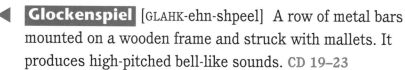

◄ **Guitar** A six- or 12-string instrument that is a member of the lute family. It has a modified hour-glass shape with a flat back. The strings are strummed or plucked. CD 19–24

◄ **Harpsichord** A keyboard instrument similar to a piano. However, unlike the piano, the strings are plucked by a quill, not struck by a hammer. CD 19–25

◄ **Koto** [KOH-toh] An instrument with movable frets and 7 to 17 strings. It is a member of the zither family and is known as the national instrument of Japan. The player sits on the floor, either cross-legged or in a kneeling position. Sound is produced when the player plucks the silk strings with a bamboo, bone, or ivory pick. The sound is similar to that of a harp. CD 19–26

Instrument Key: strings   percussion   woodwind   brass   keyboard

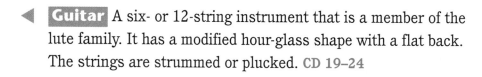

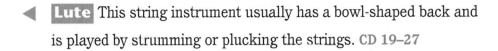 **Lute** This string instrument usually has a bowl-shaped back and is played by strumming or plucking the strings. CD 19–27

Maracas Dried seeds or pebbles fill this pair of rattles. They are rhythm instruments. CD 19–28

 **Marimba** A large barred instrument. The bars are made of rosewood and are struck with yarn mallets. Below the bars are resonating tubes that help carry the sound. CD 19–29

Native American Flute A handcrafted wind instrument made from wood, cane, clay, bone, or hollowed-out stalk of a plant. The sound of a Native American flute is similar to that of a recorder. Traditionally a solo instrument used for courtship, healing, and ceremonial gatherings, it has become popular in ensemble performances. CD 19–30

 **Oboe** A slender, woodwind instrument with a double-reed. In its low voice, the oboe may sound mysterious. These are the notes children sing. When it goes higher, the sound is light and sweet. CD 19–31

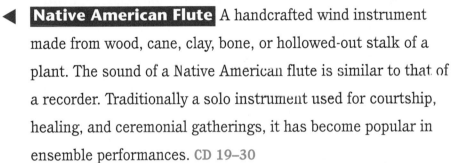 **Organ** A keyboard instrument with foot pedals and two or more sets of keys called manuals. Forcing air through pipes connected to the organ produces sound. CD 19–32

 **Saxophone** A metal-bodied reed instrument with 18 to 20 holes controlled by keys. The saxophone family consists of baritone, tenor, alto, and soprano saxophones. CD 19–33

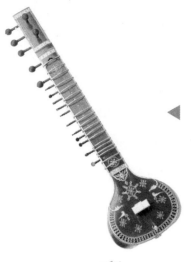

Sitar [SIH-tar] The *sitar* has seven strings over movable metal frets. Melodies are played on these seven strings. Additional strings beneath the melody strings sound the drone required of all Indian classical music. These additional strings are not plucked, but resonate by sympathetic vibration when the melody strings are plucked. The sound chamber is made of a gourd. CD 19–34

Snare Drum A small, metal cylinder-shaped drum. Metal coils are stretched across the bottom of the drum to make a distinctive sound when the top head is hit with sticks. CD 19–35

Steel Drum This instrument was originally made from an oil drum. It comes in different sizes and is played with special mallets. CD 19–36

String Bass The string bass is the largest string instrument, and it has the lowest voice. A string bass is usually taller than the average person. The player must sit on a high stool or stand in order to play it. CD 19–37

Timbales [tim-BAH-lehs] Round drums, each having a single head, often used in Latin music. CD 19–38

Timpani Large, pot-shaped drums, also called kettledrums. Unlike most drums, they can be tuned to notes of the scale. The timpani can sound like a heartbeat or a roll of thunder. The sound can be a loud "boom," a quiet "thump," or a distant rumble, depending on how they are played. CD 19–39

Instrument Key: strings percussion woodwind brass keyboard

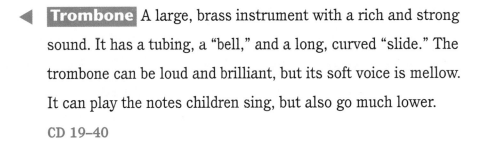

Trombone A large, brass instrument with a rich and strong sound. It has a tubing, a "bell," and a long, curved "slide." The trombone can be loud and brilliant, but its soft voice is mellow. It can play the notes children sing, but also go much lower. CD 19–40

Trumpet The smallest brass instrument, but onc with a big sound. The trumpet's voice can be loud and bright but can also sound warm and sweet. Most of its notes are the same as children sing. CD 19–41

Tuba The largest brass instrument, the one with the lowest voice. The tuba's low notes are deep and dark sounding. The higher ones are hearty and warm. CD 19–42

Vihuela [vee-WHEH-lah] A Spanish string instrument shaped like a guitar and tuned like a lute. It usually has six courses of paired strings. CD 19–43

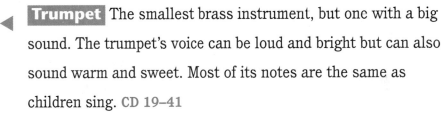

Viola A wooden string instrument played like a violin. It is slightly larger than the violin. The viola's voice is similar to the violin's, but deeper, richer, and darker. CD 19–44

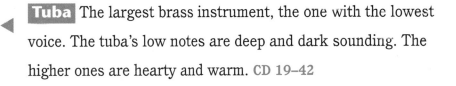

Violin A wooden string instrument held under the player's chin. The strings can be plucked or bowed. The violin plays the notes children sing, but can also go much higher. CD 19–45

Glossary

AB form A musical plan that has two different sections. p. 58

ABA form A musical plan that has three sections. The first and last sections are the same. The middle section is different. p. 100

accent (>) Indicates to play or sing a note with more emphasis than the other notes. p. 210

accompaniment Music that supports the sound of the featured performer(s). p. 36

aerophones Instruments that produce sound by vibrating air. p. 458

ballad A song that tells a story. p. 274

band A group of instruments consisting mainly of woodwinds, brass, and percussion. p. 74

bar line (⊟) The vertical line drawn through a staff to separate measures. p. 98

beat A repeating pulse that can be felt in some music. p. 12

brass A group of wind instruments, including trumpets, French horns, trombones, and tubas, used in bands and orchestras. p. 71

call and response A musical device in which a portion of a melody (call) is followed by an answering portion (response). p. 18

canon A musical form in which the parts imitate each other. One part begins, or leads, and the other parts follow. p. 357

chord Three or more notes arranged in intervals of a third, sounded at the same time. p. 163

coda (⊕) A "tail" or short section, added at the end of a piece of music. p. 61

composer A person who makes up pieces of music by putting sounds together in his or her own way. p. 17

concerto A composition written for solo instrument(s) with orchestra. p. 71

contour The "shape" of a melody made by the way it moves upward and downward in steps, leaps, and repeated tones. p. 151

contrast Two or more things that are different. In music, for example, slow is a contrast to fast; Section A is a contrast to Section B. p. 161

countermelody A contrasting melody that is played or sung at the same time as the main melody. p. 159

descant A countermelody that decorates the main melody, often soaring above the melody of the song. p. 370

duple meter A basic pattern in which a measure has one strong and one weak beat. p. 14

dynamics The different levels of loudness and softness of sound. p. 6

ensemble A group of musicians who perform together. p. 192

form The overall plan of a piece of music. p. 18

half step On a keyboard, the distance between one key and the next black or white key. p. 148

harmony Two or more different tones sounding at the same time. p. 162

improvise Making up music as it is being performed. p. 59

interlude A short musical connection between sections of a piece of music. p. 61

interval The distance between two pitches. p. 21

introduction Music played before the main part of a composition begins. p. 61

jazz An American musical style that combines elements of traditional Western music with African rhythms and melodic contours. p. 74

key signature Tells which notes are to be performed with a flat or sharp throughout a piece of music. p. 148

ledger lines (♩) Extra lines for pitches above and below the staff. p. 62

legato A term that describes music performed in a smooth and connected style. p. 88

lyrics The words of a song. p. 200

major scale An arrangement of eight tones according to the following pattern of steps or intervals: whole, whole, half, whole, whole, whole, half. p. 188

measure (▭) A grouping of beats set off by bar lines. p. 10

melodic sequence A melody pattern that begins on a different pitch each time it is repeated. p. 227

melody A line of single tones that move upward, downward, or repeat. p. 21

melody pattern An arrangement of pitches into a small grouping, usually occurring often in a piece. p. 24

meter The way the beats of music are grouped, often in sets of two or in sets of three. p. 14

mood The feeling that a piece of music gives. p. 309

movement Each of the smaller, self-contained sections (usually three or four) that together make up a symphony, concerto, string quartet, and so on. p. 155

orchestra A group of instruments usually consisting of strings, woodwinds, brass, and percussion. p. 72

ostinato A repeated rhythm or melody pattern played throughout a piece or a section of a piece. p. 76

partner songs Two or more different songs that can be sung at the same time to create a thicker texture. p. 114

pentatonic scale A scale of five notes. p. 25

percussion A group of pitched or nonpitched instruments that are played by striking, shaking, or scraping them. p. 154

phrase A musical "sentence." Each phrase expresses one thought. p. 118

pitch The location of a tone with respect to highness or lowness. p. 21

pizzicato A term that refers to plucking the strings instead of bowing. p. 90

quartet A composition for four voices or instruments, each having a separate part; a group of four singers or instrumentalists, each playing or singing a different part. p. 70

refrain A section of a song that is sung the same way every time it repeats. p. 59

reggae A Caribbean style of rock music. p. 320

repeat signs (:‖) Tells the performer to perform all the music between the signs twice. p. 316

repeated tones Two or more tones in a row that have the same sound. p. 21

rests Symbols for the length of silences. p. 10

rhythm pattern A grouping of long and short sounds. Some rhythm patterns have even sounds. Others have uneven sounds. p. 10

rondo A musical form in which the first section always returns. A common rondo form is ABACA. p. 183

root The tone on which a chord is built. p. 241

round A follow-the-leader process in which all perform the same melody but start at different times. p. 196

scale An arrangement of pitches from lower to higher according to a specific pattern of intervals or steps. p. 25

score The musical notation of a composition with each of the instrumental (or vocal) parts shown in a vertical alignment. p. 402

skip To move from one tone to another, skipping over the tones in between. p. 20

slur (♩ ♩) A curved line connecting two or more notes of different pitch that tells the performer to play or sing the notes *legato*. p. 90

solo Music for a single singer or player, often with an accompaniment. p. 18

staccato (♩) A term that describes music performed in a short and detached style. p. 88

step To move from one tone to another without skipping tones in between. p. 21

strings A term used to refer to string instruments that are played by bowing, plucking, or strumming. p. 110

strong beat Usually, the first beat in a measure. p. 12

style The special sound that is created when music elements such as rhythm and timbre are combined. p. 128

suite An instrumental work of several movements, often programmatic or descriptive. p. 376

syncopation An arrangement of rhythm in which important notes begin on weak beats or weak parts of beats, giving an off-balance movement to the music. p. 55

tempo The speed of the beat. p. 48

texture The layering of sounds to create a thick or thin quality in music. p. 34

theme An important melody that occurs several times in a piece of music. p. 223

theme and variations A musical form in which each section is a variation of the original theme p. 224

tie (♩‿♩) A musical symbol that connects two notes of the same pitch. p. 53

timbre The unique quality or tone color of sounds. p. 30

time signature Tells how many beats are in each measure (top number) and the kind of note that gets one beat (bottom number). p. 56

tonal center A pitch that acts as a resting place or "home" for all of the other pitches that happen around it. p. 26

tonic The key, or home tone in a scale. p. 106

unison The same pitch. p. 196

upbeat One or more notes that occur before the first bar line of a phrase. p. 135

variation Music that is repeated, but changed in some important way. p. 223

verse A section of a song in which the melody stays the same when it repeats, but the words change. p. 59

weak beat Usually, the second or last beat in a measure. p. 12

whole step On a keyboard, the distance between any two keys with a single key between. p. 148

woodwinds A term used to refer to wind instruments, now or originally made of wood. p. 70

word painting The positioning of pitch and rhythm patterns to resemble the meaning of words. p. 402

Classified Index

Listening selections appear in *italics*.

Choral/Part Singing

Folk, Traditional, and Regional Selections

Africa

African American

Arabic

Armenia

Australia

Brazil

Bulgaria

Canada

Caribbean Islands

Celtic

China

Cuba

Dominica

England

Poems and Stories

Recorded Interviews

Credits

Design and Electronic Production: Kirchoff/Wohlberg, Inc.

Listening Maps and Music Reading Practice: MediaLynx Design Group

Photo Research: Feldman & Associates, Inc., Kirchoff/Wohlberg, Inc., and Scott Foresman. Every effort has been made to obtain permission for all photographs found in this book and to make full acknowledgment for their use. Omissions brought to our attention will be corrected in subsequent editions.

Photograph Credits

8 Photofest 9 Laura Farr/TimePix 12 George Lepp/Corbis 12 David Stover/Stock South/PictureQuest 15 Dean Conger/Corbis 17 Bettmann/Corbis 22 (TL) Tim Thompson/Getty Images 24 © Orion Press 24 Hiroshige/The Granger Collection, New York 25 © Orion Press 26 Paul Natkin/Photo Reserve 28 Rudi Von Briel/PhotoEdit 28 The Granger Collection, New York 29 Bettmann/Corbis 30 Odile Noel/Lebrecht Collection 31 Adele Starr/Corbis 31 Christopher Berkey/AP/Wide World 32 Deborah Davis/PhotoEdit 32 Nubar Alexanian/Corbis 32 Melodie Gimple/Warner Bros. Records/Photofest 35 © Dorling Kindersley 36 Torsten Blackwood/© AFP 44 Abigail Hadeed/Visuals Concepts 41 Abigail Hadeed/Visuals Concepts 47 Photofest 48 Alain Le Garsmeur/Stone 50 Corbis 54 Lowell Georgia/Corbis 57 The Granger Collection, New York 58 David Muench/Stone 60 Chad Ehlers/Stone 62 Scott Daniel Peterson/Gamma Liaison 63 Scott Daniel Peterson/Gamma Liaison 71 © Jonathan Blair/Corbis 72 Oliver Theil/San Francisco Symphony 73 Archivo Iconografico, S.A./Corbis 74 © Danny Lehman/Corbis 74 Arnaldo Magnani 74 Tim Wright/Corbis 74 Odile Noel/Lebrecht Collection 75 © 2000 Scott Saltzman/Barefoot Photography 75 Arnaldo Magnani 77 Gerrit Greve/Corbis 78 Bruno De Hogues/Stone 79 Jack Vartoogian 80 Jack Vartoogian 80 Leslye Borden/PhotoEdit 81 SuperStock 81 Art Wolfe/Stone 84 The Purcell Team/Corbis 86 Patrick Bennett/Corbis 86 AP/Wide World 88 John P. Kelley/Image Bank 90 Karl Weatherly/Corbis 91 Archivo Iconografico/Corbis 91 PhotoDisc 92 Gerry Schneiders/Unicorn Stock Photos 97 Kenneth Hamm 104 Richard T. Nowitz/Corbis 106 Robert Gwathmey, "Children Dancing" 107 © Bob Krist/Corbis 107 Corbis 110 Dave King/© Dorling Kindersley 110 Wolfgang Kaehler/Corbis 110 Getty Images 112 Francis G. Mayer/Corbis 112 PhotoDisc 113 Paul Natkin/Photo Reserve 117 Ebet Roberts Photography 122 Grosset Simon/Spooner/Liaison Agency 123 Ousama Ayoub/© AFP 130 Daryl Balfour/Stone 132 Reuters/Fred Prouser/Archive Photos 134 Duncan Willetts 135 Jagdish Agarwal/Unicorn Stock Photos 137 SuperStock 139 SuperStock 139 David Muench/Corbis 142 SuperStock 143 Norman Parkinson Limited/Fiona Cowen/Corbis 144 Robert Freck/Odyssey Productions 145 Danny Lehman/Corbis 145 Kevin Schafer/Corbis 147 Dan Polin/Lights, Words, and Music 147 Stephanie Maze/Corbis 150 AP/Wide World 152 Iwao Kataoka/Panoramic Images 154 Chris Stock/Lebrecht Collection 156 Leo de Wys Photo Agency 156 Christopher Liu/ChinaStock 159 Michelle Wood 160 © David Muench/Corbis 166 Popperfoto/Archive Photos 166 Culver Pictures Inc. 166 Universal Studios/Photofest 167 ©/Hulton/Archive by Getty Images 168 Bettmann/Corbis 168 Dagmar Fabricius/Stock Boston/PictureQuest 169 Burke/Triolo Productions/FoodPix 169 Hulton Getty Picture Archive/Stone 169 Phil Banko/Stone 169 Joseph Sohm/Visions of America, LLC/PictureQuest 170 PhotoDisc 171 The Granger Collection, New York 172 ©Victor Englebert 173 Bonnie Kamin/PhotoEdit 174 Jane Gifford/Stone 177 Robert Freck/Odyssey Productions 177 Photo courtesy of John J. van Gool from his website http://www.lutherie-van-gool.nl 177 Kenwood House, Hampstead, London/Bridgeman Art Library, London/SuperStock 181 American David David Gallery, Philadelphia/SuperStock 188 Robert Evans/Stone 190 © Cary Wolinsky/Stock Boston/PictureQuest 190 Bob Krist/Stone 191 Tony Arrzua/Corbis 192 Kate Mount/Lebrecht Collection 193 (TL) Roger Berg, Creative Photo, Inc. Columbia, MO/Canadian Brass 193 Michael Ochs Archives, Venice, CA 193 AP/Wide World 196 Joe McDonald/Corbis 197 (CL) Jennifer Coppersmith/Index Stock Imagery 197 (TR) Joe McDonald/Corbis 198 Stephen Johnson/Stone 198 Stephen Johnson/Stone 199 Teri Bloom Photography, Inc 204 Michael Ochs Archives, Venice, CA 206 (Bkgd) Corbis 207 (L) ©Joseph McNally/The Image Bank/Getty Images 208 (TL) © David McNew/Online USA/Liaison/Getty Images 209 (TC) Diana Ong, America/SuperStock 212 Philadelphia Museum of Art, Pennsylvania/Giraudon,Paris/SuperStock. © 2002 Estate of Pablo Picasso/Artists Rights Society (ARS), New York 213 Richard Hamilton Smith/Corbis 216 © Mark Segal/Index Stock Imagery/PictureQuest 216 James L. Amos/Corbis 220 Paul A. Souders/Corbis 220 Hulton-Deutsche Collection/Corbis 222 Kent Gavin/Archive Photos 222 © Richard T. Nowitz/Corbis 223 © Dorling Kindersley 223 © Dorling Kindersley 224 © Kevin R. Morris/Corbis 225 Lebrecht Collection 226 Odd Andersen/© AFP 226 Letraset Creative Opportunities 228 (Bkgd) Donovan Reese/PhotoDisc/Getty Images 230 Barry Lewis/Corbis 231 Barry Lewis/Corbis 232 Getty Images 233 Bettman/Corbis 233 G Salter/Lebrecht Collection 234 Mary Robert/Lebrecht Collection 234 © Archivo Iconografico, S.A./Corbis 235 Astrid & Hanns-Frieder Michler/Photo Researchers, Inc. 236 (CR) Mauritius/Index Stock Imagery 237 (BR) Mike Timo/Stone 238 © Hulton-Deutsch Collection/Bettmann/Corbis 239 © Bettmann/Corbis 243 (TC) Max Alexander/©Dorling Kindersley 259 (TC) Courtesy of the Rosenberg Library, Galveston, Texas 260 David Drew/Corbis 260 Michael St. Maur Sheil/Corbis 269 The Granger Collection, New York 274 Kansas Pacific Railway Cattle Trail Map/Kansas State Historical Society 275 (CL) James Walker, California Vaqueros/The Anschutz Collection 275 (BR) 278 (Getty Images) 279 Underwood & Underwood/Corbis 280 UPI/Bettmann/Corbis 281 AP/Wide World 282 SuperStock 282 SuperStock 283 North Wind Picture Archives 283 @2000 John Running 285 J. Bryan Burton 285 John Oldenkamp/San Diego Museum of Man 286 Hulton-Deutsch Collection/Corbis 288 Joe Viesti/Viesti Collection, Inc. 288 SuperStock 289 F Good 289 B Vikander 289 SuperStock 290 ChromoSohm/Sohm/Image Works 291 AP/Wide World 292 SuperStock 293 Forbes Collection, New York City/Bridgeman Art/SuperStock 294 Michael Busselle/Stone 297 Hulton Getty/Stone 298 Susan Sterner/AP/Wide World 298 Kyndell Harkness/AP/Wide World 298 Jack Vartoogian 302 Corbis 304 Corbis 305 Corbis 307 (BL) Courtesy, Northwest Folklife and University of Washington Ethnomusicology Archives 309 David Samuel Robbins/Corbis 310 Seth Kushner/Corbis Sygma 315 Michael Damas/Music From China, Inc. 316 Sarah Stone/Stone 318 Randy Faris/Corbis 322 A. Ramey/Unicorn Stock Photos 322 Aneal Vohra/Unicorn Stock Photos 326 AP/Wide World 327 Jack Vartoogian 328 Steve Gates/AP/Wide World 328 PhotoDisc 337 PhotoDisc 340 SuperStock 343 SuperStock 343 Nancy R. Schiff/Archive Photos 344 Blank Archives/Archive Photos 344 Gary Holscher/Stone 346 Bernard Gotfryd/Archive Photos 346 Gary Holscher/Stone 348 A. Tannenbaum/Corbis Sygma 349 Michael Ochs Archives, Venice CA 349 Joseph Sohm/ChromoSohm Inc./Corbis 350 Chip and Rosa Maria de la Cueva Peterson 351 Courtesy of Henry A. Waxman; President, Earth Flag, Ltd. 352 Corbis 354 World Perspectives/Stone 354 Nigel Press/Stone 356 ©John Fortunato 356 Nigel Press/Stone 358 Bill Bachmann/PhotoEdi 358 Kim Westerkov/Stone 359 James Randklev/Stone 361 MGM/Kobal Collection 365 SuperStock 366 Dave G. Houser/Corbis 367 The Green Bay Chronicle/H. Marc Larson/AP/Wide World 372 Photo by Greg Braun, Courtesy of James Durst,www.james durst.com 372 John Warden/Stone 374 Photri, Inc. 375 Photri, Inc. 375 World Perspectives/Stone 378 Lebrecht Collection 382 (Bkgd) © Cindy Kassab/Corbis 384 (TCL) © Underwood & Underwood/Corbis 385 (BL) Jack Vartoogian for the New York Times ALL RIGHTS RESERVED/Jack Vartoogian/Photographer 388 Chritsian Pierre/SuperStock 390 Peter Harholdt/SuperStock 390 Liam Blake/Panoramic Images 392 SuperStock 398 AFP/Corbis 399 SuperStoc 400 Stephanie Maze/Corbis 400 SuperStock 401 Aldo Torelli/Stone 402 Jim Zuckerman/Corbis 402 Donald Nausbaum/Stone 404 Sorensen/Bohmer Olse/Stone 404 Trip/TH-FOTO Werbung 406 Tom Till/Stone 406 Bonnie Kamin/PhotoEdit 408 PhotoDisc 408 Myrleen Ferguson/PhotoEdit 414 (CC) Getty Images 418 SuperStock 418 Miki Kratsman/Corbis 418 Archive Photos 419 Reuters NewMedia Inc./Corbis 419 Bob Daemmrich/Image Works 419 David Young Wolff/Stone 421 Odd Andersen/AP/Wide World 421 Gavin Wickham; Eye Ubiquitous/Corbis 421 Richard Vogel/AP/Wide World 421 SuperStock 427 Victor Malafronte/Archive Photos 427 Mitchell Gerber/Corbis 428 FoodPix 432 A. Ramey/PhotoEdit 432 AP/Wide World 433 Doug Armand/Stone 434 © United States Postal Service. Displayed with permission. All rights reserved. Written authorization from the Postal Service is required to use, reproduce, post, transmit, distribute, or publicly display these images. 435 David Young-Wolff/PhotoEdit 436 William Lovelace/Hulton Getty Picture Collection/Stone 436 Hulton Getty Picture Collection/Stone 438 David Sutherland/Stone 438 Leland Bobbe/Stone 440 Brian Stablyk/Stone 468 Chris Stock/Lebrecht Collection

Illustration Credits

6 Steve Barbaria 8 Steve Barbaria 8 Michael Di Giorgio 9 Estelle Carol 9 Steve Barbaria 10 Ron Himler 12 Andrew Wheatcroft 12 Andrew Wheatcroft 14 Announshka Galouchko 16 Announshka Galouchko 16 Tony Nuccio 18 Eunice Moyle 20 Antonio Cangemi 22 Antonio Cangemi 24 Jane Dill 25 Jane Dill 34 Donna Perrone 36 Eileen Hine 37 Eileen Hine 38 Stacey Schuett 40 Stacey Schuett 44 Shawn Finley 46 Shawn Finley 50 Michael Di Giorgio 51 Fian Arroyo 53 Esther Baran 56 Elizabeth Rosen 64 David McCall Johnston 66 David Diaz 68 John Hovell 70 John Hovell 71 John Hovell 76 Rae Ecklund 92 Tom Leonard 94 Deborah White 94 Tom Barrett 96 Jean & Mou-Sien Tseng 98 Krystyna Stasiak 100 John Hovell 102 John Hovell 114 Carlos Ochagavia 116 Carlos Ochagavia 120 Gerald Bustamante 123 Gerald Bustamante 126 Carmelo Blandino 128 Carmelo Blandino 129 Carmelo Blandino 148 John Hovell 153 Michael Di Giorgio 158 Linda Wingerter 162 Nancy Freeman 172 Tom Leonard 174 Tom Leonard 178 Esther Baran 180 Esther Baran 186 Rosiland Solomon 190 Michael Di Giorgio 200 David Galchutt 202 George Baquero 210 Steve Barbaria 212 Steve Barbaria 218 Tom Leonard 219 Joe Boddy 220 Tom Leonard 222 Krystyna Stasiak 225 Krystyna Stasiak 232 John Hovell 235 Michael Di Giorgio 244 Lane Yerkes 254 Arvis Stewart 258 Ron Himler 261 Vilma Ortiz-Dillon 262 Ralph Canaday 264 Ralph Canaday 266 Larry Johnson 268 Larry Johnson 269 Tom Leonard 270 Craig Spearing 272 Craig Spearing 276 T. L. Ary 278 T. L. Ary 286 Mike Tofanelli 293 Tom Leonard 296 John Hovell 297 John Hovell 299 John Hovell 299 Vilma Ortiz-Dillon 299 Tony Nuccio 300 Donna Perrone 308 Jean & Mou-Sien Tseng 310 Fahimeh Amiri 312 Chi Chung 314 Chi Chung 318 Eileen Hine 319 Eileen Hine 322 Jerry Tiritilli 324 Jerry Tiritilli 330 Roger Roth 332 Nancy Freeman 334 Oki Han 336 Oki Han 337 Vilma Ortiz-Dillon 338 Ron Himler 340 Bradley Clark 342 Bradley Clark 342 Deborah White 346 Craig Spearing 347 Vilma Ortiz-Dillon 360 Lane Gregory 362 Tom Leonard 364 Tom Leonard 366 Alexi Natchev 367 Alexi Natchev 368 Alexi Natchev 369 Alexi Natchev 370 Bradley Clark 376 Donna Perrone 378 Dave Jonason 379 Dave Jonason 380 Susan Swan 386 Susan Swan 388 Alexandra Wallner 390 Alexandra Wallner 391 Tom Leonard 392 Tom Leonard 393 Tom Leonard 398 Jennifer Bolten 399 Jennifer Bolten 400 Jennifer Bolten 402 Jennifer Bolten 412 Nora Koerber 418 Tom Leonard 420 Tom Leonard 422 Cameron Eagle 424 Robert LoGrippo 426 Robert LoGrippo 430 Sally Jo Vitsky 432 Sally Jo Vitsky 434 Patti Green 440 Michael Di Giorgio

Acknowledgments

Credits and appreciation are due publishers and copyright owners for use of the following:

2: "Turn the Beat Around" from the Motion Picture The Specialist, Words and music by Peter Jackson, Jr. and Gerald Jackson. Copyright © 1975 by Unichappell Music Inc. This arrangement Copyright © 2001 by Unichappell Music Inc. International Copyright Secured. All Rights Reserved. 6: "Put a Little Love in Your Heart" by Jimmy Holiday, Randy Myers and Jackie DeShannon. © 1969 (Renewed) EMI Unart Catalog Inc. All Rights Reserved. Used by Permission. WARNER BROS. PUBLICATIONS U.S. INC., Miami, FL 33014. 13: "Haul Away, Joe" © 2002 Pearson Education, Inc. 14: "Gakavik" (The Partridge) an Armenian Folk Song. Courtesy of Pomegranate Music. www.Pomegranatemusic.com. English words © 2002 Pearson Education, Inc. 18: "Limbo Like Me" New words and new music adapted by Massie Patterson and Sammy Heyward. (Based on a traditional song) TRO-© 1963 (Renewed) Ludlow Music, Inc., New York, NY. Used by permission. 22: "Deep In The Heart Of Texas," Words by June Hershey, Music by Don Swander. Copyright 1941 by Melody Lane Publications, Inc. Copyright Renewed. This arrangement Copyright © by 2003 Melody Lane Publications, Inc. International Copyright Secured. All Rights Reserved. Used by Permission. 23: Orchestral Suite No. 3, BWV 1068, "Air in D," Movement 2, Listening Map by Kay Greenhaw. 25: "Tsuki" (The Moon) from Children's Songs from Japan written by Florence White and Kazuo Akiyama. © 1960 Edward B. Marks Music Company. Copyright renewed. Used by permission. All rights reserved. 26: "Waitin' for the Light to Shine" from Big River. Words and music by Roger Miller. Copyright © 1985 Sony/ATV Songs LLC and Roger Miller music. This arrangement copyright © 2001 Sony/ATV Songs LLC and Roger Miller Music. All Rights Administered by Sony/ATV Music Publishing, 8 Music Square West, Nashville, TN 37203. International Copyright Secured. All Rights Reserved. Used by Permission. 34: "Sonando" Words and Music by Peter Terrace. Reprinted by permission of Peter Terrace. English version by Pearson Education, Inc. 37: "Tie Me Kangaroo Down, Sport" Words and music by Rolf Harris. © 1960, 1961 (Renewed 1988, 1989) Castle Music Pty. Ltd. This arrangement © 2001 Castle Music Pty. Ltd. All Rights for the U.S. and Canada Controlled and Administered by Beechwood Music Corp. All Rights Reserved. International Copyright Secured. Used by Permission. 38: "Pay Me My Money Down" from Hootenanny Song Book collected and adapted by Lydia Parish. Copyright © 1963 (Renewed) Consolidated Music Publishers. International Copyright Secured. All Rights Reserved. Reprinted by permission. 44: "We Go Together" from Grease. Words and music by Warren Casey and Jim Jacobs. © 1971, 1972 WARREN CASEY and JIM JACOBS. This arrangement © 2001 WARREN CASEY and JIM JACOBS. Copyright Renewed. All Rights Reserved. Used by Permission. 54: "Rock Island Line" New words and new music arrangement by Huddie Ledbetter. Edited with new additional material by Alan Lomax. TRO - © Copyright 1959 (Renewed) Folkways Music Publishers, Inc., New York, New York. Used by permission. 58: "River" Words and music by Bill Staines. © 1988 Mineral River Music (BMI) Administered by Bug Music. All rights Reserved. Used by Permission. 63: "Hashewie" (Going Round) from Roots and Branches. Courtesy World Music Press. 66: "Riqui Rán" folk song from Latin America, translated by J. Olcutt Sanders. Copyright © 1948 CRS, transferred 1978 World Around Songs, 120 Colberts Creek Rd., Burnsville, NC 28714. Reprinted by permission. 68: "Eh, cumpari!" (Hey, Buddy!) Words and Music by Julius LaRosa and Archie Bleyer. Memory Lane Music Corporation, 1990. Used by permission. 79: "Hey, m'tswala" from The Melody Book by Patricia Hackett, © 1991. Reprinted by permission of Prentice-Hall, Inc., Upper Saddle River, NJ. 81: "Enjoy the Earth" Yoruba Poem by Anonymous, from Earthways Earthwise. Selected by Judith Nicholls, p. 78. Copyright © 1993 by Judith Nicholls. Reprinted by permission of Oxford University Press. 89: "The Happy Wanderer" Music by Friedrich W. Möller and words by Antonia Ridge, 1954. Sam Fox Publishing Company Inc. Used with permission. 96: "Osamu kosamu" (Biting Wind) Japanese Folk Song. Translation © 1993 Gloria J. Kiester. Used by permission. 102: "Cement Mixer" (Put-ti, Put-ti) Words and music by Slim Gaillard and Lee Ricks. Copyright 1946 (Renewed) EMI Mills Music, Inc. All rights reserved. Used by permission of WARNER BROS. PUBLICATIONS U. S. INC., Miami, FL 33014. 107: "See the Children Playin'" Words by Reginald Royal © 2000 Reijiro Music, ASCAP. 114: "Turn the World Around" Words and music by Harry Belafonte and Robert Freedman. Published by Clara Music Publishing Corp. (ASCAP) Administered by Next Decade Entertainment, Inc. All Rights Reserved. Used by Permission. 115: "So Is Life" Words and music by Harry Belafonte and Robert Freedman. Published by Clara Music Publishing Corp. (ASCAP) Administered by Next Decade Entertainment, Inc. All Rights Reserved. Used by Permission. 120: "Bundle Buggy Boogie Woogie" from Jelly Belly (Macmillan of Canada, 1983) Copyright © 1983 Dennis Lee. With permission of the author. Rhythmic setting © 2002 Pearson Education, Inc. 128: "Straighten Up and Fly Right," Words and music by Nat King Cole and Irving Mills. Copyright 1944 (renewed) by EMI Mills Music, Inc. All Rights Reserved. Reprinted by permission of WARNER BROS. PUBLICATIONS U.S. Inc., Miami, FL 33014 131: "The Lion Sleeps Tonight", New lyrics and revised music by George David Weiss, Hugo Peretti, and Luigi Creatore. © 1961 Folkways Music Publishers, Inc. © Renewed by George David Weiss, Luigi Creatore, and June Peretti. © Assigned to Abilene Music, Inc. All Rights Reserved. Used by Permission. WARNER BROS. PUBLICATIONS U.S. INC., Miami, FL 33014. 131: "The Lion Sleeps Tonight", New lyrics and revised music by George David Weiss, Hugo Peretti, and Luigi Creatore. © 1961 Folkways Music Publishers, Inc. © Renewed by George David Weiss, Luigi Creatore, and June Peretti. © Assigned to Abilene Music, Inc. All Rights Reserved. Used by Permission. WARNER BROS. PUBLICATIONS U.S. INC., Miami, FL 33014. 132: "T'hola t'hola" (Softly, Softly) from African Roots by Jerry Silverman New York: Chelsea House Publishers. 134: "Ochimbo" English words © 1964 Silver Burdett Company 136: "Ala Da'lona" English words © 1995 Silver Burdett Ginn 138: "Cumberland Gap" adapted by Jill Trinka © 1996 Jill Trinka. All rights reserved. Used by permission. 140: "Over the Rainbow" Words by E.Y. Harburg and music by Harold Arlen. 1938 (Renewed © 1966) Metro-Goldwyn-Mayer Inc. 1939 (Renewed © 1967) EMI Feist Catalog Inc. All Rights Reserved. Used by Permission. WARNER BROS. PUBLICATIONS U.S. INC., Miami, FL 33014. 144: "Cancion de Cuna" (Cradle Song) English words © 2002 Pearson Education, Inc. 146: "Cantando mentiras" (Singing Tall Tales) from Cantemos en Espanol by The Krones. © 1961 Beatrice and Max Krone, Neil A. Kjos Music Co., Publisher. Used by permission of the publisher. English words © 2002 Pearson Education, Inc. 152: "Ode to Joy" (Come and Sing), Words by Georgotto LeNorth. Used by permission of the author. 168: "At The Hop" Words and Music by David White, John Madara and Arthur Singer. Copyright © 1957 (Renewed) Arc Music Corporation (BMI) and Six Continents Music Publishing, Inc. (BMI). All Rights Reserved. Used by Permission. International Copyright Secured. 170: "Can You Canoe?" from Jelly Belly (Macmillan of Canada, 1983) Copyright © 1983 Dennis Lee. With permission of the author. Rhythmic setting © 2002 Pearson Education, Inc. 172: "Santa Clara" English words © 1998 Silver Burdett Ginn. 174: "Doraji" (Bluebells) Arrangement © 1988 Silver, Burdett & Ginn. 176: "La Tarara" English words © 2002 Pearson Education, Inc. 185: Piano Sonata No. 8 in C Minor ("Pathéthique"), Op. 13, No. 8, Movement 3, Rondo: Allegro, Listening Map by Kay Greenhaw. 186: "Kookaburra Sits In The Old Gum Tree" Words and music by Marion Sinclair. Copyright © 1934 (Renewed) Larrikin Music Pub. Pty. Ltd. All Rights Administered by Music Sales Corporation for the Western Hemisphere. International Rights Secured. All Rights Reserved. Reprinted by Permission. 188: "Missy-La, Massa-La" from Brown Girl in the Ring by Alan Lomax. Copyright © 1997 by Alan Lomax. Reprinted by permission of Pantheon Books, a division of Random House, Inc. 199: "Computer" from I Wish I Had a Computer That Makes Waffles, Words by Fitzhugh Dodson, 1978. Reprinted by permission of Sterling Lord Literistics, Inc. Copyright by Fitzhugh Dodson. Music © 2002 Pearson Education, Inc. 203: "Do Wah Diddy Diddy" by Jeff Barry and Ellie Greenwich, © 1963, 1964 (Copyrights Renewed) Trio Music Co. Inc. and Universal-Songs of Polygram International, Inc. This arrangement © 2001 Trio Music Co. Inc. and Universal-Songs of Polygram International, Inc. All Rights Reserved. Used by permission. WARNER BROS. PUBLICATIONS U. S. INC., Miami, FL 33014, and Hal Leonard Corporation. 203: "Do Wah Diddy Diddy" by Jeff Barry and Ellie Greenwich, © 1963, 1964 (Copyrights Renewed) Trio Music Co. Inc. and Universal-Songs of Polygram International, Inc. This arrangement © 2001 Trio Music Co. Inc. and Universal-Songs of Polygram International, Inc. All Rights Reserved. Used by permission. WARNER BROS. PUBLICATIONS U. S. INC., Miami, FL 33014, and Hal Leonard Corporation. 206: "America" Words and Music by Neil Diamond. © Bicycle Music Co. 210: "America, the Free" Words and Music by Phyllis Wolfe-White (adapted). © 2000 Heritage Music Press, a division of The Lorenz Corporation. Reprinted by Permission. 215: "El rancho grande" (The Big Ranch) Words and music by Silvano Ramos. © 1927 - Edward B. Marks Music Company, Copyright renewed. Used by permission. All rights reserved. English version by Pearson Education, Inc. 219: "Bones" excerpted from Bone Poems. Text copyright © 1997 by Jeff Moss. Used

Index of Songs

and Speech Pieces